SIRENS

How to Pee Standing Up:
An Alarming Memoir of Combat and Coming Back Home

Laura Naylor Colbert

Dear Bridgit,
Keep fighting the
right fight. With gratitude,
LC

WARRIORS PUBLISHING GROUP
NORTH HILLS, CALIFORNIA

SIRENS

A Warriors Publishing Group book/published by arrangement with the author

PRINTING HISTORY
Warriors Publishing Group edition/October 2019

For information address:

Warriors Publishing Group
16129 Tupper Street
North Hills, California 91343

Library of Congress Control Number: 2019950181
ISBN: 978-1-944353-26-1 (hardcover); 27-8 (paperback)
The name "Warriors Publishing Group" and the logo are trademarks belonging to
Warriors Publishing Group

10 9 8 7 6 5 4 3 2

PUBLISHER'S NOTE
The views presented are those of the author and do not necessarily represent the views
of the Department of Defense (DOD), its components, or its personnel.

**The stories in this book reflect the author's recollection of events. Some names,
locations, and identifying characteristics have been changed to protect the
privacy of those depicted. Dialogue has been re-created from memory.**

To my husband and children.

And to all my past and future students.

The war was always there, as undeniable as the jagged little black lumps of shrapnel which spent a lifetime worming their way out of his hard old body.

—Tony Parsons, *Man and Boy*

Contents

PART I
THE INTRODUCTION

"Did you look under the lip of the sink?" Wes asked.

"Yup, I didn't find anything. Do you mind checking the ceiling tiles?" I responded.

"You bet." Wes—the school resource officer—stepped onto a ladder. He lifted the lightweight drop-ceiling tiles and ran his finger around the edge. He continued to the next stall and did the same thing. In the meantime, I opened the metal paper towel dispenser—my fingers blindly searching for incriminating evidence. I pulled the thick black plastic trash bag out of the tall gray receptacle. I shook the bag and crunched the soggy used brown paper towels, hoping to feel a hard JUUL pod. I got on my knees and explored under and around the toilet crannies. *Thank goodness I'm doing this in the morning when this space is relatively clean. These kids are crafty when it comes to hiding their e-cigarettes. If only we could find a pod or the charging device—something to prove that the last student in here was vaping and was the culprit who left the fruity odor behind him.*

"Did you find anything?" Wes asked—interrupting my train of thought.

"Nothing. Our search is in vain; the e-cigarette smoker won this time."

Wes joked when we were walking back to my office, "You oughta write a book about this crap. You can't make this stuff up. If I would have told my wife that I would be searching ceiling tiles in the middle-school boys' bathroom, she wouldn't have believed me."

"Ha! I hear ya. Who would have thought my military police training would be so pertinent as a middle-school administrator?" I chuckled.

My name is Laura Naylor Colbert. I am an American citizen and a veteran. I imagined I would do something extraordinary in my life, being an overachiever and an adventure seeker from the start, but never—not in a million years—thought I would go to war.

I grew up in a small town in central Wisconsin in a typical American family. Along with various pets, I have two brothers and two amazing parents. My parents are still happily married and are proof that hard work, love, and faith in God can do great things. I owe so much to them. They are my heroes and role models. Both of my parents were civil servants, and all three of their kids ended up working in the same field. My mom, who is now retired, worked at Head Start for almost two decades. She is smart, giving, and fun to be around. My dad, who is also retired, was a self-employed family and business consultant. He consulted for many different organizations, including the State of Wisconsin, where he facilitated the Wrap-Around program, which creates teams centered around at-risk youth. He's intelligent, kind-hearted, funny, and he keeps our family grounded.

As a freshman at UW-Madison, I signed up for the Army National Guard on March 6, 2001. I did it to help pay for college, to have adventures, to serve my country, and as a reason to stay in shape. I had no idea war was on the horizon. When I was debating whether or not to sign up, my friend Rachael Murray said, "Do it. What's going to happen in the next six years?"

We all know what happened six months later on that somber September 11th day.

I left for basic training the summer of 2001. It was two months of madness. In August 2001, I returned to college for my sophomore year. The following summer, I went back to Fort

Leonard Wood for Advanced Individual Training to become a Military Police officer. Most troops conduct their basic training and AIT at the same time, but I was given the option to split my training since I was a college student.

In front of my temporary up-armored Humvee in Camp Flacon before a run to the IP Stations. This is prior to putting on my 40-pound vest and Kevlar. I wore this black beanie to collect the sweat and keep my hair out of my face. June 2004.

THE BEGINNING OF MY SOLDIER SELF

At basic training....everything is associated with killing and
after a while, you want to do it....you create this internal anger
towards an unknown enemy and you have this drive to kill
that enemy whoever it may be. You are prepared on the most
intense psychological level.

—*The Ground Truth*

Basic Training. June through August 2001: the first time in my
life I strived to be invisible. I didn't know a thing about the
military. I didn't know the difference between a general and a
sergeant, between a team and a platoon—I was ignorant in the
ways of the military. I tried my hardest to stay out of trouble
and under the radar, but as you can imagine, being a six-foot-tall
female did not bode well for me. Overall, the drill sergeants left
me alone, but once in a while, they picked on me because of my
height. At college, with 45,000 other students, being tall wasn't
a big deal. I had just finished my novice year on the crew team,
where my height was considered average. Suffering through
years of trying to find a tall-enough guy to date or jeans that
didn't look like capris was bad enough, but I caught grief from
the military as well. About a month into Basic, Drill Sergeant
Harger came up to me in the chow line and whispered, "Private,
get down to my level."

I bent at the waist until I had shrunk to his 5'7" stature.

He shook his head, smirked, and then hissed, "No, Private.
Bend at the knees."

I straightened my waist and then bent my knees until my eyes
were level with his determined steel-gray eyes. I was practically
squatting. My thighs burned while he grilled me on my family,

my college career, and my friends. He finally told me to stand at ease. My knees creaked in pain when I returned to a standing position. My legs trembled and almost crumbled beneath me when I stepped forward in the line.

On a dark and muggy Missouri morning, we prepared to go to the rifle range. The oppressive humidity made it feel like the air was being sucked out of our lungs. Sweat beaded our brows and soaked our t-shirts before we even lifted a finger. I felt like I should be catching frogs by a swampy shoreline instead of getting my gear ready for the range. While in my sleepy and groggy haze, I must have gotten too close to a drill sergeant. Drill Sergeant Lencki barked, "Get away from me, Private!"

I responded, "Yes, Ma'am," instead of, "Yes, Drill Sergeant." Oh boy, did I tick her off. She balled up her fists, her face turned red, and she spat when she bellowed, "What did you just call me?"

"I said, 'Yes, Ma'am,' but meant Drill Sergeant." My voice trembled in fear. *Holy hell, the red of the rising sun is making her look like the devil incarnate. Her face is glowing! Are those horns protruding through her hat!?*

She laughed like the devil itself and hissed. "That's what I thought! Don't ever call me ma'am again. I work for a living. Now get down and push!" Instantly, I got down and pushed. Anything to get away from the she-devil. Within seconds, she was distracted by other soldiers and drill sergeants, and I was forgotten as I exerted myself by her feet. Lencki stood about five-foot-eleven, a large, broad woman with a voice to match. She exuded confidence and self-assurance and had the swagger of a CEO. As the Head Drill Sergeant, she needed it. She was the last person I wanted to see me make a mistake.

Finally, after minutes of pushing, she said in a neutral tone, "Get up, Private."

Exhausted, I replied, "Yes, Ma'am." *Wait, did I just say that? How could I have done that after pushing for that exact same reason?* My stomach did a nervous flip, my heart skipped a beat, my sweat took on the disgusting stench of fear. If you want to see a drill sergeant at her worst, call her *ma'am* twice. Without being prompted, I slinked to the ground to conduct more pushups on my already rubbery arms. She didn't forget about me this time.

Lencki stood above me with fire coming out of her ears and mouth. Her eyes were red with anger. "I can't believe how stupid you are. You certainly must have ridden the short bus when you were in school. I bet you didn't even graduate from high school. You're probably here because you can't hack it in the real world, huh? Well guess what, Private! You're not doing too well here either, are you?" On and on she went, sometimes talking directly to me, and sometimes talking to other soldiers about me as they hustled past.

Finally, I was able to stand up. She must have gotten sick of hearing my grunts and seeing my exhaustion. I finished with a "Yes, Drill Sergeant" and skittered back to my platoon, feeling like a failure.

On the first day of training, my company, which consisted of about 120 troops, had to sit in silver metal cattle cars to transport from the processing center to our barracks. Yes, cattle cars—the same metal trucks that drive down the highway with small air slats just big enough to catch a smattering of black and white and the audible melancholic mooing. Humans that are supposed to be fighting for this country plopped into cars designed for animals traveling to the slaughterhouse. Little did I know the accuracy of this metaphor until I was in a war zone.

Over 100 squeaky-clean troops jammed into cattle cars fit for less than 50. The drill sergeants yelled incessantly, "Get friendly with your neighbor!"

"Private, put your head down; how dare you look at me!"

"You think you're good enough to have space in here? You got another think comin'."

"You better not make eye contact, Private!"

"Oh, lookie here! We have a smart-ass who's too good to look away. You think you're better than me? I'll show you what you're worth for the next two months. I got your number, Private."

They chastised us, making us feel like we were about to be shocked and tanned like the bovines meant for the trailer.

Ten minutes after my company arrived in front of our barracks to fits of yelling and instructions, we were allowed to put down our two brimming duffels and our one personal bag. The Drill Sergeants lined us up in our first formation, challenging with over 100 novice soldiers scared out of our wits. None of us were trying to disobey orders, but the drill sergeants nitpicked and forced us to push for the littlest indiscretion.

With their green crisp-and-pressed uniforms, round hats, and booming voices, the drill sergeants berated us to prove their superiority. With condescending passion, they pressed their faces right up against our scared, self-doubting, green ones. If we dared to make eye contact, we were ordered to the ground to push. My headgear fell off my head as soon as I hit the dirt. When I got on my knees to replace it, Drill Sergeant Harger tore through the line of soldiers and screamed in my right ear, "Look what we have here. Another female that can't do push-ups. You're so weak you gave up already, huh? You better start pushing before I make you do something worse."

Without a word, I resumed my pushups.

Out of nowhere, Drill Sergeant Stinemates approached my left side and yelled, "Private! What are you doing out here without your headgear! Do you think you're above the rules? Are you an idiot or something?"

I didn't know what to do. I wanted to throw my hat in Stinemates' face, slap Harger, and say, "Screw you and all this crap!"

Instead, I bottled my welling frustration, put my headgear on, and continued pushing, seething inside. I would do whatever they told me—I did not need to be treated like dirt in the process.

After an eternity in the hot and humid summer sun, my company was finally shown our Vietnam-era barracks. Brown. Our new home oozed the color both in sight and feel. The other 30 or so females and I were herded into first-floor barracks and divided into our platoon's areas. The ferocious smell of freshly polished floors and hyper-sanitation hit us as the drill sergeants spat orders in our faces. Sanchez and I were shoved into our own private room. I stood frozen, hoping this sliver of humanity would persist. The quiet, creamy cinder-block walls and slate-gray beds became our oasis away from Basic's chaos. The ghosts of soldiers past were etched in the stained and sagging mattresses with stacks of starched white sheets, army-green wool blankets, and well-used feather pillows on the foot of the bed. The females of first, second, and third platoons were ordered into the large open bay of the barracks, their bunk beds lined in perfect rows. The seven of us in fourth platoon obtained three dorm-sized rooms down a bleak, dark hallway. When the drill sergeants tore into the barracks, we were awarded a few extra seconds to tuck our bedding in tighter, hide our contraband, or get ourselves in order before they screamed into our rooms.

The first night we were ordered to line up outside the showers. To further objectify the fresh meat, every female had to strip and spin in front of Drill Sergeant Stinemates to show her our identifying markers. She checked for offensive tattoos and piercings and then sent us into the lukewarm running showers. Drill Sergeant Lencki stood at the other end of the shower stalls, moving the troops through in an assembly line, giving us three demeaning and stressful minutes to clean our bodies. The drill sergeants roared as tired and dazed troops rushed with shoulders slumped and heads down.

At last, my head hit the pillow. I murmured a good night to my new battle buddy, Sanchez. I spent the night in fear—facing the ceiling with my brown glasses firmly planted on my face—not knowing when or if the Drill Sergeants were going to wake us up to continue their torture.

Those dreaded glasses. All the new troops at Fort Leonard Wood, Missouri, spend the first two days at the Processing Center before our cattle-car adventure. The hotel-like rooms were pleasant, and the military personnel treated us with dignity as we were issued our gear and administered various shots. I was able to forgo the painful butt-cheek penicillin shot because of prior allergies, which turned out to be a good thing. The rest of the soldiers sat lopsided and grimaced with pain for the rest of the day. We were issued BDUs—battle dress uniforms—boots, and eyeglasses. It didn't matter if we brought our own glasses or contacts. We were forced to replace our civilian spectacles with the issued 1980's nerd-club glasses for the next two months. Everyone called the thick, brown glasses BCGs—birth control glasses—because they were so ugly no one wanted to sleep with you. The BCGs were the worst during physical training—PT. I couldn't see through the thick fog on my glasses while running in humid 100-degree temperatures. Sanchez snuck in her contacts and wore them through basic training. I, on the other hand, was not that brave.

I instantly connected with my battle buddy, Rais Sanchez. Like me, she was tough, energetic, driven, and wouldn't take crap from anyone. My bond with Sanchez grew throughout the two months as we broke down the Army's machismo facade. We often talked into the night as best friends do. Sanchez and I bonded with the other five girls in our platoon, claiming polter-geists as our common connection.

Thompson, Sherman, and Miller shared the last room at the end of the hallway. An identical double-sized room sat directly across from Sherman, Thompson, and Miller. It was being used for storage of old beds, chairs, and other miscellaneous furniture. During our first moment of downtime, Sherman went into the storage room to explore and walked out white as a sheet a few minutes later.

"What's up with you?" I asked.

In a hushed voice, she responded, "There's something weird in there. I can feel the temp change. I think this place is haunted."

"Right, sure. Uh-huh. Whatever." I walked away, shaking my head.

I am not susceptible to ghosts. I've never seen a ghost and don't think I ever will. Thompson agreed with Sherman. There was an entity in the back of the barracks. Within the week, strange things happened. Sanchez ran into the barracks during one of our breaks to use the bathroom. As she entered the bathroom, she stood face-to-face with an eight-year-old black girl wearing a green dress. When Sanchez blinked, the girl was gone. A couple of weeks later, another soldier, Thompson, saw this same girl standing in the hallway outside the storage room at the end of our hall. Same girl, same dress, same look. Two weeks after that, Sanchez and I heard rustling and stifled screams. We found Thompson quaking on the top bunk. She had been sleeping when she bolted awake, choking. A huge overall-clad white dude had his meaty hands wrapped around her neck. After struggling for a moment, the giant had vanished and we had rushed in to find out if Thompson was OK. *Something weird is going on.*

Basic Training dragged on with more belittling, smoking sessions, and yelling drill sergeants. My company spent the first couple of weeks in a classroom, learning about the history of the military, the ranking system, and traditions. Next, we explored rifle training, the gas chamber, ruck marches, orienteering, bayonet training, and the brainwashing that motivated us to kill.

We conducted PT until we were on the verge of puking every morning except for Sunday. We got up before the sun and ran or did an hour of push-ups and sit-ups. I went from having little faith in my running skills to joining the top running group with a sub-six-minute mile. After PT and a quick shower, we rushed to the chow hall and scarfed our food in five minutes flat. Often, I created a pancake or French toast sandwich with bacon, eggs, and syrup in the middle, then inhaled it while downing a belly full of juice and water. After this eating insanity, it's still difficult to eat at a normal pace almost two decades later. Lunchtimes were unpredictable. They ranged from 1000 to 1400, which made it imperative to eat our fill at breakfast so that we could make it for the next three to seven hours before we had our next meal.

The ruck marches were the bane of my basic-training existence. Not the marches themselves, but the requirement that we wear the dreaded gas masks. On average, we marched six miles through Ft. Leonard Wood with a full uniform, flak vest, Kevlar, and a loaded 40-pound rucksack. I didn't mind the distance or the weight of the gear—those things only made me stronger. I often zoned out in a hot and exhausted haze, marching to the same rhythmic footsteps as those around me. The sound of our gear lulled me into a trance. The metal rifle tinged against our flak vest's clips, our boots scuffed across the rough road, our Kevlars bounced up and down in sync with our strides. Then, without warning, the international sign for chemical warfare rippled through the ranks. The soldiers looked as though they were trying to take flight by flapping their arms up and down after donning their masks. The second after I had my own mask sealed, my heart rate jumped from claustrophobia and I was shocked into paranoid alertness. I was aware of every breath I took, every step I tread, every inch of earth we had yet to cover before we reached our destination. The lack of peripheral vision and the steam rising from my face on the hot and humid summer days decreased my vision to a mere shadow. Breathing through the filter was comparable to breathing through a thin cocktail straw. My lungs couldn't fill to capacity, and I gasped for breath with every step. I coached myself through the insanity until we received the "all clear." *You got this, Laura. You can do this. Put one step in front of the other. Think of something else. Slow your breathing down. They can't force us to keep these on forever. We'll take them off eventually. Come on, there you go. You'll be OK.*

The gas chamber was the single-most talked about and dreaded aspect of Basic. All of us wondered what the torture would be like. We stood in a single-file line, anticipating the worst physical experience imaginable. The compact 15-by-20-foot cinder block chamber held a chemical stove, two opposing doors, and zero windows—an ominous cement box reminiscent of King Tut's sarcophagus. Eight fearful soldiers entered at a time. I was in Fourth platoon, at the end of the line, and I watched as my fellow troops staggered out of the chamber drooling, pouring snot, crying, and struggling to breathe. By the time it was my turn to don the mask and shuffle into the chamber, my palms were sweating, I reeked from my own nervous perspiration, and I couldn't shake the feeling that I was about to voluntarily enter my own coffin. Once all eight of us were inside, the chamber doors shut, enclosing us in the dimly lit solitary room. Sgt. Moyer stood in front and ordered us to conduct jumping jacks, push-ups, and other PT exercises. *OK, this isn't so bad. I can totally breathe through this thing.* At some point, Sgt. Stinemates snuck up behind us, which was easy since we didn't have peripheral vision. As we listened to Sgt. Moyer, Sgt. Stinemates yanked off our masks one at a time. Before she got to me, I could tell something was happening to my fellow troops, but I didn't dare stop my PT to take a look. I could hear them gagging for air, but I thought it was because their masks had unsealed from the strenuous PT. I had no idea I was about to join them. I tried to hold my breath when Stinemates finally took my mask off. But I couldn't because I was winded from the PT. I coughed, hacked, and struggled to breathe as the thick, gray tear gas billowed out of the stove like an ancient spirit trying to tear out my soul. They made us continue our PT after our masks were removed. At last, the doors opened and the life-saving fresh air beckoned us outside. My throat and eyes were on fire. My lungs felt like someone lit a match and moved the flame along every bronchiole. My eyes were thick with tears; I could barely see. The second I stepped outside, I felt immediate relief, even though my body kept assaulting the foreign CS gas. My eyes continued to water and that darn snot wouldn't stop coming out of my nose. I must have looked awful because Sgt. Harger ran over to see if I was going to make it. I laughed and told him I was fine. Within ten minutes, my body had fully recovered.

The most profound brainwashing occurred during bayonet training. The bayonet—a long knife fixed to the front of the rifle—is meant to be combat's last line of defense. Shortly after breakfast, my company took our rifles and bayonets and hiked to an open field dotted with rubber dummies stuck on metal poles. Each of us fixed our bayonets to our rifles and stood face-to-rubber-face with our dummies. On command, we stabbed our green dummies, yelling, "Kill! Kill! Kill!" at the top of our lungs. We were becoming conditioned to slay our enemies. Our cadences about smashing little birds' heads, shooting holes into humans, and trading in your beauty queens for M16s were slowly changing our passive selves into killing machines.

Sgt. Stinemates shouted, "What makes the green grass grow?"

Like robots, we shouted back, "Blood! Bright-red blood, Drill Sergeant!" We stabbed and shouted over and over until we were winded with effort. We enjoyed every second of the vicious attacks. Our urges to slaughter were manifesting themselves during this brutal training.

Halfway through Basic, my company qualified with our M16 rifles. It took two weeks and a variety of ranges to finish the extensive training. When we weren't shooting, we cleaned and explored the killing machine, learning to disassemble and assemble the weapon at record speed. *Forest Gump had nothing on us.* I was frazzled and stressed from the pressure on the ranges. I was as novice as they come, having never shot a weapon in my life. Night and gas-mask ranges proved the most difficult with the pop-ups providing lifelike excitement. The Drill Sergeants knew the added stress required less intense interactions from them, which increased bonding among the company troops. They let us relax in the shade and enjoy ourselves to diminish the heightened state of the ranges. I remember lying under a lush deciduous tree, watching the clouds pass in the bright-blue sky, listening to my new-found friends laugh, joke, and share tidbits about their lives.

When the M16 qualifications ended, my company went to other ranges to expand our weapon skills. We trained with the SAW M249—a squad automatic weapon—the MK19 Grenade Launcher, and hand grenades.

Unlike other weapon systems, the grenade was the most volatile. My insides turned into nervous knots the second I pulled the grenade pin. My athletic hands felt shaky, clumsy, and awkward—as if they weren't even mine. *What if I messed up and the grenade slipped from my white-knuckled fist? What if the grenade malfunctioned? What if I threw like a little boy*—see what I did there?—*and I didn't clear the wall?* The range consisted of 15 holes that were about seven feet deep and wide enough for two people to hurl grenades over the edge. I climbed into the hole with Sgt. Eller. He coaxed me through the process. "Hold down the lever, pull the pin, and lob the grenade over the dune as far as you can," he commanded.

"Yes, Drill Sergeant," I said, feigning confidence.

After my throw, Sgt. Eller said, "Wow, you must play softball, huh?"

I said, "Yes, I have. Why?"

He answered, "That was a beautiful throw, Private."

My hands became mine again and my nervous knots fluttered away. Sgt. Eller left me with more confidence than I had before I stepped seven-feet-under.

Without skipping a day, we jumped into Humvee training after weapons completion. Military Humvees cannot compare to the comfortability of civilian Hummers. The military versions, with thin metal floors and walls, allowed the road and engine noise to penetrate, making it impossible to carry on a conversation. The seats, also made of stiff, flat metal, possessed a square-foot pad no thicker than an inch. With massive radios, five geared-up soldiers—including a gunner sitting in the middle of the turret—there was barely space for oxygen. The windowless hatch in the back meant the driver depended on the side mirrors, a ground guide outside of the vehicle, or the gunner to help navigate when reversing.

Basic ended with a three-day camping trip. The Drill Sergeants dropped us off in the middle of nowhere and ordered us to dig foxholes. Each hole was deep enough to hold our prone bodies and long enough for our height. Once Sanchez and I dug our hole, we lay side-by-side in the cold dirt while people scurried around us. Some shovels had broken against the tough soil, some holes were dug above huge boulders and had to be moved, and some battle-buddies did not work well with each other. Being efficient, hard-working team players, Sanchez and I burrowed in and pulled security as everyone else finished up. We were amply entertained during that time as we watched our fellow soldiers bicker, cry, fight, and complain. Thank goodness I had Sanchez at my side. After three hours of lying there, laughing, whispering, and nodding off 63 times, we were ordered to erect our tiny A-frame tent. It was a green canvas tarp held up by two poles and a couple of stakes just large enough to shelter two prone bodies.

The three-day excursion included middle-of-the-night ruck marches and constant war scenarios. Sleep was an elusive stranger—having only the second night as a night to rest. However, the cold ground and snoring bodies left me twisting and turning until the sun rose in the distance. The third and last night included a six-mile ruck march back to our barracks. I could barely keep my eyes open as I approached the bottom of a large hill. Sleep must have overcome me as I marched, because a moment later, I found myself at the top of the hill and didn't remember ascending its incline.

Once back at the barracks, we dropped our stuff and stripped our muddy, dirty, stinky clothes off our rank bodies and jumped into the warm showers. I had never enjoyed a shower more. When we entered the bay, the smell nearly blew me over—like my grandpa's old pig barn. Our body odor reached a new level of disgusting that exceeded any of my old sports locker rooms. Johnson, a girl in my platoon who was complaining of blisters, showed me the bottom of her foot where a massive blood blister had formed on her heel. Blood and pus oozed out of her tender, swollen foot. I don't know how she made it the six miles with her entire heel encapsulated in blood and pus.

By August, I was a lean, mean, fighting machine. I had blood on my mind and was ready and willing to kill the next person who pissed me off. *Watch out, crazy college professors; civilian Laura has been replaced by a soldier.*

I came home two weeks before my second year of college. Then came that fateful September morning when I realized my military life wasn't going to be filled with fun and games, peace-keeping missions, and national emergencies. My bright-yellow bubbly radio was perched on the back of the toilet and was blaring NPR while I was showering on September 11th, 2001. An emergency announcement interrupted the broadcast. A plane had crashed into the World Trade Center. With a towel wrapped around me and my hair dripping wet, I ran into the living room and watched as the second plane hit the other tower. My world shattered before my eyes. *What have I done? I might actually have to go to war.*

In shock, I walked to class like a zombie. In a time when cell phones were the size of bricks, publicly taboo, and texts were a thing of the future, I had an obligation to explain my predicament to the instructor.

"Professor, is it OK with you that I leave my cell phone on my desk? I'm in the National Guard and I'm not sure if they're going to call me or not."

"Oh, my goodness. Yes, that's fine. Do what you have to do."

With pride, I placed my phone on the desk, awaiting a call from my team leader. I was too preoccupied to pay attention, and the class passed in a flash. No call. I went about my day as normal as possible.

My twin brother, Andy, called at noon.

"Hello?" I answered.

"Laura, are you doing OK?" he asked.

"Yes. Are you?" *Holy crap, what have I done? What is my enlistment going to do to my family?*

"Oh, my gosh. Do you think it's terrorists? What the hell just happened?" he asked.

"I don't know, Andy. The news said it's terrorists. Must be."

"Do you think you'll have to go to war?"

"I don't know. I thought I would have gotten a call by now. Maybe that's a good sign."

"Laura, I don't know what I would do without you. What am I going to do if you and Joe both go to war?" Joe—our older brother by two years—was in the military full-time as a medic in an Infantry unit stationed out of Ft. Riley, Kansas.

"I don't know, Andy. Try not to think about it. It probably won't happen. There's no way we'll get deployed at the same time."

"I can't imagine celebrating Christmas without you," he said with an audible cry. Our family's funny man was reduced to tears. Although he could contort his face into odd shapes, mimic any accent, and make me smile when my world fell apart, he had lost his own joy.

"Don't get ahead of yourself. Let's take it one day at a time. For all we know, this won't even result in a war. Let's not stress about it yet."

Our normal family was becoming unhinged.

For a while, my 32nd MP company out of Wisconsin continued to drill normally as many other military companies prepared and deployed to Afghanistan. The 32nd was based out of Milwaukee and Madison and was made up of five platoons. Rumors and assumptions spread like wildfire as the drill weekends intensified: our company was going to get deployed—no one knew where or when, but it was going to happen. The next nine months flew by, and I finished my sophomore year of college.

The summer of 2002 rolled around, and once again, I shipped to Fort Leonard Wood, Missouri for my AIT—Advanced Individual Training—in the Military Police Corps during June, July, and August. AIT drill sergeants were more relaxed and humane than they were in Basic.

My new Company, starting their second phase of training, welcomed me and 30 other soldiers who had opted for split training. By the grace of God, Sanchez was one of the 30. I joined fourth platoon, while second platoon absorbed Sanchez. Instead of Vietnam-era barracks, we stayed in double-wide trailers barely a few years old. The brightly lit room housed all the females without a wall of privacy. The blue and red specks in the cream-colored linoleum floor provided the only color. Our light-gray bunks and warm white walls were a far cry from the brown of Basic.

Having learned my lesson, I hid my BCGs in a pocket of my civilian jeans and used a Tylenol container for my contacts. I had to wait until I was in a bathroom stall to fix my blurry vision. I only changed the solution a couple times throughout AIT to avoid getting caught. Ruining my eyes was a small price to pay to avoid the BCGs.

AIT was heavy on classroom work. Policing includes a lot of legalities and reports. We learned proper use of force, searching procedures, police terms, apprehending a subject, hand-to-hand combat, proper handcuff use, how to search buildings, and the rights of our alleged criminals. Instead of spending weeks at the M16 ranges, we qualified with our 9mm Berettas—the MP's favorite pistol.

Our company still conducted PT every morning, and I got stronger and faster. I was still in the "A" running group and was one of the top three fastest females.

AIT offered more downtime, which meant more monkeying around in the barracks. Sanchez and I made up barracks baseball and motivated most of the females to join. We put the PT mat around our arm and used that to bat at our rolled-up socks. Even with a lookout, somehow Drill Sgt. Martens snuck in and caught us. We walked away with a tongue lashing in lieu of a smoke session. Halfway through AIT, I was cracking a girl's back by standing above her prone position when Sgt. Holman caught us by surprise. He asked, "What do you think you're doing, Private?"

Feigning confidence, I replied, "Cracking her back, Drill Sergeant."

"What gives you the right to do that? Don't you think you could hurt somebody?"

"I'm studying to become a chiropractor, Drill Sergeant," I said without hesitation.

He quickly turned around and said under his breath, "Carry on."

I graduated AIT more fit than ever, muscles rippling under my flesh. My parents and Andy attended my graduation, and then we drove to Ft. Riley, Kansas to spend a couple of days with my older brother before we headed north.

When I returned home in August 2002, my company was already planning for an impending war with Iraq. The following seven months were an anticipatory jumble. Knowing that a deployment was imminent, I tried my hardest to enjoy civilian life. My junior year of college started off with a bang. I lived across from UW-Madison's football stadium, Camp Randall, with three social roommates. The prime location meant almost constant company and many parties. My classes specialized around my physical education degree, and my professional network was expanding. I was tentatively anticipating my first college summer.

My team leader, Sgt. Hart, started to personally prepare Murray—the gunner on my three-person team—and me for deployment during our December drill. Sgt. Hart was an impressive man with the memory of an elephant and the personality of a stand-up comedian. He stood slightly over six feet with an average physique, a balding head, and interestingly enough, his baby teeth, which looked slight and gapped in his adult mouth. He could remember every detail about the military. He knew the guns' weights and effective ranges off the top of his head. He could remember directions to every location by glancing at a map, knew all the crazy military acronyms, and could remember details from every military book he'd read. I was blessed to have him as a team leader because I always felt safe when he was in charge.

Sergeant Hart's wit, though, was what set him apart from everyone else. His magnetic personality brought many joyful moments during the throes of war. Sometimes the jokes were at the expense of others, but any added laughter and humor was welcomed with open arms during combat.

My teammate Murray, on the other hand, was shy. His short, light hair was balding, and he was slightly overweight. He was a simple man in his early 30s from rural Wisconsin with a passion for guns and Harleys. His quiet demeanor and my vivacious and social disposition caused a perpetual rift. We got along well but never became good friends or confidants. Murray had a huge heart, but our chemistry rarely worked. His fading hearing meant that there were times when both our tempers flared because he couldn't hear what I was saying. While driving, I often needed information expeditiously, and if he couldn't hear me, the situation could become cataclysmic in a heartbeat.

My amazing team at a FOB in Baghdad shortly after we had eaten an MRE. We had heated it by setting it on our hood. The engine heat and blaring sun heat it within two minutes. Hart is on the left, Murray at his SAW, and I'm on the right. September 2003.

Orders had not yet been given, but my company knew deployment was imminent. The preparations had begun. With full ranks and up-to-date equipment, we had become ideal candidates for deployment. By January 2003, we started our anthrax and Hep B vaccinations. Thanks to the military, I was now getting my unnecessary third Hep B series. Prior shot records meant nothing in the eyes of the military machine. My company's weekends evolved from boring, monotonous lectures and training drills to sitting inside our supply cage and poring over our gear. Everything was coming to a head and pointing to war. Inventory was the top priority. We tried to envision the upcoming enigmatic war while checking serial numbers of night-vision goggles, weapons, flak vests, Kevlars, and gas masks. Glenn and Daniels, the captain and first sergeant, based training on assumptions and fabrications of a war that didn't yet exist. The lectures shifted to the Middle East because we knew we would be headed in that direction.

Our company commander, Captain Glenn, was a well-educated, 30-something man, with full lips, a pointy nose, and soft blue eyes. He had brown, thinning hair and a pale complexion. Outside of the military, he was a politician and a lawyer, which made motivation behind some of his combat decisions questionable. We speculated that some of our missions were meant to give him fame and a political platform upon his return home.

First Sergeant Daniels was the perfect leader. With five daughters back home, he possessed the patience and common sense necessary to maintain a level head when our company needed him most. His sympathetic demeanor, toughness, and ability to work-hard-but-play-harder made him approachable— even through the military's rigid chain of command. His thick, gray mustache, caring blue eyes, and heartfelt smile further enhanced his charm and friendliness—like a midwestern Sean Connery.

Sgt. Hart called on February 14th, Valentine's Day, and without any small talk, he clipped, "I have to read your orders verbatim. Are you ready?"

I hesitantly responded, "Ah, OK."

"Laura Naylor, this call is to notify you that you are now on standby. You may receive orders to report to active duty in a short period. It is recommended that you get your life in order. That includes your finances, job, schooling, and family. Laura, did you hear and understand what I just read?"

Finding my voice, I cleared my throat and responded, "Yes, Sergeant."

With the seriousness that the moment required, Hart said, "Goodbye," and hung up the phone.

I am going to war.

On March 1st, while looking for decorative flowers in a La Crosse, Wisconsin craft store, I received the most pivotal phone call of my life. The instant I heard Sgt. Hart's mechanical voice, I knew. I was told using cryptic military jargon to report to active duty on March 15th to prepare for war. I don't remember my emotions coming to a screeching halt. I remember my heart thumping, my mind racing in response to all I had to do and who I had to tell, but my emotions vanished. I was on autopilot. No adventure-driven dip in my stomach. No flutter of antici- pation. No thrill of the unknown. *Is this survival mode?* My body instinctively knew what to do—but my feelings didn't. I didn't even remember leaving the store.

Somehow, I drummed up the courage to tell my family. Thankfully, my parents and I were visiting Andy in La Crosse, so the only phone call I had to make was to Joe. I could see my parents shrink from the weight of the unknown. Andy cried. I thought I was prepared for the news, but nothing could have prepared me to have my life torn out from under me.

Two weeks. *How am I supposed to prepare for war in two weeks?* When I returned to Madison, I packed up my belongings and called UW to end my current semester of college. With their van and trailer, my heroic parents assisted in the move out of my Madison apartment.

While packing, my parents and I debated whether or not my company would cross the ocean. There was a chance we would replace a stateside MP company who was to head overseas, or perhaps pull rear security in Kuwait. If Iraq was my fate, we had no idea what my job would even look like: constant fighting, searching buildings, apprehending bad guys? Or sitting at the base and twiddling my thumbs as the infantry went out, day in and day out? President Bush had yet to invade Iraq, my company did not have a specific deployment location, and Saddam might still hand over his weapons of mass destruction. The many variables in play helped with my optimism and hope. There was still time.

Halfway through the day, I peered out of my window with nostalgia and scanned the stadium looming across the street. From the corner of my eye, I saw parking enforcement writing my mom's van a ticket for exceeding the two-hour parking limit. I spun around with anger and defiance and barked at my mom to run outside before it was too late. Parking enforcement officers are the curse of downtown Madison. Parking tickets are a way of life, and everyone jokes about their ghastly prices.

Faster than you can say ticket, my mom bolted for her van. With luck and sympathy on her side, my savvy mom avoided the $30 fine.

A couple of hours later, I hugged my roommates goodbye, got in the van with my parents, and drove north. I watched as UW blurred by, not knowing if I would ever come back to this life.

I couch-surfed the following week as I said goodbye to various friends and family. While out for drinks, Emily Cooper casually mentioned she was getting a funnel to pee with during our deployment. I wanted to laugh, but the more I thought about it, the more sense it made. *How else were females supposed to pee while at war? Squatting with our exposed butts for all to see?* The funnel would provide privacy and aim—just like that of our male counterparts. Even if stores, restaurants, and public facilities were in reach, they might be a dangerous lair, housing our enemies. The next day, I went to a hardware store and picked out a 99-cent blue auto funnel for myself and for Chloe Kirking, a fellow squad member.

Eccentric Emily Cooper. Her pixie hair and five-foot-two, petite stature created a false facade of weakness. I leaned on her for advice when I first joined. Her oddities and capriciousness provided a respite from the seriousness of war, which is why I valued her company.

On March 15, 2003, I reported for active duty in Madison, where my company spent three days before leaving for Fort McCoy on the 18th. While in Madison, we packed our gear and PMCSed—Preventive Maintenance Checks and Services—our vehicles. We sat around and waited for orders while counting and cleaning our equipment to make the days go by faster.

Before leaving Madison, my company had a farewell ceremony at the Wisconsin National Guard Headquarters. My parents and Andy came to the emotional event. While sitting in the front row, their signs, "God Bless the 32nd" and "We love you, Laura," shone like beacons as I marched past. Cpt. Glenn spoke of our company's importance to assist in the cause. *What is the cause, exactly, and how important are we with an absent mission?*

We were given a few moments to say goodbye after the commander and National Guard officers were done droning. I cried as I hugged my parents. They, too, were shedding tears as they said, "We love you, Laura. We're proud of you. Put your faith in God. This is His will." The latter sentence became my mantra as mortars flew through the air and bullets rained down. If I thought it was hard to hug my parents, it was even harder to say goodbye to Andy. My tears were more for him than for myself. I hated myself for my selfishness when I enlisted two years earlier. He did not deserve to lose a twin. My parents now had two active-duty children. My dad had cried three times in the last month over his little girl. Before my deployment, the only time I saw him shed a tear was when his father died five years earlier.

My stoic dad, about five-foot-eleven, was sentimental and soft-spoken. He had been a Military Police Officer during the Vietnam War and was one of the lucky few who didn't have to go overseas. He'd tell you that, like Chico Escuela, "Baseball's been berry berry good to me." He was asked by his First Sergeant to join his unit's baseball team, and he was given an administrative position so he could stay and play. When his MP company was off training, he could stay behind to play. He was able to personally avoid the tragedies of war, but wasn't able to protect his own daughter.

Prior to deployment, my dad had said, "Believe it or not, I think this war is going to be harder on me than you." I had thought vanity had overtaken my humble dad. How could he possibly know the ramifications of a war zone versus staying stateside? I finally understood his sentiment when I returned home and Joe was still deployed. I cringed every time the phone rang, fearing it was my parents calling with bad news. Now that I have my own children, I can't fathom the agony my parents must have gone through with not just one, but two children deployed.

My mom and I were clearing off the table after a leisurely Sunday lunch about a week before the Farewell Ceremony.

My dad had asked, "Laura, could you please join me in the sunroom?"

I knew this was going to be an emotional experience by the look in his eyes and his somber tone of voice. I told him, "I'm not going in there if you're going to make me cry." I looked into his eyes and saw tears start to swell, breaking my heart into a million pieces.

He asked, "Can you please sit down on the couch?" He sat down next to me on the light-green sleeper sofa, pulled out his wallet, slid out a two-dollar bill, and said, "When my father died, I found this bill in his wallet. It was his lucky two-dollar bill. I want you to have it and carry it with you throughout your deployment. The one stipulation is that you give it back when you get home."

I broke down and gave my dad a warm embrace and said, "I'll take good care of it and give it back to you as soon as I get home." I kept that sentimental two-dollar bill in my uniform's front pocket throughout my deployment. The rarity of the bill was a constant connection to not only my dad, but my sweet, tender-hearted grandpa who left this earth too quickly. I cherished that bill as if it were a rare gem.

TRAINING

After the farewell ceremony, my company convoyed two-and-a-half hours to Ft. McCoy in western Wisconsin. To get our minds off the pain of leaving our friends and families, we bantered back and forth in the loud Humvee. My unique platoon of 13 females and 20 males split a full-sized barracks, with females on the first floor and males on the second. First and Second Platoons had seven females each, and Third Platoon only had four. The decade-old barracks had a white exterior and mass-produced cheap craftsmanship. Each squeaky bed was placed five feet from the one next to it within the open floor plan. I dropped my meager belongings at the foot of my assigned bed.

I was drained but had to stay in uniform and awake until our 2145 platoon meeting. After the meeting, I took a quick, cold shower, thanks to the insufficient water heaters. At about 2300, I finally crawled into my saggy, old mattress and fell into a deep sleep.

Kirking's smallpox shot a week after inoculation while at Ft. McCoy. We had to keep a Band-Aid on the entire week, and when we took it off, it oozed pus and blood. March 2003.

The following days were filled with early mornings, training, and mandatory Soldier Readiness Processing—SRP. SRP included a physical, more shots, a dental exam, and other preparatory actions. My third set of anthrax shots were the most painful. The first shot starts the dosing schedule with a second shot two weeks later, then one on the fourth week, then six months, twelve months, and 18 months, followed by an annual booster. Some soldiers in my company had terrible swelling around the injection sight. Their joints and muscles were affected, making it difficult to lift their arms.

After dinner, on the second day at Ft. McCoy, I returned to the barracks to relax and to wait for President Bush's decision on whether or not to invade Iraq. About nine of my fellow 21st-century soldiers and I huddled around a tiny, archaic FM radio. I felt like I was transported into a World War II war movie. How were active-duty soldiers preparing for war not privy to information before the public?

We were eager. Our nervous energy skittered across the tiled floor and bounced off the white walls. What would President Bush do? Sgt. Hart was adamant. "We're going to war no matter what. Even if Saddam comes forward, we've already invested too much in this war to back out now." Ssg. Verbsky—my fearless squad leader—and Sfc. Phair—my attractive platoon sergeant— nodded. I kept my mouth shut, hoping and praying they were wrong. *How could Saddam let our military crush his country? He needs to stop the insanity and protect his country and his people.* After Hart's proclamation, we sat in restless silence swimming in our own thoughts and prayers.

With anxious glances, we accepted our fate as it was broadcast over National Public Radio. President Bush's words will forever be etched in my memory: "The United States has invaded Iraq."

I. Am. Going. To. War.

Ironically, a wave of relief washed over me. The guessing game was over. Everything I'd trained for would come to fruition.

My company's conversations were abuzz. Will we stay stateside, fight in Iraq, or sit in Kuwait as reinforcement?

The training took on a new meaning and became our central focus. Unfortunately, the Vietnam-era training of range cards, running through wooded areas, and training on foot didn't mirror our mission. The military, being slow to change, couldn't foreshadow appropriate scenarios fast enough to adapt our training before our departure overseas.

In every facet of my life, I've strived for equality with my male counterparts. It all started when I tried to keep up with my brothers in grade school. *I can play tackle football with the rest of them.* It loomed into High School. *I deserve to be president of the class, just as much as Silly Simon does.* Then into college. *I, too, can be an amazing PE teacher and coach. I don't need to be a ripped jock to succeed in the gym.* The military was filled with sexual stereotypes. *I can lift the 73-pound MK19 onto the Humvee without assistance. Half the men and barely any of the other women in my company can do that.* Screw the PT gender differentiation. Hello, 45 push-ups in one minute—meet Soldier Laura—she can kick your butt. Even now, as a school administrator, I have to prove my worth among the good-old boys.

Fascinated with medicine and having majored in pre-med my first year of college, I volunteered for Combat Lifesaver training with 20 other soldiers. I perfected administering an IV, applying a tourniquet, splinting broken bones, treating a collapsed lung, and many more healing skills—tangible techniques to save lives instead of taking them away.

After two weeks at Ft. McCoy, it was time to conduct my own training. That bright-blue funnel taunted me every time I peeked into my footlocker. I stood in front of the urinal with my pants still over my behind and the funnel jutting out through two opened buttons in my pants. As my bladder emptied, my pants began to feel warm. *Oh, no!* I adjusted the funnel by pointing the hose end down and urine flowed out into the proper receptacle. A quick shower and embarrassing uniform switch soon followed.

Beyond training and SRP, we received Southwest Asia briefings. During one of the briefing breaks, my platoon congregated outside in the cool March morning. Spring in Wisconsin was wonderful, filled with the smell of raw vegetation and fresh air. The birds chirped near to bursting. When the warm sun shined, it was heaven on earth.

While taking in this wonderful morning, Sgt. Hart spat on the ground. I laughed and taunted, "You call that spitting?"

"What are you talking about, Naylor? You think you can do better?" he prodded.

"I *know* I can do better," I said confidently. Being the goalie on a winning high school soccer team allotted me a lot of downtime. On my lonely and boring end of the field, I practiced line dancing for P.E. and taught myself how to spit...far...

"Hey guys, get over here! Naylor says she can spit farther than me. Let's find out!" Hart yelled to Phair and Verbsky, his best friends.

"I *can* spit farther than the rest of you," I said, defending myself.

Both Phair and Verbsky chuckled and meandered over. "There's only one way to find out," chortled the tall, tanned, toned, confident, and flirtatious Phair. "Let's have a competition." Verbsky, who was gorgeous with a body of a Greek god and blond, curly hair, was already drawing a line in the gravel with his foot. I smiled, knowing I was going to win. There are two unsuspecting talents I possess—spitting and chugging. Hart and I stood behind the line, gathered our spit, and on the count of three, propelled our saliva forward. I beat Hart by a landslide. Actually, I hit the side of the building. *Aren't you proud, Dad?*

Hart's flabbergasted glance went from my spot on the building to my face, and then—without a word—he got down on the ground and pushed. Verbsky and Phair, who fed off one another in humor and intelligence, laughed at Hart's failure. Verbsky, caught in the moment, said, "I dare you to choke Sergeant Hart."

I looked at Hart who was red-faced from knocking out 20 push-ups, felt pity, and shook my head. "No," I said, wondering about the origins of that peculiar request. I also wondered why I could never break through Verbsky's tough exterior shell and get to know him on a personal level.

Hart, surprised I refused Verbsky's order, demanded, "Get down and push, Specialist. You just disobeyed a direct order." While pushing, the three amigos stood above me, laughing and joking with a jovial atmosphere. At last, Hart ordered me to stand.

After I joined their circle again, Verbsky looked at me and ordered, "Choke Sergeant Hart." Having no other choice, I did.

"Get down and push, Naylor. You can't choke me," Hart barked as I wrapped my hands around his neck.

I shrugged, deflated by the absurdity. My pride and self-worth disappeared. *How did our joking around turn into mocking and belittlement?*

When we got back to the barracks, Sgt. Hart said, "Naylor, I'm putting you on curfew. You need to be in the barracks by twenty-one-hundred every night."

"What? Why?" I asked, flabbergasted at his newfound authoritarian rule. There was no reason for this. I was a good soldier who never got in trouble. I had a good relationship with Hart and always did what he asked.

"Don't ask questions, Specialist. Do what you're told," he bellowed. I walked away without any acknowledgment. *Where did this come from? He's never pulled this kind of degradation before..* The only explanation I could figure out, was that I was dating a guy from third platoon. I don't think Hart liked him, and he was trying to protect me from him.

I was insulted. I was an independent, self-sustaining 21-year-old. I paid for everything on my own—car, apartment, college, food, fun. I decided everything on my own. I never had a curfew, even under my parents' roof.

My emotions took a dive the following day. My world shifted from a social college student to a soldier preparing for war. Moments of darkness intermittently clouded the subsequent days while at Ft. McCoy. Manipulation, degradation, and the loss of independence were like prison: rigorous schedules, piss breaks, chow time, bedtime, wake-up, constant accountability, mail call, visitation hours—or lack thereof—close-quarter sleeping, and community showers. My moods and emotions bounced through my mind like a pinball game. Joy abounded with the various adventures, exciting training, teamwork, and bonding. Then, in an instant, a crash, a falling, I would enter an oppressive state, yearning to get out. Every twinge of negativity opened a depressive abyss a little wider until my fear was tangible. Regardless of my faith in God, my human instinct brought insecurities.

I had been so naive. A true pacifist wouldn't have been ignorant enough to join. Why had I? *Am I willing to kill? To give my life for this country?* I couldn't justify homicide as a Christian— even in war. It wasn't my job to take another human life. I couldn't do that to their loved ones. What if the person or people I killed were innocent bystanders caught in the crossfire? Basic Training tried to beat these sentiments out of me, but I had a mind of my own and was adamant that war solves nothing. The only thing I could do at that point was to keep telling myself my new mantra: This is God's will.

Thanks to Kirking, I knew I wasn't alone. Kirking and I told each other everything. I valued her as a friend and a kick-ass soldier. Her baby face, blond hair, and short stature could fool you. Her sponge-like brain, quick wit, and bluntness held its own. Just like me, she had her moments of weakness. One night, her fear focused on the realization that this war was for real. I worried about Kirking, who was only 19—the youngest person in our platoon.

Shortly after the spitting match, we had a party in the barracks. We could drink in the barracks for the first time. Hart and I were hanging out, and he asked, "So, what do you think about women being in the Navy Seals and in the military in general?"

I took a second to respond, trying to be thoughtful with my answer. "I think that women should be allowed in any military branch. After all, I know that I could handle anything they throw at me."

Hart nodded with a deliberate look on his face. "OK, I understand *you* can handle it, but what about most women? Don't you think you're the exception?"

I chuckled, slightly taken aback by his compliment. "I don't know. I'm sure there are a lot of women who couldn't handle it, nor would they want to, but I'm sure there are lots of men who fit in the same category. I bet if push came to shove, women would do really well in all branches of the military. It's human nature to survive, and we all do what we have to."

"Yeah, I suppose. I'm just glad I got you and not some other woman who couldn't handle herself," smirked Hart.

"Thanks. I'm glad you're my team leader. At least you know what you're doing, and I can trust your decisions," I said as I winked at him. "Do you think men are ready to have women in the military?" It was Hart's turn to look surprised. I continued, "Do you think men are afraid to admit their nurturing skills may come into play when they see a woman struggle? Might this become a distraction on the front lines? Also, what about romantic relationships?"

"I'm not sure," he shrugged. "I guess we'll have to wait and see. I can tell you that I wasn't too excited to have a woman on my team at first, but now I know it's not a big deal."

I felt validated as my head hit the pillow that night. At least I knew Hart had faith in my ability as a soldier, even if I felt like my mind was playing tricks on me with its high highs and low lows.

We had many company briefings and squad meetings while at Ft. McCoy. One time, the commander gathered the company together to tell us about our potential mission. He claimed, "Our mission, as of now, will be very dangerous, and the pucker factor better be high. We're preparing for war, so we need to start training like it. We will be spending a couple of weeks in Kuwait, and then we will head north to Baghdad. We will be under the First Armor Division and attached to the Eighteenth MP Brigade out of Germany. This information is confidential and subject to change. I don't want to see it in the newspaper or hear it on the news. Please do not share this information with your family. That is all."

I got a rush of adrenaline-filled anxiety like it was a blind date. I kept asking myself, *When will this start to feel real?* I felt like I was still playing cops and robbers in the backyard with my brothers and their friends instead of training for war. Perhaps— since I had never been to war—I had no idea what that feeling embodies.

Subsequently, Glenn had a handful of other briefings covering varying degrees of the same message. My company had become a pawn in the game of Operation *Iraqi Freedom* chess. I was an insignificant cog in the military wheel.

Our nightly squad meetings divulged further details in a more intimate setting. During one such squad meeting, Verbsky reported multiple soldier deaths in Iraq. I felt sick to my stomach—as though someone had kicked me in the gut— as I reflected on those soldiers' deaths. I saw surprised and fearful expressions within my squad's huddled circle. After that briefing, I committed myself to the training and reacted to the environment around me with a new lens—a combat soldier's lens.

Like any job, military work can be frustrating. About three weeks after my company arrived at Ft. McCoy, a local news station came to conduct a story on troops getting ready for the impending war. Glenn, being the go-getter that he was, ordered us to go outside in subfreezing temperatures in a show of toughness. My platoon worked on traffic-control points, walking formations—lines and wedges—anything that kept us moving. Western Wisconsin's unpredictable spring weather brought frigid temperatures, and we were subjected to them for four painstaking hours. Sick of working in the cold, Phair went to check on the reporter's whereabouts. When he returned, he was irate. He ordered, "Stand down. The cameras left two hours ago. The rest of the company forgot about us out here." With Phair in charge, we were in good hands. He never entered into unnecessary danger as other leaders appeared to do for their own personal gain.

After giving us barely enough time to thaw, we were ordered to load everything into the vehicles by 2200. This news did not sit well with me. I asked Hart many questions to figure out the extent of the order. No one could explain what "load everything" meant. *Should I pack all of my possessions, including personal gear? Bedding? Toiletries? Was this an overnight mission? Did I need my contact solution? Would we be outside the entire time? Should I pack all my layers?* After a few hours of agitation and complaining, Sgt. Hart told me to lock my personal gear in my tote and pack a day's worth of stuff. *At last, some answers!* When our vehicles were loaded and ready to go, we stood down until morning when the vague mission was to commence. I pulled 0200 to 0300 guard duty with Hart. The loaded vehicles had to be manned overnight because of the sensitive material. In my humble opinion, they could have been loaded in less than ten minutes after we woke up instead of disrupting our sleep to watch nonliving gear.

Even though we had loaded our gear the night before, we didn't leave the barracks until 1400. We sat around all morning. We talked with each other, snacked, napped, and waited for something to happen. The mission consisted of a two-and-half-hour convoy through Ft. McCoy. All the fuss for a meandering drive. I rode in the uncomfortable turret seat—a three-inch-thick nylon strap that squeezed my thighs together and dug into my rear end. To make matters worse, it snowed the whole time. I had 30- to 55-mile-per-hour winds whipping across my upper body in subfreezing temperatures. For someone who suffers from Raynaud's Syndrome—in which arteries that supply blood to the skin constrict excessively in response to cold—it was pure torture. My hands and feet had been numb since the first ten minutes.

The day ended with a silver lining. We turned in our weapons and were given the night off to enjoy the only Ft. McCoy bar, naturally named "McCoy's." It had been 17 days since our last night off with permission to consume alcohol. I hadn't realized how much I needed a break until we were dancing the night away.

The next day, I met my parents and twin brother at a restaurant off base and later went to the park. Five days after that, we had another 48 hours off—our apparent last hurrah before we were shipped overseas. My parents picked me up on Friday and took me home. It was a bittersweet weekend. Not knowing if this was the last time I would ever be home, I took it all in: the pine trees' deep aroma, the giant rock we used to explore as kids, the tree stand that passed from hunter to hunter through the generations, brightly colored blooming flowers from my mom's many flower beds, chirping birds—chickadee-dee-dee, chickadee-dee-dee—chattering squirrels—even the red ones that my dad eliminated on sight because they were destructive to our property—and the wind through the Chinese elm trees. I explored my grandparents' old farmstead next door and took in the smell of the lilac bushes and the old grease from my grandfather's rod-and-reel repair shop. I ate delicious food and laughed the nights away with my family and friends.

When my parents dropped me off, our hugs and kisses were clouded with the unknown. *Will I ever see them again? Will I be the same person the next time they see me?* Our hugs lingered a bit longer than normal, and they said, "We're so proud of you, honey. We know that God will watch over you and protect you. We'll keep you in our prayers. We love you so much. Call when you can."

I mostly nodded and said, "I know, I know. I will call when I can. I love you, too. Keep an eye on Andy for me. I know this isn't easy on him." I stood outside my barracks, watching them drive away until the swirling dust settled.

Our departure date continued to be postponed. Unsure of how to proceed, our company admin gave us the following weekend off as well. Instead of going through the emotional turmoil of saying goodbye to my parents, I went 40 miles south to La Crosse where my twin brother lived. Wendel—my brief boyfriend from third platoon—Korb, and her civilian boyfriend joined me in staying in a hotel close to the UW campus. We soaked up every last second of civilian life by exploring the city, hanging with my brother, and swimming in the pool. Korb, a fellow fourth platoon female, had lush, dark hair, dark eyes, and was one of the best friends I had while deployed. I don't know what I would have done without her and her rabble-rousing.

After being on active duty for 46 days, we were finally issued desert camo, tan boots, and updated sleeping bags for our deployment. During a briefing a few days later, Glenn said, "We're leaving for Kuwait within forty-eight hours. Our deployment shouldn't last longer than six months. Our vehicles and larger gear will be put on a ship and will meet us there. You will be given twenty-four hours off to say your final goodbyes." *Finally! We have been at Fort McCoy for too long. I'm ready and excited for this adventure.*

After our briefing, Hart pulled me aside and said, "Sorry, Naylor. You've been put on Commander's Quarters—CQ—duty for the next twenty-four hours."

"What? Twenty-four hours? The shift has never been longer than twelve hours since we've been here. How come I get the shaft?" I said, devastated.

Sgt. Hart shrugged and said, "Maybe someone can split it with you or something."

"Yes, Sergeant," I replied, defeated. Everyone else was given an opportunity to see their family and friends one last time, but I had to stay back in the dark, damp CQ building answering phone calls, delivering messages, and conducting random tasks for our company. After a few hours of pleading with soldiers in my company, Wendel volunteered to take eight hours of my shift so I could see my family one last time.

The next day, my parents picked me up, and we drove into Sparta, ate at Subway, and then sat at a park where we played catch with a softball and talked. It was a sobering yet nice afternoon. My dad asked, "How are you doing, honey?"

"I'm OK. I don't really know what to expect, so I'm not too worried or scared."

"That's normal. Perhaps it's better that way. Now you can go in with an open mind and create your own opinions without anything to fear."

"Yeah, I guess so. I just can't believe that my life went from wearing red Badger gear to a desert camo uniform. I don't feel like this is real."

"I'm sure it will once you get over there."

My mom kept giving me sad, compassionate looks as the afternoon crept to an end. Our final goodbyes were tearless. We had shed enough tears over my deployment. Now it was time to leave each other with positive and brave sentiments in case this was our last memory together.

The next night, Andy came to get my civilian stuff and say goodbye. Overwhelmed and emotional, I handed him my cell phone, civilian outfits, a blow dryer, and other amenities while avoiding looking in his eyes. I felt like I was betraying him. We had no idea when or if we would see each other again. He didn't stay long. I let out a sigh of relief as he drove away, and I'm sure he did the same. And with that sigh of relief, I transformed into a full-time soldier.

LEAVING THE USA

We flew to Kuwait May 10th, 2003, my 57th day on active duty. Hundreds of soldiers joined us in the pristinely clean hanger. The gray cement floor had turned into a sea of moving camo. Most troops sat on the ground with their buddies and hung out. Some napped, some read, and some played cards. The current of energy morphed back and forth from excitement to sadness to eagerness. Fifty-seven days—every single 32nd MP was ready for the next step. Finally, at 2130, we loaded the plane—a United Airlines 747. As I walked towards the plane with my M16, 9mm, and all of my battle gear, I felt like I was in an ominous movie.

Stephen King couldn't have depicted an eerier scene: The night approached and the distant sound of thunder rumbled through the massive black clouds billowing overhead. The air was filled with static electricity both from the storm and from our own pulsing emotions.

As we marched out of the hangar in a snaking, single-file line to climb into the belly of the plane, a bolt of lightning streaked the sky, followed by a booming thunder, and then rain began to dampen our uniforms.

Being the last squad to load the airline, I could see the 130 other soldiers from our company spread out over 100 meters, trudging one person behind the other through the storm to the huge plane that awaited us.

We were on our way to war, and I couldn't think of more suitable weather to foreshadow our future.

The flight to our layover in Amsterdam took a little over seven hours. The airline attendants treated us like royalty. They let us walk around throughout the flight, including takeoff and landing. I stood as we landed just because I could. They let us keep our seats and tray tables in whatever position we wanted, and we never had to buckle up. I slept through most of the flight, thanks to the Dramamine that I had taken. We stopped briefly in Amsterdam to refuel and then headed to Kuwait.

When we landed in Camp Wolf, Kuwait, it was midnight and the weather was a balmy 80 degrees. It did not feel like the dry heat they briefed us about. I could have sworn I disembarked onto a humid Florida tarmac. My skin was wet with perspiration within minutes of stepping onto the soft sand.

We were ushered into a massive canvas tent after unloading the plane. We had a briefing and then were put into a smaller holding tent until 0600. My team attempted to get some shuteye, but the heat's intensity and excitement of the moment prohibited it.

Like clockwork, we loaded local buses to take us to Camp Virginia, Kuwait, at 0600. The Kuwaiti buses transported us into an alternate culture. The deep-red velvet curtains with their tassels reminded me of Aladdin's flying carpet. Beautiful Arabic language and foreign music blared from tinny speakers. The wind started to howl an hour into the three-hour drive. Soon, the sky began to darken, and a wall of sand rose from the horizon. The small sand particles slammed into our windows, sounding like someone was tapping tiny pins against the glass. As we entered the storm, our visibility diminished to mere inches. The sand's thickness made it impossible to see the bus in front of us. Miraculously, our driver trucked on like nothing was happening.

The sandstorm was still kicking up a lot of dust as we pulled into Camp Virginia. We wore goggles and any cloth we could find to cover our noses and mouths while we unloaded our equipment into the tents.

My company dispersed into three different tents. My tent included all 65 soldiers from third and fourth platoons. We crashed the second we were done unloading our gear, drained by the unforgiving heat and lack of sleep. We tried to relax with sweat pouring down our bodies. After leaving the Wisconsin spring, the 125-degree air felt like a raging inferno. Since our cots were thousands of miles away on a ship, we slept with our PT mats and sleeping bags directly on the sand-covered wood floor. As I rolled on my side, gobs of packed-in sand scratched my earlobes like fingernails. I went outside with a rag and brushed off as much sand as I could and then went to sleep. That was the last time I left my ears exposed to sandstorms. With no air conditioning and the unrelenting heat, we left the tent doors open, hoping for a cool breeze. Unfortunately, the occasional breezes brought malicious sand. Waking up with granules in my hair, ears, eyes, nose, and every other crevice I was blessed with was not a pleasant experience.

After a while, my squad and Phair mustered up enough energy to go to lunch. The chow hall was a half-mile walk through thick, loose sand. Camp Virginia didn't need roads, as you could drive anywhere you wanted across the desert terrain. Putting on our full uniform and trudging under the scorching sun was torment. At that point, I didn't even care about food—I would have rather starved than hiked to the chow hall for every meal.

Inside our tent. My bed is the one on the right. I have my poncho liner up as a sand block.
Murray is on the left with Hart next to him. May 2003.

KUWAIT

You have not converted a man because you have silenced him.
—John Vicount

The Kuwaiti desert wasn't like the common image of rolling sand dunes. Kuwait's barren lands were as flat as Illinois farmlands, dotted with an occasional tumbling thorn bush. The constant, cursed winds provided a Catch-22—a respite from the oppressive heat, with dreadful, blowing sand. The perpetual dust in Kuwait's sky was comparable to that of Los Angeles smog. Even on cloudless days, the sky was nowhere near my hometown Wisconsin blue, but rather tan from flying sand. The sand's fine texture was like weightless Turkish coffee and white flour, creating disastrous sand walls. Imagine the mess of one bag of flour. Now multiply that by billions, and that's what Kuwait was like.

Our tent's floor lay about three inches off the ground. All kinds of critters claimed the dark quarters underneath: insects, rats, mice, snakes, and scorpions.

My deep sleep was interrupted around 0330 on one of the scorching-hot nights. A mouse had crawled onto the floorboard by my tousled brown hair. I opened my eyes to find Hart, Phair, Verbsky, and Freier lurching over my sleeping area with their knife blades shining in the flashlights' faint glow. They were on the hunt for the mini-mouse as if it were the insurgents who were slaughtering our fellow troops. I could see their thirst for blood in their vengeful eyes, crinkled foreheads, and their defensive posture. They were hurling gear left and right and were hissing orders at each other. "You, get over there and flank him," "I think I just saw his tail, bring me the bucket to catch him," "Phair, he's headed your way, be ready!" "Quick, throw the pillow here to scare him out!"

Instead of getting up to help, I rolled my eyes and turned on my side to gather more shut-eye. Their shuffling feet, angry whispers, and sporadic flashlight beams didn't keep me up for long. Sgt. Hart said to me the next morning, "Naylor, I'm in trouble, if that's how you sleep."

"What do you mean?"

"You slept through the entire mouse hunt. You didn't move a bit."

"Trust me, I didn't sleep through it. I decided not to get up because you guys were acting like crazy, blood-thirsty lunatics. I didn't want to get in the way of your cops and robber game," I responded.

"Well, that's good—because I don't want you sleeping through a fight or something," he said, cracking a smiling.

Returning his grin, I said, " You don't have anything to worry about. But if four burly soldiers can't even catch a little mouse, that doesn't bode well for me, now does it?"

Finding it uncomfortable to sleep on the centimeter-thick sleeping pad, I went to the PX a few days after our arrival to purchase a $15 foam mattress and $4 pillow. The comfort was well worth the investment. A few weeks later, while scrounging through a heap of goodies other soldiers had left behind before they convoyed north to Iraq, I found a six-inch tall wooden box that fit my mattress perfectly. The acquisition of these items, plus our newly acquired AC, provided the perfect sleeping conditions. At last, I could recover after the daily heat-induced daze.

On one typical sunny day, a wall of sand dropped on us without warning. Most sandstorms approached from the distance giving us time to prepare, but not this time. I had just returned from chow before many of my fellow tent-mates. As I settled down to read my book inside the tent, I could hear the wind pick up outside. The sand whipped against the canvas, begging to come inside. The dozen of us in the tent hustled to secure the flaps on our doorways. The atmosphere's electrical energy inten-sified, making my hair stick straight up. Within seconds, the air conditioner's metal vent sparked against one of the center poles, audible over the hum of the storm. Our tent flapped wildly in the wind, causing the vertical poles to come out of their designated holes. With three soldiers to a pole, we braced them against the flapping canvas, tearing circular holes in the tent every time it slammed onto the poles' tips.

Slowly, the rest of my sandblasted, disheveled, pissed-off tent-mates stumbled in from chow. Most of them were caught in the storm without protection. A lucky few climbed under vehicles to wait out the storm.

My living space was just big enough to hold my gear and sleeping box. I slept between Murray, the pack rat, and rancid-smelling Welch. At times, the smell was strong enough to make me gag. To combat it, I erected a wall of empty water boxes. It worked, and as a bonus, it made my area private and cozy. I had a bona fide wall!

Scrounging was taken to a whole new level when Sgt. Henry and Spc. Fairbanks—our treasured ingenious duo—claimed an old rundown Iraqi bus. It sat next to our company's AO for about a month without anyone taking ownership. Being the innovative fellas that they were, they hot-wired it and drove it in circles because the steering wheel was chained to the floor. Eventually, Henry—with his blazing red hair and stocky short stature—used his Leatherman to saw through the chain. Soon after, Henry and Fairbanks gathered up fourth platoon and took us for a joy ride around Camp Virginia. We waved, hooted, and hollered at everyone we passed. We pulled over at an old Humvee graveyard. Henry used his brawn to crawl inside an upside-down Humvee. His red face matched the color of his red hair, his thick fingers turned white from clinging to the steering wheel so that they wouldn't hang to the ground, and his face was elongated oddly from earth's gravitational pull. It was one of those silly moments in life when everyone was laughing uncontrollably. Fairbanks—fourth platoon's primary auto tinker—kept the energy alive with his whoops, winks, and a giant grin. This valiant, optimistic, and courteous man made him one of my favorite people.

Without laundry machines, the dirty clothes piled high until we were forced to sit outside and hand-wash them using a bucket of sudsy water. I used laundry detergent I had put in an old Gatorade bottle while back home.

Like pioneers using rivers to wash their clothes, Kirking and I grabbed our dirty, sandy, soiled duds, buckets, and detergent and hiked over to the shower trailers. A Kuwaiti man sauntered over to us with a shit-eating grin on his face. Treating us like fresh meat, he flirted with his broken English by flowering Kirking and me with compliments.

"You beautiful. You movie stars? You marry Iraqi, it be me, OK?"

We were flattered, but after refusing to flirt back, he lost his mojo and dejectedly walked away. Moments later, a nasty, old sergeant from a different company came over to seduce us. Kirking and I refrained from making eye contact and maintained quipped responses to motivate the man to leave. Unable to recognize social cues, it took him forever to move on.

One time, Sgt. Hart accompanied me on a laundry adventure. We were having a great time laughing and joking around when he pulled out his underwear with a skid mark on them. I asked, "Are you a grown man or a toddler?"

He looked at me with his eyebrow raised. His grin turned into a sneer as he said, "Guess who's going to wring them out when I'm done washing them."

My surprised eyes met his as I pleaded, "You're kidding, right? There's no way in hell I'm touching those disgusting boxers."

"Specialist, that's an order. You will wring out my underwear, or you will deal with the consequences," he said authoritatively.

Trying to not let his crazy antics get to me, I gave in and said, "Yes, Sergeant." After wringing out his boxers, I scrubbed my hands in my own soapy water.

Even though it was degrading, it came with benefits. Hart was in a good mood for the rest of the day and even begged me to tell my parents about the underwear incident in the letter I was writing before bedtime.

Living in a multi-gender tent was challenging. Most of the time, I changed down to my skivvies in the wide open. I became a professional at changing my bra and underwear under my clothes or under my blankets. On really hot nights, I wore my sports bra and PT shorts. That didn't last long. Modesty beat out comfort. After a few weeks, we received strict orders to cover sports bras and boxers. The rules became even more restrictive when we were banned from reading *Cosmopolitan* and *Maxim* magazines because they were considered offensive. My hunch is they upset our overly conservative commander.

As if these inane restrictions weren't enough, we females were sick of being treated as though we didn't have minds of our own. Along with the underwear washing, we couldn't go anywhere without another soldier, and sometimes that soldier had to be male. At the same time, the men could go anywhere they wanted by themselves. Imagine being a self-sustaining adult one minute, and the next minute, you had to ask for permission to go to the bathroom, to shower, to walk to chow, to go for a walk. It was demeaning. Except for the lieutenancy, men had every leadership position in our platoon. It was maddening considering our numbers were virtually equal. Our inexperienced female lieutenant, Weir, lacked the know-how and courage to advocate for the rest of us. We finally asked Phair for a meeting. Speaking on behalf of the other eleven females,

I said, "We feel like we're being treated like children. We have no independence. We're getting told what to do everywhere we go by random sergeants. We can't go anywhere by ourselves because we're female, which is ridiculous because we're on a safe American base."

Sfc. Phair's response wasn't what we wanted to hear. He said, "I hear what you're saying, but you need to get used to living this way because it's not going to change. It's the way the Army works, especially when preparing for war."

I responded, "You understand, this double standard is going to wear us down, right? We need some autonomy to have self-worth."

"I get it, Naylor, but you have no idea what kind of pressure I have on me to always make decisions. It's exhausting."

And things didn't change for the duration of our deployment.

We didn't turn the AC on during the day because it didn't make a dent against the excruciating heat. With an average temperature of 130 degrees and the scorching sun, the inside of the tent reached around 150 to 170 degrees. We built a "porch" on the backside of our tent as a cooler option. We stretched camo netting overhead, built a plywood floor, and set up abandoned cots for seating. I drew a cribbage board and checkers on the floorboards, and we used different colored bottle caps as our pieces. Miraculously, over time, we acclimated to the heat and our energy levels returned to normal.

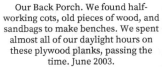

Our Back Porch. We found half-working cots, old pieces of wood, and sandbags to make benches. We spent almost all of our daylight hours on these plywood planks, passing the time. June 2003.

There was no getting used to going to the bathroom in that heat, though. The porta-potties, clumped in threes, reeked in the scorching daylight heat. We were forced to buy our own toilet paper, as Camp Victory didn't supply any. Instead of wasting my money, I stole napkins from the chow hall to wipe my undercarriage. *What kind of military ships soldiers to war without providing this basic necessity?* The constant sweat made it nearly impossible to pull my pants up and down. My uniform felt like sweat-soaked cling wrap. My utility belt made it even more difficult to pull my pants back up. I was short of breath after every trip to those hot-boxes. Without proper bathrooms, I used bottled water to brush my teeth, a wet wipe to wash my face, and I put my contacts in while they sat on my lap.

Oh my, the sweat. It was nonstop. When the blessed winds were strong enough to dry us off, salt crystals covered our limbs and clothes. I could wipe the white powder from my body. Even though I drank about ten liters of water a day, I barely peed and my funnel lay idle all day, collecting the Kuwaiti dust.

The lack of provisions didn't end with toilet paper. During our stay in Kuwait, my company would intermittently send small convoys to Camp Doha for additional supplies. Camp Doha resembled a U.S. military base with its fast food restaurants and huge PX. I was allowed to go twice during my time in Kuwait. The first time I spent over $100 on army essentials. I bought another pad to put in my helmet, socks, undershirts, sunglasses, sunscreen, and gloves. We should need for nothing, being the richest country and best-equipped army in the world. That, however, was not the case. At the onset of the war, we had machinists from back home producing metal plates to fit into our vests. Later in the deployment, we hired Iraqis to install metal diamond plates onto our unarmored vehicles.

Our time in Kuwait was routine and regimented. We woke at 0600 every day. Once in a while, I chose to wake up at 0500 to go to aerobics and yoga for two hours. The classes were led by other soldiers at Camp Virginia. If I arose at 0600, I put on my DCUs, ate a Power Bar, brushed my teeth, and cleaned weapons. Next, we attended a two-hour class led by our company's leaders. The classes were designed to keep us busy, but most were poorly planned and boring. We learned Arabic from a non-Arabic speaking civilian who worked on the base, and tactics, map reading, arm and hand signals, and other monotonous skills. After class, I either sat around until lunch or signed up for the computers and ate at a sub shop. After lunch, I entertained myself until supper by reading a book, watching a movie, attempting to call home, or playing games. I took my showers after supper and attended our 2030 squad meeting. Lights out was at 2200. I chose to shower between 1730 or 1800 because there was never a line. Showers were almost as difficult as using the porta-potty. For about a week, nothing but a drizzle oozed out of the shower head, and at times the water flow would stop abruptly, leaving us full of soap suds for minutes at a time. The humidity made it impossible to dry off. The second I toweled off, I began to sweat. One night, I walked out of the trailer into 106 degrees and got chills because of the intense heat and humidity from a moment before.

Verbsky's mundane squad meetings were usually the perfect lullaby to coax me to sleep, but sometimes we received noteworthy information, like the Rules of Engagement—ROE. The ROE in Iraq stated that U.S. soldiers could not shoot until shot upon. "Wait a second," I asked. "Does that mean that even though we know who our enemies are, we can't kill them until they start shooting at us?"

Ssg. Verbsky looked at me and replied, "Yes, Naylor. That's exactly what that means." There was a palpable inhalation as my fellow squad members internalized the information. Although

Verbsky's the kind of leader that every soldier wants—cool, calm, collected, and honorable—even he couldn't alter orders.

Murray growled under his breath, "Screw that." Beyond Murray's quiet objection, no one said a word because orders were orders.

At one of the more alarming squad meetings, Verbsky said, "Soldiers are dying on a daily basis by either sniper or grenade. The Military Police and Infantry are having a hell of a time developing the Iraqi police force and army because they have to start from scratch. Additionally, the former Iraqi Army that disbanded a couple of days ago said that if the U.S. doesn't give them their pensions in one week, they are going to re-band and take Iraq back."

I left the meeting with a sour taste in my mouth. I repeated my mantra: *This is God's will.* I hoped things would be different by the time we arrived in Baghdad.

The staggering amount of downtime was tedious. I had a five-day stretch without a book to read. I sat staring at the sand, the camo netting, the others quietly talking, reading, or resting. I silently waited for someone to talk to, tried to invent something to do, begged others to play checkers with me, roamed around the patio area, anything to make the time move faster. My wandering mind pined for home, and I wondered if other soldiers had the same yearning. *How are they coping?*

To avoid another book drought, I proactively created a library by my bunk. All 65 soldiers in our tent caught wind and were swapping books left and right, thanking me for the ingenious idea.

Shortly after I established our tent's library, Camp Virginia erected a small tent for MWR—Morale, Welfare, and Recreation—which contained a TV, books, games, and four olive-green decades-old rotary phones. We were given 15 minutes maximum to call home, including the time it took to dial the phone card and hassle with the conversation's three-second delay. Sometimes, I waited in line for two hours to call home. Hearing my parents' voices made it well worth the wait. I felt revived and optimistic after our conversations.

As my company's tenure in Camp Virginia lengthened, so did our missions. We were ordered to contribute to the various duties that kept the camp running smoothly. My first duty on base was guarding the AHA or ammo holding area. I reported to a tiny hut outside the AHA at 0730 with my M16 in hand. I sat with Lyons, a soldier from second platoon, for eight hours, observing the world. Camel herds of all colors meandered through the desert. Large, flying black and red ants four times bigger than those from Wisconsin crawled and flew around me. Two gargantuan black beetles the size of a badminton birdie burrowed through the sand. A Chinook helicopter landed 100 meters away from the hut. The bombardment of swirling dust lasted for 30 minutes. I couldn't see the tip of my nose through the thick cloud. I put on my goggles and breathed through a handkerchief until the air was clear.

After I was done with my shift, I went to the center of Camp Victory to watch a USO cover-band called US Express. The United Services Organization caters to troops with concerts and MWR amenities.

My next gig brought me to the convoy gate. I stood in a tower and checked with the lead vehicle in every convoy. I inquired about and annotated their unit and number of troops and then sent them through. The convoys varied from five to 100 vehicles. Each one sent the powdery dust into endless cloud cover.

The last job I had in Kuwait was guarding the perimeter in a tower with Sgt. Henry. His zest for life and various passions surprised me. I assumed Henry was a shallow, muscle-headed flirt, but when he unpacked scientific magazines and we talked about his love for scuba diving, I realized my first impression was wrong. Beyond Henry's entertaining personality, the 12-hour tower duty dragged on like a never-ending day. I had looked through his magazines before half of the day was through and ran out of interesting conversation before that. I spent too much time in my own head during the silences between our conversations. What a waste of energy and manpower. There we were, in the middle of a desert in a friendly country, waiting to get attacked by a non-existent enemy. AHA duty proved more entertaining with its various little critters. The only fauna from tower guarding was a bat I found in our cooler, which I threw in the dumpster to feed off the garbage. Thank goodness Sgt. Henry was there to break up the monotony. They might have found me dead from boredom had I conducted the duty on my own.

At last, on May 27th, 74 days into our deployment, our mission was finalized. During our nightly squad meeting, Verbsky said, "We're headed to Baghdad to conduct law and order and train the Iraqi police officers." *I knew it! I am destined to go to Baghdad. Wow, I'm actually excited.* "But," he continued, "it's really dangerous in Iraq right now. Every convoy going from Kuwait to Iraq is getting shot at, and two more soldiers died today. Apparently, there are motorcycle gangs in Baghdad, and the gangs use anything to hurt the U.S., including grappling hooks, of all things." My excitement deflated to an anxious flutter.

Our vehicles finally arrived from the states on June 23rd, 101 days into our deployment. It took our vehicles a month and a half to get to Kuwait. The first ship they used out of Texas started to sink. The Humvees were unloaded, transported by train to the Carolinas, put on a different ship, and then that ship got caught in two different tropical storms. It was a miracle our vehicles survived at all. Their arrival meant one thing: we would soon leave for Baghdad.

Knowing that our departure was quickly approaching, I wrote the following cryptic email home:

I wanted to let you all know that we may be leaving this area shortly. When we leave here, communication is going to be limited. I really wish I could tell you where I'm going and what I'm doing, but I can't. I bet if you think about it hard enough, you know where the center of the action is, and what my job is. You'll figure it out. My team may be going on a pretty cool mission first. It's getting to the point that it's all I think about, which is good because I need to get into the mindset of it all. Goodbye for now.

To my parents, I added:

I just wanted to thank you for raising me the way you did and for being such wonderful people. I am the luckiest person I know. Thank you. This is the last email I will send out, so I wanted to tell you how much I love you, and how much you mean to me. It's indescribable. I'll be safe and take every precaution—don't worry. Sgt. Hart is very careful and he will do all he can to ensure that we are safe. The place we're going is the safest part of the city, as far as we know. So it could be worse. Remember that. Take care and say goodbye to grandparents and family. Thanks.

I called home two days later to say my final goodbyes, not knowing when or if we would get a chance to call again. There were spilled tears and many "I love yous."

The next day, my team and I prepared our vehicle for the trip north. We took our time loading the Humvee and trailer. Hart and I concocted a bungee-cord hanging mechanism for our CD player. It was unsuccessful. No matter how much cushion we provided, the Humvee was too rough, causing the CD to skip. I found a good spot for my funnel, which we dubbed the PUD—Personal Urinary Device. We wrote our alias names on the vehicle with chalk. My name was Xena, the warrior princess.

Our Humvee was all set, the sun was setting, and I was ready to call it quits and get some rest before our trek north. Then, our ammo arrived. We had to count and divide the bullets, explosives, and pyro with the beams of our flashlights over the precarious sand. Then our armorer, Aber, passed us each our share as the night enveloped our tired minds. We filled our magazines and loaded our weapons. *Bring on the enemy. We are ready.*

Just when I thought I could finally get some shut-eye, Glenn ordered our company to line up the 55 vehicles in preparation for the next day's convoy. I cringed and mounted up. It took 30 minutes to corral the giant circus. We thought we were all settled, and then Glenn had us do it again. *Argh! Sometimes I hate the military.* Headlights pierced the dark desert terrain for another 30 minutes, shining their lights this way and that until once again, we were in a single-file line. Finally, at 2130, the drivers were released to get ready for bed. I dragged my bed box next to the truck, brushed my teeth, wiped my face with a baby wipe, and fell into a staggered sleep around 2300. Murray slept on the roof of the Humvee, and Sgt. Hart slept on the hood. My alarm cut through the pitch black at 0300. It was time to PMCS the vehicle and prepare to move north.

My platoon of proud Wisconsinites in Kuwait, right outside of our living area. I'm the fifth soldier from the left in the back row. Notice the camo netting behind us. This was to block most of the sun, but let the breeze through. May 2003.

PART II
LIBERATION

"The soldier above all other people prays for peace, for he must suffer and bear the deepest wounds and scars of war."
~ *General Douglas MacArthur*

IRAQ

Gradually, we 32nd MP company soldiers rose from our slumber, prepared our vehicles, and sat in the convoy line with our vehicles humming to life. The dark morning was illuminated by each diesel vehicle starting its engine. The sound of a bee swarm interrupted the pitch-black silence. The anticipatory energy grew. Seriousness was etched on our faces and echoed in our conversations. This was it. We were stepping over the line from soldier to veteran.

At 0430, our vehicles started the parade north. As the rear vehicle, my team watched the convoy stretch out in front of us like a growing earthworm. I was all jitters when I pressed my foot down on the gas. I had the same nervous energy as I did at a game-clinching ace, or a save in the soccer net. My competitive nature kicked in, and I promised myself I wasn't going to lose this time, either.

Three hours later, we entered Iraq. A measly trench measuring about 15-feet deep and ten-feet wide was all it took to enter into a war zone. As we ventured across the border, I whispered to myself, *Game on.* I grew electrified and tense. The elusive enemy could be anywhere.

Within seconds, we approached a small village. Shepherds herded their sheep adjacent to the road, children waved and ran alongside our convoy as if we were in a parade, adults stood up eyeing our convoy with apathy, camels grazed in the distance, and wild dogs ran rampant. A solitary man stood five feet from our passing vehicles. He leered and presented his middle finger. Our first taste of hatred.

A tiny, dirt-covered four-year-old girl was standing in a garbage-laden field. Trash rose from the ground and swirled in small cyclones while our massive convoy zoomed past. The girl's dark, ragged dress barely covered her dusty, spindly knees. Her knotty black hair looked like a bird's nest while she hunched over to pick up the garbage. She ignored us as we sailed past, her tiny little arms filled to capacity with pieces of cardboard, colorful plastics, and cans. *What kind of wretched country allows their daughters to stand amid such filth? This is why I'm here. I'm here to help little girls like this live a better life.* My journey took on a newfound relevancy and meaning. I was fighting to better the Iraqi lives.

I was comfortable dodging the animals and humans who haphazardly crossed the roadway after a few hours of driving. I could not, however, wrap my mind around the eerie Iraqi or two walking through the desolate desert hundreds of miles from civilization. Like a mirage, they would appear on the horizon waving as our monstrous military machine flew past their barren existence.

After driving for 14 hours, we stopped at a guarded refueling station, Camp Cedar, to rest for the night. Our vehicles pulled about 20 feet off the main thoroughfare, leaving a wide enough berth for military vehicles to pass us as we slept. Exhausted and sore, soldiers emerged from the metal beasts. My squad gathered for a supper of MREs and small talk. On the verge of collapsing, I dragged my cot out of the Humvee and lay down. For the second night in a row, we slept under the stars. Convoys drove past us as the hours melted away, covering us with blankets of dust.

Once again, my alarm jolted me upright at 0300 to begin my PMCS routine. I cringed as I shook the dust off my things, wondering why my arms burned. Scores of red welts covered every inch of my exposed skin. Bug bites. I was their feast through the night. What more could my weary body handle? To make matters worse, Verbsky told us that terrorists were more likely to attack us during the next leg of the drive north. My heart was racing and my mind was filled with fearful thoughts and what-if scenarios as the convoy got underway.

Day two tested my driving skills. Thirty miles of highway had been bombed beyond repair, causing my company to drive off-road. We crept forward at 20 miles per hour. It was treacherous navigating the pockmarked earth as clouds of swirling dust enveloped our vehicles. As though driving through dense fog, the visibility was reduced to mere feet. After 15 miles and a few near misses, we stopped to rest, refuel, and empty our bladders. I was standing next to my Humvee with the door open using my PUD to pee in privacy when a long convoy drove past. Once again, the dust cloaked us in powder. The three vehicles in my squad, including my own, pulled rear security. We were about 100 yards away from the rest of our company's vehicles. When the air cleared, we realized our company left without us. We were left in the dust with the rest of the 32nd miles ahead of us.

The huge, three-foot-deep potholes, thick sand, and obstacles around every bend whizzed past us as my squad doubled our speed to catch up. It was imperative that I maintained a 20-foot distance from the vehicle in front of me. If I got too close, I risked rear-ending them. If I got too far away, the impervious cloud would conceal the Humvee's hazy silhouette, and I risked losing their trail. We did not want to be a lone Humvee in the middle of a hostile country. With the help of Murray and Sgt. Hart, I stayed on the right path and avoided a collision.

After we caught up to our company, the drive became rather pleasant. When we got to our fuel point, we saw our first Iraqi

Bazaar, which we affectionately called a Haji Hut. Most of the soldiers in Iraq used the slang term *Haji*—which is a term used for Muslims who made the pilgrimage to Mecca—to describe an Iraqi. The Haji Hut was full of Iraqi men beckoning us to buy their crap. "Hey, misses; hey, mister." I had never been to a bazaar and didn't know the etiquette. Their incessant squawking was making the tension in my chest rise. To alleviate my throbbing head, I slid around my Humvee to the far side. I needed to get away from the constant flow of Arabic and broken English to find peace of mind before I embarked on another stressful leg of our journey. I yearned for a quiet cool place to find solace and sanity. Instead, I leaned against the side of my rough, hard Humvee in the sweltering heat with 50 pounds of gear squeezing my insides and shut my eyes to escape into my delightful imagination. I let the cool waters of Marl Lake cascade over my festering body, hoping to find some respite in my own thoughts. The pressure in my head, my bones, and my muscles melted away.

South-bound troops approached us to chat and jolted me out of my daydream. They had gotten into a firefight with the Iraqis just north of our location on the same route we were using. The pain in my head returned in full force. I could feel my eyes pounding and my blood pressure rise. *How can driving get any worse?* Somehow, every leg of the journey proved more difficult than the one before.

A few short hours after we hit the road, my bladder was ready to burst. I couldn't stop the entire convoy just to pee. I had to either piss myself or come up with an ingenious solution. After much deliberation and planning with Sgt. Hart, I used my PUD and a water bottle.

I told Murray not to look down while I unbuttoned two buttons on my pants and inserted the large end of the funnel. The other skinnier end found its way into an empty water bottle. I hoisted myself a little higher in the seat to have a better angle to pee downwards. Lacking cruise control, I kept my foot on the gas and had Hart help with the steering as I relieved myself in the bottle. I did it. Without a drip in my pants, I peed into a bottle while driving. After I was done, I handed the bottle to Sgt. Hart who threw it out his window. That's what he gets for making me wring out his filthy underwear. *Welcome to the brother/sisterhood bonds of war.*

The Iraqi nothingness with the shadow of my Humvee. I took this during our second break in the middle of nowhere. I asked Murray to pose at his gun. Notice how he's facing backward due to us being the last Humvee in the convoy. 6/27/03

BAGHDAD

You don't know where to focus your anger and hate. It gets
focused on every single Iraqi.

~*The Ground Truth*

Baghdad's beauty surpassed that of the barren desert. The abundant vegetation offered a much-needed distraction from the monotony of driving through sand for almost 30 hours in two days. My sight was starved of greenery the last two months, and I soaked in the landscape as we drove along the Tigris River. The smell of lilacs and foliage wafted through the air.

Our first destination was Baghdad International Airport—BIAP. Our Command Sergeant Major—CSM—briefed us. He said, "Welcome to Baghdad. I hope you had a safe journey. I'm sure you're exhausted and ready to settle into your compound. Your new AO—area of operation—will be in the Green Zone. Take a few days to get established. In the meantime, I'll be in contact with your Commander to explain your mission. You may go when your company is done refueling." We left within 30 minutes to settle into our new home, which was a resort formerly owned by one of Saddam's identified henchmen.

The Green Zone included two of Saddam's palaces, his parade grounds, multiple army compounds, and some Iraqi homes. It was located in central Baghdad and surrounded by 15-foot-tall cement barricades. We unloaded our personal and sensitive gear after arriving at 1800. Six other females and I were directed to a nine-by-twelve-foot cinder-block room with one door and one small window that was about two by three feet. With six soldiers, our personal gear, totes, and cots, there wasn't an inch of space left in the room. Our six cots extended across the width of the room with our gear piled high at the foot of our beds. Our new home quickly took on the funk of our body odor, sweat, and lack of showers. Sleeping in the stifling heat was often interrupted by others' elbows and knees as we rolled over to find a comfortable spot. I dozed in out of sleep while lying in my own pool of sweat.

The south side of our compound housed the main resort building, which sustained damage from two large U.S. bombs at some point before we arrived. Four ballroom-sized guest rooms, a kitchen with a dumbwaiter, and many other nondescript bombed-out rooms occupied the main floor. The intact portions of the resort building oozed wealth with their lavishly ordained marble ceilings, floors, and walls, and ornate crown molding. There were rooftop rooms as well. Four of the steps going to the roof were missing large chunks, but the rest of the staircase maintained its integrity and was safe to use. The stunning rooftop view of the Tigris River looked like a postcard with its date-filled palm trees, calm waters, and the stately buildings running alongside the historical estuary. The building's grounds had two fountains and a carport. A bit farther north in our compound, a large pool was filled with a thick, green-brown liquid, and two dead birds floated in the filth. Within a month and a half, hired Iraqis cleaned out the pool and got it running. I became addicted to swimming and sunbathing. The refreshing water offered a sense of freedom in the land of hell.

A pool house lined the west side of the pool and a smaller building sat on the north side. This is where our tactical operations center—TOC—was located. Twenty small buildings occupied the northernmost part of the compound, which was most likely where the workers, butlers, and maids had lived and was where we stayed the first night at our compound. After the first night, the three other platoons lived in this region of the compound for the remainder of our time at Camp Mustang, with three to four soldiers in each building. In between the pool and the southern buildings was a tree grove and another small building where our commander and first sergeant lived.

The pool in our compound. This photo was taken within the first two weeks of our Baghdad stay. The pool is still a gross, green, murky liquid. The locker rooms are on the far-left side of the diving board. I took this picture while standing on the steps of the building where we lived. July 2003.

Let's rewind a bit to our first morning in Baghdad. After tossing and turning in my sweat all night and defending myself against my cot-mates' probing limbs, I woke up because of an intense urge to defecate. I had no idea where to go. Being from the Northwoods of Wisconsin, I went to my comfort zone, the tree grove. I leaned up against a tree, relieved myself, and picked up some old leaves and bark off the ground to wipe. Later in the deployment, Rausch, a soldier from first platoon, had mentioned that there was a lot of poop back in the tree grove. I smiled and laughed. Apparently, I wasn't the only one that needed a toilet that morning.

I returned to the stinky, overcrowded room to find my company hustling around me. I had no idea what was going on, but everyone was running around like they had an important mission to do. I was the only one who appeared to be out of the loop. I asked Sgt. Hart, "What's going on?"

"Nothing. Just getting ready." he curtly responded while hustling away. Again, I looked around me, trying to figure out what I missed.

I asked Murray, "Dude, what's going on?" He simply walked away in a trance.

After bugging Hart one more time, I sat down, dumbfounded. He came back a few minutes later and said, "Gather your stuff and put it in the vehicle." You know how I feel about obscure orders...I bitterly grabbed my stuff and methodically packed the Humvee like we had been doing for the last two days. Hart ran over and said, "Just throw it in, and let's get going."

I took a deep break and asked through gritted teeth, "Can you please tell me what's going on?"

"Naylor, relax. We're just driving to the south side of the compound to move into the large building. Load up and let's go," he answered. Relief set in, and my frustration floated away. *Why couldn't he have said that from the get-go?*

Our Humvee looked like a hillbilly mobile as we haphazardly threw our cots and totes in any groove and crevice they might fit. Our hatch was wide open, and our personal effects were busting out. We gingerly crept the tenth of a mile toward the south side of the compound—careful not to lose any of our possessions. Phair assigned the males from the three squads to three different rooms, yet crammed the 13 females into one space. The rooms were huge, but not mammoth. At this point, it didn't matter that the max number of men per room was seven and we were packed like sardines. We were determined to make our new abode with a beautiful marble floor, a burned charcoal-black ceiling, and two marbled walls our home. The other two walls had been blown out from the bomb's blast months ago. Our nonexistent back wall looked into the interior of the building, which was littered with burned debris, chunks of marble and cement, and metal poles. The front of the room faced our unmanicured, grassy lawn with shards of glass, bricks, metal, and marble jutting out between the sweet, green blades of grass.

Pieces of the building were embedded in the tough palm tree trunks that surrounded the complex.

The second day in Baghdad, we cleaned our room and moved in. We swept and washed the floor, found some shelves in the rubble, and pulled down parts of the ceiling, which would have posed a sleeping hazard.

In the process, Fairbanks and Henry were busy engineering two shower stalls and a wash point. Their two concocted showers were made out of ponchos that were wrapped around four long pieces of vertical scaffolding that had blown from the building during the bombing. Then, Fairbanks—being the genius that he is—connected a piece of hose to the irrigation system in the yard. We put the hose inside the ceiling-less ponchoed water stalls, and *voila*: we had a shower! After the U.S. helicopter pilots figured out that females showered with no roof over their naked bodies, the pilots flew slower and lower to catch a sneak peek. This happened to me on multiple occasions, but all I allowed them to see was the bird. Our wash point was made from a sink we found in the basement. We attached a hose and then propped a mirror on it.

Our shower stalls. Thanks to Kirking for her *Where's Waldo* pose. Notice how we put the shower stalls conveniently next to the outdoor water fountain. This was how we found the water supply, and it also offered a nice shelf to place our toiletries while showering. July 2003.

After putting our showers and sink together, we cleared a small yard space in front of our room, eliminating the safety hazards previously mentioned.

Two gunshots interrupted our domestication. Being new to war, we couldn't decipher the proximity and distance, so we instinctively went into combat mode. Phair, Hart, and Verbsky yelled, "Get down and stay down!"

Hart bellowed towards me, "Naylor, grab your gun and follow us. Stay back about ten meters and pull security." The four of us ran to the front gate, located on the opposite side of the building we occupied—a good 150 meters away. Crouching, I scanned around me, even though I couldn't see over the 13-foot plaster perimeter surrounding our compound. It wasn't until we reached the gate that we could look across the Tigris River, where we assumed the gunshots had come from. Phair ran to the entrance and peered around it with the muzzle of his rifle ahead of him. My heart raced. *Action already? We just got here!* We sat there for 20 minutes, waiting for something to happen. It didn't. We never figured out where the shots came from, or if they were aimed at us. The intermittent gunfire became all too familiar as our time in the Green Zone lengthened. We barely noticed it after a few weeks in.

Before the day's end, I toured the rest of our building. I walked down into the chasm-like basement, with its silent marble walls. Our army-issued flashlights barely pierced the ominous pitch-black air. It smelled like a damp cave, but with a hint of burnt particles. The basement was mostly intact. It included a movie theater with reels of film inside the reel room and nearly 75 lush, green padded seats. There was a slew of magnificent rooms with soaring ceilings, crown molding, and marble floors, six bathrooms, and a large kitchen.

The heat and day's work left me dehydrated and weak. I drank 11 liters of water and only used my PUD twice the entire day. It's a miracle humans can survive in that environment.

The weather mirrored that of Kuwait, with an average daytime temperature of 120 degrees or so and about 90 degrees during the night. The sky was clearer in Baghdad, but not as blue as back home.

Two of our initial rooms. The females were the center opening and third-squad males on the left. Notice all the building ruins piled in the foreground. You can also see the sunlight pouring into the back of our room due to the roof's holes. The gated window between our rooms housed a beautiful marble bathroom where we stored our extra ammo and gear. July 2004.

After enduring heat-induced insomnia for a couple of nights, I moved my cot outside to the sidewalk adjacent our room. I suspended a mosquito net over my cot to protect my skin from annoying critters. I also soaked my cot with water to cool down by evaporation. It was the only way I could lower my core temperature to find respite from the heat.

Struggling to fall asleep one night, the city came to life with gunshots. I watched through the mosquito net from the comfort of my cot as the sky lit up with tracers that crisscrossed the black expanse like sinister fireworks. *How many people were going to die during this spattering of gunfire? The bullets have to fall down at some point.* Going into the room to avoid falling bullets would have been the smart choice, but I didn't care. Transfixed, I enjoyed the show for two hours, knowing full well that for every tracer I saw, there were twice as many invisible bullets being shot without the glowing tip. The following day, we discovered that Saddam's sons, Uday and Qusay, had been killed, inspiring the celebratory shooting. The Iraqis often used that lethal mode to portray their joy or anger. Many times throughout our deployment, we heard gunshots that were not a product of war, but rather of emotions—a death in the family, a soccer win or loss, a family wedding, or some other celebration known only to those involved.

Once we switched to night shift, I moved back into the room to avoid sleeping under the hot Iraqi sun. I complained to Hart and Reynolds, "I hate being in the female hooch. The day-shift girls make a lot of noise and keep me up. It's hard enough to get any sleep when it's a hundred and thirty degrees, but now I have their constant noise to deal with."

Phair said, "You should move your cot into our hooch. We're all sleeping at the same time. It would only make sense for you to sleep in there as well." Hart nodded in agreement.

I laughed and said, "Yeah, right," thinking he was joking around.

"No, I'm serious, Naylor. You should do it," Phair responded.

"No kidding," quipped Hart. "It would save you a lot of headaches."

"Uh, OK. I will. Thanks!" I said with hesitation, unsure if they were messing with me.

When we returned that morning, I moved my cot into the back of the men's hooch and woke up refreshed after a solid five hours of sleep. It was bizarre waking up with seven guys around me while I slept in my bra and underwear, but the awkwardness was worth a good night's sleep. When I woke up, Phair passed by and said, "You look sexy and miserable all at the same time." He knew when to maintain his professionalism and when to flirt.

His authoritative and friendly demeanor wasn't an easy balance to maintain in the military.

Halfway through August, we were given the "all clear" to sleep in the cool, bug-free basement. In hindsight, I hope the air quality won't leave us with lasting effects. I can't imagine it was entirely safe to sleep in the basement of a bombed-out building for seven months.

I was very excited about moving into my area in the basement. I had built my shelves out of 550 paracord and old boards that I had found. I also found a broken mirror and put that on the wall. My pillowcase is an old t-shirt and all the food on my shelf is what my friends and family sent overseas. August 17, 2003

Now, for my favorite part—our toilet. Within a few days of our Baghdad arrival, Sgt. Hoyord built a three-stall pooping toilet out of plywood. We put thick, black garbage bags in each hole. Even though we only changed the bags every couple of days, it didn't smell too bad because we continued to pee between a row of shrubs and the plaster wall that surrounded our compound. A piece of plywood acted as a bridge to walk over the dense shrubs and a clothes hamper held our soiled toilet paper. We received a glamorous porta-potty—the Rolls Royce of bathrooms—a month into our time in Baghdad. A month later, our tushes lucked out further when we finally fixed the plumbing in the basement. Using a real toilet felt like a forbidden luxury the first couple of times I had to go. I basked in the bliss of flushing and enjoyed the omission of human excrement odor lingering in the air.

Our meals also improved after our arrival. After a week of MREs, we got a mobile kitchen trailer—MKT. It only lasted a week or so before it broke. The cooks waited for parts that never came. The MKT provided a hot breakfast and dinner chow. It wasn't the best cuisine, but at least it was close to our AO, and it wasn't the preservative-filled MREs. A few days after our MKT crapped out, we started going over to Camp Viper, our Battalion's AO, to eat supper. Finally, edible food! It tasted fresh, had variety, and included healthy options. I equate a chow hall to a high school cafeteria—mass-produced food, but at least we had a choice in what we ate.

Camp Viper was a 10- to 15-minute walk from our compound. Nepali fighters, called Gurkhas, resided in a compound between us and our Battalion. Most days, we only had time to eat supper at Viper. I religiously ate a Power Bar for breakfast. For lunch, I either ate an MRE, Iraqi food, or food sent from home, which consisted of SpaghettiOs, Easy Mac, cans of soup, granola bars, and other preservative-filled snacks that could withstand the two-week trip.

Of course, the local food far exceeded the taste of Army food. I ate Iraqi pizza, kabobs, rotisserie chicken, pita bread with veggies, falafels, tikka, lamb, or eggs in a pita, and vegetables stuffed with rice in an oily sauce. I haven't found a falafel or eggs in a pita quite like the ones I enjoyed in Iraq. The Iraqis drank copious amounts of black tea, which they call chai. They consumed this hot beverage in tiny cups with a ratio of two parts tea to one part sugar. Their chai should not be confused with the traditional spiced chai tea. The flavors are worlds apart.

Our first mission outside the wire occurred on our second full day in Baghdad. We escorted our battalion Command Sergeant Major to Camp Marlboro—an army base in Baghdad about 40 minutes away. I felt more like a tourist than a soldier while driving through the diverse parts of Baghdad. Our convoy took us to the ghetto—otherwise known as Saddam City or Sadr City—and to the wealthy parts of Baghdad. Most of the kids in the ghetto liked us, but there were a few who didn't. The ones that didn't like us yelled at us in Arabic or chanted "Bad America." They threw rocks at us and gave us either a thumbs-down gesture or the middle finger.

Before we left Mustang base, we loaded our rifles—put a bullet in the chamber—so that we could use them instantaneously while driving through the city. That meant that as we entered another military installation, we had to unload our weapons to avoid an accidental discharge. I had only learned how to unload my weapon "basic training" style and not "war zone" style. With furrowed brows and a hissing voice, Sgt. Hart showed me how to pull out the magazine, unload the chamber, and put the magazine back in, ready to use in a moment's notice on his own rifle. He did all of this as the CSM watched with an amused expression on his face. *I'm such a frickin' idiot! I fed his bias against women and looked helpless when this is not who I am. I get stuff done, and I get it done right.* To make matters worse, when I attempted to clear my rifle, my magazine jammed. I couldn't pull it out of the M16. Hart assisted by pulling the magazine out while I held onto the loaded rifle. He sounded like pissed-off Batman when he asked, "Why the hell did you use a magazine that stuck in your rifle?"

Red-faced and guilt-ridden, I humbly responded, "I don't know, Sergeant." *Um...probably because I've never loaded my rifle with this magazine and didn't know its ramifications.* I tried to keep it together for the rest of the mission and managed not to screw things up again.

Baghdad was the perfect storm of a third-world country colliding with modern amenities, causing pure insanity. People rode on top of cars, families of four and five commuted on mopeds, people walked in the middle of streets, and rode bikes and horses as vehicles whizzed past them going 55 down major highways. Garbage covered every square inch within the slums, and donkey carts ran rampant. We even saw a festering dead horse lying in the middle of the road.

A few times gunshots rang through the air close to our convoy, but we cruised on, never knowing if they were meant for us or someone else. Relieved, I took a deep breath when we returned to Mustang Base, let out the stress, and reflected on the amazing cultural differences.

AL SHA'AB

My platoon's first official mission was to monitor the Al Sha'ab Police station 24 hours a day in two 12-hour shifts. My squad was put on the day shift for the month of July and night shift in August. Typically, I awoke an hour before we left Mustang Base to PMCS the vehicle and get ready to go. My team led the three-vehicle convoy. The 45-minute drive was nerve-wracking as I watched for garbage, potholes, and crazy drivers—by far, the most stressful time of day.

Imagine a city with the same population as New York City, but with complete anarchy and chaos: congested streets, continuous blaring horns, Iraqis shouting in Arabic, cars driving down the wrong side of the street, people walking across major roadways without looking both ways, drivers disregarding road lines of all kinds, and donkeys and horses woven into the city traffic.

The Iraqis were infatuated with honking their horns. They pimped their rides with fun melodies and amplified blasts. Many times, I had a horn go off for sport right next to my vehicle, causing my heart to leap out of my chest and my hand to instinctively reach for my pistol.

I had two cars driving toward me while I was driving down the main highway at 55 miles per hour. I thought I was going to have a head-on collision, but the cars separated just enough for me to squeeze through. Iraq taught me how to be a vigilant driver—ready for Nascar upon my return home. Those giant, elephant-sized Humvees didn't slow me down.

Regardless, accidents and collisions still occurred. As I was squeezing through traffic on the first day, I scraped the side of a bus and bent its mirror. Sgt. Hart was proud. He had wanted me to hit several other vehicles to get them out of our way, but I didn't want to lose the hearts and minds of the Iraqis. Not yet. My goal was to be safe, quick, and agile.

Hart enjoyed when I hit Iraqi vehicles. We all needed an outlet in the war, and hearing metal on metal was Hart's. He liked it enough to create a reward system for me. His wife, Lori, sent over car stickers, and when I hit a car, I put a sticker by the visor in my Humvee with the date and initial. By the time we were done using the Humvee, the entire flat panel across the top of the vehicle was covered with stickers.

Over time, the Iraqis learned to give us the right-of-way, and driving became easier through the busy streets. This wasn't always the case. One day, on the way home, I was the lead vehicle, going 60 miles per hour in the left lane of a three-lane highway. A quarter mile ahead, a vehicle was hogging both the middle and the left lane. I honked my horn as I was trying to sneak between the car and the cement barricade that separated the ongoing traffic from our lane. Instead of moving over, the car got closer to the left lane, closing off my thoroughfare. I slammed on my brakes, causing the Humvee behind me to do the same. The third Humvee lost control, hit the barricade, and while correcting the orientation, almost tipped over. I could have killed my squad, based on an assumption that the Iraqis knew the new rules of the road. Hart berated me the rest of the commute, and by the time we got home, I was in tears. Thankfully, the vehicle didn't sustain damage and no one was hurt.

Stoplights rarely worked. The City of Baghdad could not provide enough electricity for the entire population at one time. The solution was to divide the city into grids and give each grid equal electricity throughout the day with a total of about 12 hours during a 24-hour period. The sporadic electricity inadvertently caused drivers to stop heeding the traffic lights. Intersections became treacherous and jammed. They were safe for only the bravest and toughest of vehicles—namely, our military ones, which meant we would get the right-of-way most of the time.

My first impression of Al Sha'ab Police Station, located in the northeast part of Baghdad, was disbelief. How could professionals function in such disrepair and repulsive conditions? Garbage surrounded the two-story, tan building. A sewage leak in the back released a green, odorous liquid. One useless intact window stood out among its jagged-edged or nonexistent counterparts. Half the station had burned ceilings and smoke damage. The bathroom was two holes in the ground, one hole slightly resembling a squatting toilet. The other three-inch hole emitted a pungent sewer stench. While defecating one day, I witnessed a rat squirm out of the sludge in the hole and scamper off. A small pipe—considered the tap—hung out of the wall about ten inches above the small hole. Without soap, I typically passed on the tap because I was afraid my hands would get even dirtier from the rising fumes.

The worst part about our squatter was that it lacked a flushing mechanism. The plumbing used gravity to move our business through its pipes. My bowel movements sat there until someone else went on top of it and pushed it down the pipe. We used a community toilet paper trash bag. Once the bag filled up, we burned it. The smell in the bathroom reached a potency that I wouldn't wish on my worst enemy.

After a few weeks, we rigged a sittable toilet by replacing the seat of the chair with a toilet seat. This lasted for about a month until we procured a one-legged prisoner, and he needed it in the jail cell in order to defecate.

Phair grabbed me shortly after we arrived at the station on the first day, and said, "Your job is to clean up this shithole."

His directive pissed me off, and he could read it on my face.

Phair continued without skipping a beat, "And that guy over there is Mr. Clean. You tell him what to do and he'll do it." He pointed to a 30-something IP, with a middle-eastern Afro.

"Uh, OK," I stammered. *How the hell was I going to tell Mr. Clean what to clean when we don't speak the same language?* I mimicked cleaning gestures and we got by. But Mr. Clean did not like following orders from a female. I pointed at the floor on the main level and made a sweeping motion. He stared at me defiantly, not moving an inch. I smiled, exhibited kindness, and once again acted out my request. He tsked, shook his head, and reluctantly began to sweep. Out of spite, he swept the pile under the stairwell and left it there. I approached Ra'ad, one of the lead police officers, and told him what Mr. Clean did through an interpreter. Ra'ad stormed over to Mr. Clean, cuffed him on the back of the head, and yelled Arabic at him. From that point on, Mr. Clean did what I asked.

The police station had a small jail where we briefly detained prisoners. They were transported to BIAP each week. The jail was disgusting. The squatter toilet routinely overflowed and emitted a repulsive odor. That, combined with unwashed prisoners' body odor, a haze of cigarette smoke, no air circulation, and rats running rampant, created a vile and inhumane environment.

I also fortified the security surrounding the station on the first day. I filled sandbags for the fighting positions and laid concertina wire around the perimeter. As I bent over to extend the circular wire, sweat dripped from my Kevlar like a slow tap. My poor PUD sat neglected all day because I peed more from my head than I did down under.

Hart worked with the civilians. He recorded their reports, facilitated prison visits, and coordinated meetings with the IPs.

Throughout the day, I met the IPs and three interpreters. It was impossible to discern who the IPs, interpreters, and civilians were at the station. The IPs and interpreters didn't have uniforms or I.D. tags. The men sat in front of the station, chatted, smoked copious amounts of cigarettes, and drank their chai. Nada, a female interpreter, was the only other female besides the women in my squad. Her olive skin, wise brown eyes, petite stature, and wavy black hair gave her an exotic look. Her western façade and principles demonstrated the vast differences between Iraqi ideals. Most women wore burkas, only left the house with a male, and refused to make eye contact. Nada didn't wear any Muslim garb—not even a head scarf—and she moved about the city on her own accord and spoke with confidence while giving eye contact. She brought a unique perspective that I wanted to investigate. I asked her, "Why are the laws seemingly unenforceable?"

She said, "The Iraqis don't know how to deal with freedom. They had never been able to express themselves freely because they were under constant threat of persecution and death under Saddam's iron rule. Once Saddam's regime was gone, the Iraqis thought they could do whatever they wanted, whether or not it was wrong. If they could get away with it, why not? Why not loot the museums and stores? Why not drive down the wrong side of the street? Why not drink in public? Why not wreak complete havoc in all of Iraq? No one was around to take their lives for small infractions."

I nodded in astonishment, thankful for her viewpoint.

An infantry platoon helped with the PD's security for our first 35 days. Their 24/7 presence was meant to give us peace of mind, but instead, my concern amplified, knowing how dangerous our sector was. With a squad of six to ten soldiers, they helped pull security on the roof and second story. It was a good day when they brought additional soldiers because that meant we had company while attending our own fighting positions. It helped break up the monotony of sitting in one place for hours. The infantry was a godsend, both for our safety and our sanity. When their time with us came to an end, their absence left a black void as the never-ending hours crawled by.

Hadi, one of the translators, approached me on the first day while I manned the front of the police station. He reached the height of my collarbone and looked like a balding garden gnome with a mustache. "I'm going to call you Moon," he said curtly.

"Why?" I asked, amused.

With a twinkle in his eye, he smiled and said, "Because I look up to you, you have a round face, and you are beautiful—just like the moon."

Taken back by his answer, I said, "OK, I can handle that. Thanks." From that point on, almost everyone at the station called me Moon. Later, he told Kirking he was going to call her Apple. When she inquired why, his response was, "Because your face is round and you're always red." I think I got the better end of the deal.

Toward the end of our shift, Hadi sauntered over with an IP who was six-one and had a large, grotesque nose with crater-sized pores. His red pockmarked face contained a thick black mustache.

"Yes?" I questioned.

Hadi said in a serious tone, "This is Ali, and he wants you to be his wife."

I looked at both of them, dumbfounded. "Are you serious?" I laughed.

"Yes, you must stay here and be his wife," Hadi ordered me.

Not sure how to deny Ali in a diplomatic way, I said, "I'm here to conduct a mission and nothing else. I'm from America and fully intend on returning there as soon as our mission is complete. I'm flattered, but no thanks."

The following day, Ali brought me a blue satin fan with gold trim, attempting to sweeten the deal, but failing miserably.

I grew to dislike the loitering children. Normally, I love kids—*love them*—but the Al Sha'ab children were beyond irritating. Usually, between five and 15 children stood yelling at our gate. Most of them wore raggedy and stained clothes with flies swirling around the sores on their bodies. They were dirty and starved for attention. It sounded like an elementary school playground, but instead of innocent children playing, they were trying to distract us. They begged for food, water, money, and attention. They yelled in Arabic and broken English, screamed nonsense, waved if they thought we were looking at them, blew kisses if we made eye contact, and brought us dying flowers or dirty candy. At first, we viewed their intentions as positive and innocent. They screamed, "Hello Missus; you beautiful! I love you."

We realized they were the only English words the kids knew after they repeated them hundreds of times, and it was an attention-seeking ploy. They taunted us for hours when we were at our fighting positions. A disturbed eight-year-old boy made sexual gestures at me while I was in a fighting position. Twice, he flashed me with his penis. It was heart-wrenching to see all the children run through the city without parental guidance, school, and family support.

The IPs were also concerned about the children's constant presence. The children would be caught in the crossfire if we were attacked. We tried everything to get them to leave: sent an interpreter, had the IPs speak with them, and yell at them. We pointed our weapons at them, we gave them food and water, we smiled and waved, told them to *Ishta*—go away—and *Imshi*—keep walking. The IPs even threw rocks at them, which caused them to scatter like cockroaches and return a few minutes later. Ignoring them was the only way to get them to go away.

The five jobs I held at the station were guarding the front gate, sitting at the fighting position on second floor or roof, monitoring the front desk, training IPs, and RTO—radio/telephone operator. Typically, we stayed at each position for two hours and then rotated.

FRONT GATE

These children were outside of the Shleck police station the morning after Saddam was captured. They were crowding around during the morning before too much chaos ensued.
12/15/03

The busy front gate offered the most entertainment, which helped the time go by faster. We talked to the Iraqi civilians, IPs, and MPs. We, the female MPs, searched the women before they entered the station. Due to their religious principles, we took them around a barricade where it was more private. One time, a woman thought I was a man as I searched her. She slapped my hands away and appeared distraught. After the search, she screamed at the IPs, wagged her finger in my direction, and shot a murderous look at me. She cooled down when they explained to her that I was a female. Another woman thought I was a male until I took off my sunglasses and showed her my ponytail. Overall, most of the women were compliant when I searched them, but the occasional woman squirmed as my hands probed for weapons.

We also worked with and trained the Iraqi Police in real time. For example, two cars crashed a block from the station. It was lucky that only two civilians were involved in the crash. It could have been an Iraqi clown-car with multiple family members in tow. When the crash occurred, the IPs stared at the scene behind our sand-filled barricades called Hescos. With my hands, I beckoned them to go to the scene. They looked at me, looked at the scene, looked back at me, looked back at the scene, and stood there. Helpless, I yelled at the Iraqis, "Get out there and help those people! What are you doing standing around staring at the accident?"

Again, the Iraqis looked back and forth. They didn't budge an inch. Ssg. Verbsky burst from the station when he heard my temper. Within a split second, he caught on to the dilemma. Even though he motivated the Iraqis to move, it still took them a whopping 15 minutes to go a block away.

The IPs came back ten minutes later with two guys in the bed of a truck, one of whom had a bleeding head wound and a minor concussion. The other had first- and second-degree burns on his arm, neck, and face. Instead of taking the wounded men to the hospital, the IPs escorted them into the station to question them.

Mr. Head Wound admitted to having money in his car during the questioning session. Eager, five IPs escorted him to his car to get the money. The money was gone. Either one of the IPs pocketed the money while he was searching the vehicle, or a bystander took advantage of the disabled and abandoned vehicle and walked away richer. In the end, the IPs never took the injured men to the hospital. They sat outside an IP office until my shift was over.

A few weeks later, from the roof, I witnessed a motor-cycle-versus-pedestrian accident in front of the station. One of the two passengers on the motorcycle flew about ten feet through the air and the other skidded about 50 feet with the bike after colliding with a male pedestrian. The pedestrian slammed into the pavement on impact and didn't move. Dozens of Iraqis flocked to the accident within seconds. One of them had the nerve to pick up the broken bike and walk away with it.

Once again, the IPs were idle. They *watched* as the injured men suffered in the street. They *watched* the traffic pile up. They *watched* the civilian steal the bike.

I could hear Ssg. Verbsky's volume increase as the seconds ticked by. Within a minute, he appeared at the tea shop across the street on the side of the IP station. He screamed, "What the hell are you doing? Get off your lazy asses and get over to the accident!"

His voice resonated to my second-story position. The defiant IPs moved at a snail's pace to rebel against Verbsky's temper tantrum. Their first move was to catch the bike thief. They skirted past the injured men and ran after the guy who carried the bike away. Once they retrieved the bike, they meandered over to the three men sprawled on the cement and aided them to the station. An IP who we called the Greasy Commish carried Paul-the-pedestrian like an infant. He dropped Paul, who looked dead by now, in the station's threshold without remorse. Paul had a broken leg and arm from the accident; both were compound fractures. The IPs wasted 13 minutes before they left for the hospital. They looked like chickens with their heads cut off as they shuffled around the police station, accomplishing nothing except postponing the trip to the hospital.

Both of the men on the bike had minor injuries: cuts, bruises, and scrapes. The IPs who remained at the station delayed taking the men to the hospital for an hour because they wanted to question them. Within two hours, the IPs returned from the hospital with the bandaged driver to throw him into jail. When Verbsky asked them why, they responded with a plethora of false allegations: "Maybe he's drunk, maybe he doesn't have a license, maybe we won't be able to find him later, and maybe we should keep him until the pedestrian says that he can go."

The last reason caused us to pause. *What kind of warped policing is occurring right under our nose?* After much persuasion from us, the IPs let the driver go.

On a different and less dramatic day, we arm-wrestled. I was dragged into the competitive atmosphere because the IPs wanted to see how strong I was. To appease them, I joined the fun and arm-wrestled a couple of the IPs before I beat one. The young, baby-looking-IP, Aban, was skin and bones at about 125 pounds and inches shorter than myself. It wasn't a fair fight. Since he lost to a female, the IPs pretended to kick him out of the station. They took his badge, kicked, and harassed him until he was past our gate. I laughed and played along, but could tell that my victory upset Aban.

DESK

This IP and I are posing prior to him beating me in arm wrestling. Hadi is standing directly behind that man. Ali is on the far left. I cannot identify the other two IPs. This picture was taken before the PD was remodeled. We questioned the Iraqis on the other side of the sandbags piled behind the plywood wall. 7/15/03

Working at the front desk included writing down Iraqi statements, complaints, questions, and even compliments. Here are a few of the unique statements: my brother just kidnapped my daughter; my husband is prostituting out my pregnant daughter; and the government is trying to steal my land, but the Americans promised I could keep it. All we could do was write statements down, have the linguist interpret them, and then let the IPs know. What they did with that information was beyond us. Most of the IPs shrugged off the information and continued to sit there and smoke. When I asked Hadi why the IPs didn't care he said, "The majority of the complaints are made up, and you shouldn't believe the people."

"What?" I asked, "Why would anyone make up such lies? What would be the point?"

Hadi looked at me, as though I would never understand, and shrugged.

RTO

As the RTO, we sat by the SINCGARS—single channel ground and airborne radio system—and monitored the Net. When we first arrived at Al Sha'ab, our RTO position was located inside a Humvee that was parked on the front lawn, but after a couple weeks, we hooked up a radio in the safest corner of the police station, which became our MP office. That was the only location where we were allowed to write letters and read.

The date was July 7th, ten days after we arrived in Baghdad. At 1400, I was outside in my Humvee, parked in the front of the station on RTO duty. One of the IPs meandered over to talk to me. They all tried to talk to me with various levels of success, either through interpreters, a kind of international pidgin language, or broken English. Then, abruptly, I had my first war experience. In a flash, I was on the ground next to my vehicle, hiding behind the tire well. There had been a thunderclap, a cannon, or a bomb exploding. Whatever it was, it was damn loud. The continuation of the staccato bangs meant it was most likely a drive-by shooting. The bastard shot ten rounds before speeding away. As the first shot rang through the air, time sped everything into a blur. Because our Humvees weren't up-armored, I ducked low and slid out of my vehicle to take cover behind the tire well. Realizing I had left my rifle sitting in the vehicle about seven feet away, I crawled back into the vehicle, snatched my rifle, and scooted back to the tire well. Then, the IP, still jabbering to me, tried to grab my rifle out of my hands. I looked at him like he was insane and yelled, "Imshe!" *Get the hell away from me!* Iraqis were yelling, and soldiers were running for cover. Palmer, an awkward male SPC in my squad, booked it into the entrance, tripped and fell, but made it inside. By that time, I was the only MP still outside. My heart was beating outside of my chest, and my head spun with nervous anticipation, wondering what my next step should be. Within seconds, my trusted team leader emerged to try to kill the henchman who was long gone. Sgt. Hart asked if I was OK. I nodded. I was more than OK. I was ecstatic. For the first time in four months of active duty, I had war stories. The three amigos—Hart, Verbsky, and Phair—crept along the station wall waiting to retaliate if the gunman revealed himself again. The silent seconds ticked by while we waited for further chaos. After an eternity, we collected ourselves and checked for injuries.

As I stood up, Mustang Base called for Charger 6 or Charger 7—our LT or Platoon Sergeant. I responded, "We are under attack. They'll call back later." Pride flooded over me. I had just stepped into the world of the front lines. My eyes lit up, I grinned slightly, and I felt like I could go home with a story. A bona fide war story. After years of anticipation and months of training, my time at war felt complete.

Five hours later, the station was attacked again while the night shift was there. They had a ten-minute gunfight. The soldiers at the station killed three people—one terrorist and two civilians. The two civilian bystanders, Mohammed Isa—age 16 and Ali Toma—age 24, were caught in the crossfire. Three IPs and one interpreter were injured. The following day, BBC, CBS, CNN, and an Italian news station reported from Al Sha'ab about the incident. The rest of Al Sha'ab must have sensed the tension that had blossomed since the attack because it was a ghost town. The streets were less traveled by cars and pedestrians, the children stayed home, the marketplace had half the normal customers, and some shops didn't even open.

A few days after the attack, Mohammed Isa's four brothers vowed revenge against us—the U.S. soldiers. The tension was high at the station. We laid out more wire, erected more Hescos, and sandbagged our fighting positions on the second floor and roof to further fortify the station.

Allegedly, the Isas were going to strike the next day, either between 1200 and 1500 or around midnight. The infantry brought out tanks and added security during those times. The brothers said they had RPGs and AKs. Their plan was to use the RPGs to break into the station, attack, and kidnap the "weaker female soldiers." *Good luck trying to find "weak females" at the station!*

In preparation for the onslaught, the infantry borrowed Palmer's ammo case. Inside, they found candy instead of ammo. Palmer left the ammo under his cot back at Mustang Base and packed candy to feast upon while sitting in the boring fighting positions. Imagine our anger when we realized our gunner proved useless in our time of need. Phair and Verbsky gave him a good tongue-lashing, and Palmer never lived it down with the rest of us.

We waited and waited and waited, but were never attacked. The next day, the Isas came to talk to the MP boss. Phair talked them out of an attack by saying, "Your retaliation would cause more bloodshed, and we want to avoid another deadly confrontation. We are beyond sorry for the loss of your son, but there is nothing more we can do now besides move on peacefully without causing more bloodshed." The family understood that peace was the best solution to their U.S. hostilities. According to Phair, the Isas were on our side after their meeting. *Such a smooth talker.*

Later that day, Ali Toma's family showed up. Phair had the same conversation with them, and they, too, agreed not to retaliate. Our PD returned to normal.

Back in the States, there was animosity against the war, and I wanted the U.S. civilians to hear a soldier's point of view. It broke my heart that people didn't see the value in the time and energy we were putting into Iraq. I wrote a letter to the editor during RTO duty and had it published in my hometown newspaper,

UW-Madison's newspaper, and the city of Madison newspaper. This is what I wrote:

I usually describe myself as a college student, proudly proclaiming the fact that I belong to the fine University of Wisconsin-Madison. As a member of the National Guard, I have always considered myself more of a civilian than a soldier.

Things have changed. I have changed. After spending a short five months overseas, my life will never be the same. I now see myself as a soldier—a proud American soldier. Every day I drive on the dangerous streets of Baghdad, hear the distant and not so distant gunfire, and see the lack of regulated laws. I feel bad for the people who have to live like this all the time.

People may not agree with us being over here. They may think it is a waste of time and money. I can honestly say that it was hard to leave my family and friends behind. To stop school dead in its tracks. To basically put my life on hold for the unknown. However, I want everyone to know that I am blessed. I am experiencing something very few Americans can grasp. I will be able to go home and fall in love with my life all over again. Every little detail will mean the world to me. The smell of grass, the falling rain or snow, my own bed, a flushable toilet, picking out my own clothes, and the ability to go anywhere at any time without fear for my life.

In other words...Freedom! This is the very reason I am here, so the people of Iraq can understand what it feels like to be free.

Every day at work I see a sadness in the Iraqis' eyes. I've seen brothers betray brothers, neighbors shoot at neighbors, and kids alienated from their parents. This city is garbage-laden, with no government to help clean it. I see police officers too afraid to answer calls or help their own people. It is amazing that this city can still function and that somehow, the people find enough courage to persevere through the hard times.

I ask you to take a moment and relish the fact that you are blessed. You live in a great nation. A free nation with regulated laws and leaders who care about your daily well-being. Take a moment and wish this freedom on the whole world. Now you know the reason why we are here.

When I wrote this, I was adamant and optimistic that our deployment was making a difference and that we were in Iraq for bigger reasons than ourselves. How ignorant these sentiments were a short six months later.

FIGHTING POSITIONS

I dreaded manning the fighting positions more than any other job. My brain felt like it was deteriorating from the endless hours without being able to read, listen to music, talk to someone, or write. All we were allowed to do was wait for an attack. Thankfully, our station was next to a large marketplace. Later in the afternoons, after the scorching midday sun and heat, the bazaar owners opened their shops. The market was busiest around 1900 and typically closed between 2100 and 2200. The hours dragged by while I watched the shadow angles change throughout the 12-hour period. To this day, I cannot sit idle without intrusive feelings of my time at Al Sha'ab. When the boredom became too tedious, I secretly took out my tiny pocket-sized notebook. I collected data on popular car colors, wrote my favorite baby names, and listed the guys I had kissed. I did anything to stimulate my brain before it turned to oatmeal.

About a month into our mission, I was sitting at the second-story east-side fighting position. Across the intersection, a man appeared to have an RPG pointed directly at me. *Holy shit, I'm going to die.* I got the same tingling sensation I get when I see my own children about to hurt themselves. The ground fell out from underneath me. My lungs closed in on themselves, making it hard to breathe. I made a split-second decision. Since our ROE stated that we couldn't shoot until shot upon. I put him in my sights, flipped my weapon to fire, put my finger on the trigger, and waited for him to shoot the RPG. My hair-brained idea was to pull the trigger when I saw him ignite the rocket and then dive for cover. An RPG flies slower through the air than a bullet does. Because of this knowledge, I naively assumed that I could pull my trigger after he ignited the rocket, kill him, dive for cover from the RPG, and save myself.

While these thoughts raced through my head, the man adjusted his position and set down his weapon—sewage rods. It wasn't an RPG after all. He was a plumber, carrying around rods that he shoved down clogged pipes. Thank God for the ROE, because I might have shot an innocent civilian.

Sgt. Kennedy, one of the infantrymen, joined me during a long night at the fighting position. My first impression of him did not bode well. His short stature and round, pockmarked face made me think he was another guy trying to make up for his height by carrying a big gun. I couldn't have been more wrong. He was intelligent, down to earth, and a keen conversationalist. We talked about every subject under the sun, including our missions, Iraqis, our families, and education. The talks reinvigorated me. I'm sure he felt the same way since there weren't females in his company.

One night, Sfc. Phair joined us and took this odd opportunity to tear me down, a common theme throughout the deployment. He quipped, "Did you know that you're my property?"

Stunned by his abrupt assault, I said, "I'm no one's property. Especially not yours." My body tensed in defiance.

"Yes, you are, and I can do anything I want to you. You are mine," he jeered with a smirk on his face.

"Screw you," I said, hoping to not get in trouble for the disrespectful comment. He hit a nerve, and my anger was growing. I wanted to say F-you and slap him in the face, but that would have crossed the line.

He laughed, and like a taunting bully, he asked, "What do you think G.I. stands for?"

I shrugged.

"It means government issued. You are issued to me, and I own you," he stated proudly. He looked at Sgt. Kennedy, hoping for an affirmation of his depreciation. Kennedy maintained a neutral expression and avoided eye contact.

I'm sure I looked angry. I do not have a good poker face. I was overwhelmed with the Army's shackles, and here he was worsening the situation by comparing my value to a piece of military equipment.

Sgt. Kennedy spoke up, trying to lighten the mood, "Speaking of property, the tall shop owner across the street from the station requested to marry you for a night. He offered my team a satellite phone and a scooter as payment."

Phair and I both laughed. It worked. Kennedy saved the day. Phair walked away and took my anger with him.

"So that's my bride price, huh? A satellite phone and a scooter? Better make sure my future husband knows," I joked.

After our busy 12-hour days at the front gate, desk, RTO duty, and the fighting positions, my nightly routine was as follows: drive to Viper, eat dinner, refuel, drive back to Mustang, receive mail, clean weapons, shower, write in my journal, write letters, and sleep. This routine repeated with no more than two days off in a month.

On Al Sha'ab roof with almost 70 pounds of gear on me. The SAW weighs 12 pounds, the ammo is six on the SAW, and I have six pounds of M-16 ammo hanging on my vest. The vest itself is about 40 pounds. The Kevlar is three, and the night vision goggles add a few more. You can also see my hip holster for my pistol wrapped around my upper thigh. All this gear, full uniform, and over 100 degrees on a daily basis. August 2003

TRAINING A DIFFERENT CULTURE

About half of the IPs had never been police officers before the U.S. liberated them from Saddam's regime. They were unemployed Iraqis looking for a constant paycheck of $100 per week. The other half had served as police officers prior to our occupation and brought their vastly different way of policing with them. Not a day went by when I wasn't surprised by their actions, words, or lack thereof.

The IPs worked a 24-hour shift and then had 24 hours off. Instead of policing at night while they were supposed to be on duty, they slept. They claimed the "city was too dangerous." *How can we change this mindset? How can we force the Iraqis to get in their squad cars and leave the station to patrol?* It was impossible. While we were on night shift during the month of August, this mentality shifted a hair. There were a few Iraqis who agreed to patrol, and the number of hours the Iraqis slept decreased. Verbsky and Phair helped by stomping around the prone bodies, sometimes tripping over the men and their makeshift beds. The IPs used various techniques to soften their sleeping surface. We dubbed the broken-down cardboard box the *featherweight mattress*. Some Iraqis had enough foresight to bring a foam mattress with them, and some used empty sandbags or nothing at all. They slept on desks, benches, and on the floor—anything that was flat.

Through Adnon—an interpreter—I questioned the best-looking IP. We called him Hollywood. He was tall, slender, muscular, had a perfect five-o'clock shadow, and great hair. He did not have the infamous Iraqi comb-over or neglected dental hygiene like the majority of the IPs.

"How come the Iraqis don't police to our standards?" I asked.

He bluntly retorted, "We're afraid of getting attacked when you're not around. Since you don't leave the station, we don't want to either. Plus, you only gave us two squad cars. We need at least ten to have enough IPs to go on a call. And we don't have a radio in the squad cars to communicate with the station or with each other."

"Ten squad cars? Don't you think that's excessive? I do agree with you about the lack of communication. We should work on fixing that. Is this why you refuse to work at night?"

"Yes, we need your protection. The community has no respect for us, which is bad if we're in a dangerous situation. We can't tell if the civilians are on our side. The IPs agree that once you aren't working at the station anymore, we're going to quit because we don't feel safe."

"Don't you think it would be a good idea to go out into the community to gain the respect that you deserve while we're here, instead of trying to do it after we leave?"

Hollywood nodded and took it into consideration. Then he flashed me his charming smile and walked away.

Adnon holds a very dear place in my heart. He's intellectual, Kurdish, and Christian. Adnon and I spent hours discussing politics, literature, and philosophy. Even though we held a few fundamentally different beliefs, our bond strengthened with every moment we were together. He brought me reading materials, showing me "scientific proof" from the '50s, claiming that women were intellectually inferior to men. I did everything in my power to prove him wrong without access to legitimate data sources.

Adnon had a son and a daughter but rarely saw them because he and his wife were separated. He didn't think they would get divorced because of his religious and cultural affiliations. He was slight in stature, standing at 5'8" and about 140 pounds. He had a gentle demeanor and a handsome face. Adnon was one of the few men in Iraq without a mustache. Like Hollywood, he didn't have a comb-over or rotting teeth.

Adnon—my favorite interpreter—is sitting in the newly remodeled, sparkling-clean entrance way into Al Sha'ab. Notice how the windows are intact. This lasted only a few weeks. 8/30/03

One day, we were talking about the Coalition's occupation of Iraq. I asked him, "What do you think we should do? Do you think things are getting better or worse since we've arrived?"

He simply said, "I think Iraq would be better if the U.S. left."

"Why?"

"Because you don't understand us," He quipped.

Stunned by his reaction, I didn't pursue the conversation any further. I didn't know how to react. If Adnon, a friend and supporter, felt this way, how did the rest of Iraq feel?

A couple days later, I asked Hadi the same question. He said, "The U.S. should definitely stay."

I felt a little better about our occupation knowing that a few Iraqis depended on us to make their country a better place. Then I remembered how Hadi's interpreting skills weren't always on par with Adnon's, and I second-guessed his understanding of my question.

Our patience often ran thin with the differing cultures. Sgt. Hoyord's anger, for example, went too far when he hit an IP. Hoyord was a portly fellow who ate an abundance of junk food. He was religious, but sometimes his pessimism and anger masked his beliefs. Hoyord struggled with leading his motley team, which consisted of Taylor and Saunders. On this specific day, Taylor—his driver—told an IP named Asif to stop pulling the trigger on his unloaded pistol. Mohammed, a different IP, asked Asif why Taylor yelled at him. Instead of explaining the situation, Asif showed Mohammed what he did by pulling the trigger. Sgt. Hoyord was watching from a distance. When he saw Asif pull the trigger again, he whirled around and smacked Asif on the side of the head and yelled, "I told you over, and over, and over again, not to do that."

Obviously, we were not allowed to touch the IPs. Hoyord received a letter of reprimand and was no longer allowed at the station. To make matters worse, Taylor had to write a sworn statement against Sgt. Hoyord, her own team leader.

Taylor was a beautiful person both inside and out with beautiful straight brown hair, penetrating dark eyes, and a figure to die for. She was quiet, unassuming, and a wonderful friend.

During one of my many conversations with Adnon, we talked about the IP corruption. We—the MPs—knew that the IPs lacked integrity, but never knew the extent of it. He said, "If Iraqis were arrested for stealing, they would pay the IPs a fee or give the IPs some of the stolen loot to avoid a conviction. They might have been charged with a crime, but it would be closer to a public disturbance conviction, as opposed to robbery." He went on to tell me, "We have prisoners in the jail without reason, and when the IPs impound criminals' cars, they sell them off to their friends or keep the cars for themselves."

The following stories further demonstrate the IP corruption:

During peak market hours, a two-person civilian fight erupted across the street from the station. Our confident IPs, Moley—nicknamed because of the large mole on his face—and Asif, ran over to pull the two men apart. Within seconds, a mob of onlookers gathered around the melee and closed in on the IPs. Moley shot his gun four times into the air in a state of panic to disperse the crowd. Disperse the crowd, it did. It also meant we had to confiscate his gun because he unnecessarily discharged his weapon. We could tell Moley was crooked from the start with his evil and cunning laughter.

A few days later, it had just gotten dark, the market had shut down, and the streets were calming to a few cars a minute. I was manning a fighting position on the roof and trying to find as many stars as I could in the darkening sky. My gaze moved down to the pavement when three IPs—Moley, The Greasy Commish, and The New Guy—raced across the street to the adjacent corner. This alone was odd, because the IPs don't run. Ever. The three IPs screamed and yelled at a horse-drawn cart trotting toward them. Then they shot off four rounds. In a flash, they were back at the police station. Moley grabbed an AK, they jumped into a squad car, and they burned rubber towards the horse and cart. The IPs caught up to the cart two blocks away and shot at it again. They shot about 20 rounds within five minutes as they maneuvered through the dark streets beyond our view on the other side of two- and three-story buildings. Just as quickly as it vanished, the squad car peeled back into the station and everyone jumped out. The Greasy Commish was replaced by a boy named Jovan, who was the original cart driver. The Greasy Commish appeared moments later, driving the horse and cart like a madman, laughing hysterically. He parked haphazardly next to the police station and pulled the bolt back on his handgun to clear his gun. The bullet flew out from the chamber, and he caught it in his mouth. Jovan rushed away from the squad car towards his cart to make sure the IPs didn't steal his possessions. He discovered that his money was missing after rummaging through the few plastic bags and moving around leather containers that were in the seat. With fists clenched and his chest puffed, he stomped to the station entrance. There he argued in Arabic with the many IPs that had congregated. Jovan was on the verge of tears as he pleaded his innocence and claimed his money was stolen.

Mahdi, the passenger in the cart at the onset of the madness, marched to the station with his uncle named Saad. At the same time, Al Sha'ab's Captain, Emad, emerged from the station to assess the madness. Emad forced The Greasy Commish to empty his pockets to prove his innocence. The Greasy Commish pulled three wads of cash from his pockets. Emad smelled the money. The boys in the cart worked with kerosene, which caused their money to obtain that odor. According to Emad, the three wads smelled like kerosene. The IPs turned on The Greasy Commish, pissed that he lied. The front of the police station turned into a cacophony of yelling IPs and crying Cart Kids. The Greasy Commish tried to express his innocence, claiming the money was his. The IPs pooled together a couple dinars and reluctantly gave it to him. Then The Greasy Commish gave the three kerosene wads back to the Cart Kids—Mahdi and Jovan.

After two hours of mayhem, the IPs let the kids go. Moley, The Greasy Commish, and The New Guy were fired.

On a different occasion, a distraught girl staggered into the station, begging to speak with someone. I was working at the front desk and was able to speak with her. She said, "I usually intercede when my dad beats my mom, but I was locked out and could hear my parents fighting. I ran all the way here, fearing for my mother's life."

After much persuasion from us, the IPs went to investigate. They were hesitant because their fear of getting hurt overrode their sense of duty. They soon returned with the detained husband and wife. Within minutes, the husband and wife reconciled their differences. The IPs were grateful and let them go home. The husband received no warning, ticket, or jail time for his domestic violence.

The corruption spread from the newest hires all the way to the veteran bigwigs. At the beginning of August, we arrested Al Sha'ab's Captain, Cpt. Baha, because he accepted a bribe from a prisoner named Salazar. The prisoner paid Baha to keep his sister, Dahlia, out of jail. After accepting the bribe, Baha still allowed Dahlia to go to jail. Irate, Salazar turned Baha in to us—the MPs. Both Baha and Salazar found themselves in jail. The only positive attribute was that we had one less rat in the Iraqi Police Force.

During one of my many philosophical conversations with Adnon, he shared that Iraq was westernized before Saddam came into power. The women seldom wore burkas or other traditional Muslim garb and even wore swimsuits at the pools. It's hard to believe that a single ruler could change the mentality of a country. I was also surprised to hear that Iraq had a functioning 911 system—an impossible feature in Iraq's current state.

After our conversation, and reflecting on the lack of IP professionalism and the abundance of corruption, the Coalition Forces should have used some kind of international police force, perhaps like Bosnia's plan or Interpol or something brand new, to create stability in Iraq. We could have cleaned out the criminals with a legitimate police force instead of hiring criminals as the police. We were between a rock and a hard place without a promising solution to rid Iraq of terrorism.

My Favorite IPs. Ra'ad is far left, Hollywood is in the plaid in the middle, Ali is on the right and another Ali is kneeling in front. Salar and Umar are in the back. I can't remember if I asked for a picture with them or if they wanted a picture with me. I do know that I am in many of their personal photographs. July 2003

DEAD BODIES

The guilt and moral tension many veterans feel are not necessarily being dubbed as Post Traumatic Stress Disorder (PTSD) any longer, but Moral Injury. Moral Injury refers to the emotional shame and psychological damage incurred when a soldier has to do things that violate their sense of right and wrong. Black humor and laughing about situations that would normally disgust them.

~ *Benjamin Sledge*

Yippee, a DB! It sounds morbid, but without anything constructive to do while at the station, we welcomed the dead bodies with open arms. They were our TV, our Netflix, our Hulu, and our movie theaters. They were entertainment.

One day, the Iraqis opened their squad car trunk to reveal a dead body—DB—on ice. They moved it into the station to "observe it." These men weren't doctors, morticians, or coroners. *What do they need with a dead body?* I never found out, as our shift came to an end, and the body was gone by the time we returned to the station.

On a different day, Sgt. Hart and I were pulling guard out front when the IPs rolled up to the station and popped open their trunk. Both men walked to the back of their squad car and pulled out a body.

As I was heading to the squad car, I yelled over to Hart, "Hey! Sgt. Hart, DB!"

He stopped what he was doing, grinned mischievously, and followed me to the trunk of the squad car. To our surprise, the IPs pulled a live person out of their trunk. *What the hell? How could they put a live person in their trunk?* Our astonishment grew as we looked at the man's wrists. A profuse amount of blood was pooling onto the cement. The damned IPs cuffed him too tightly. He had an IV tube on one wrist and a flexi cuff on the other that were digging into his flesh. All I had to do was glance at Sgt. Hart to know we were on the same page. He unsheathed his multi-tool, took out the knife, and cut the cuffs off. When the man brought his wrists forward, we realized they weren't the source of bleeding. The only part of the body on top of the pooling blood was the man's rear end. Sgt. Hart, once again, grabbed his knife, slid the blade between the man's back and his sweatpants and gently pulled the pants away to reveal his gluteus maximus. The man's butt cheek looked like ground beef. He had been shot in the butt, and both the entry and exit wounds were next to each other. Hart said, "Let's call him Hamburger Ass."

"That's a perfect name," I responded, laughing.

In a flash, Sgt. Hart's demeanor turned serious. He looked at the IPs and said, "Get this dying man to a hospital right now." They stood there, staring at us, pretending to not understand the meaning of Hart's words. Exasperated, Hart called for Waleed—an interpreter. He told Waleed, "Get these IPs to take Hamburger Ass to the hospital."

Waleed translated, but again, the IPs didn't move. They spoke back to Waleed, appearing to get upset. Waleed looked at Hart and said, "They don't want to get any more blood in their squad car. They aren't going to take him."

Hamburger Ass was delirious. His words were slurring as he suffered from shock and blood loss.

Ssg. Verbsky, who had joined the party a few minutes earlier, shouted, "Take Hamburger Ass to the hospital immediately, or you will be fired." His face turned beet red.

The IPs looked around, spoke a few words, picked up Hamburger Ass, opened their trunk, and were about to drop him in when Verbsky, Hart, and I yelled, in unison, "Nooo!!!"

Flabbergasted, they took Hamburger Ass out of the trunk and dropped him on the ground, right on his injury. With every fiber of patience he could muster, Verbsky gritted his teeth and said,

"Waleed, please explain to these men that they need to treat this man with kindness and put him safely in their squad car. If he dies on their watch, they will not have a job here anymore."

Waleed shared Verbsky's request.

The IPs huddled together and then dispersed. *What are they up to?* Within a couple of minutes, they had found a civilian to transport Hamburger Ass to the hospital as they escorted him.

I headed back to the PD entrance. Waleed was waiting for me. His dark silhouette was illuminated from behind by the police station lights. His raspy voice penetrated the darkness, "The IPs are lazy, just like the niggers in America." Sgt. Hart and I looked at each other with disbelief in our faces. Our jaws dropped.

I said, "No, Waleed; that's not OK. People of color are not lazy, they are humans just like you and me, and you cannot say the N-word anymore. It is simply not OK."

He looked at me startled and asked, "Really?"

"Really," I responded definitively and shut the conversation down. He had crossed a line with me.

Waleed looked like Jay Leno's Iraqi doppelganger. His thick head of hair had a white streak going through the center, similar to how Leno had a dark streak that penetrated through his gray. Just the week before, I searched a homely-looking woman and Waleed had made us bust out laughing when he said, "That's the most action she'll see all year." Most often, the conversations with Waleed had vulgar comments. People don't get much dirtier than military folk, but somehow, Waleed managed to surprise me. At one point, he declared that his name was Red Octopus. From that point on we called him Red. He loved every minute of it.

At the end of August, an angry demonstration had assembled within a mile north of our station. A local sheik had died, and the Iraqis were forced to close their shops in the Al Sha'ab area. Some shop owners, who did not agree with the forced closure, retaliated against the sheik's family and his supporters. They marched to the sheik's house, killed two men, and caused two other men to surrender. Imagine more death and bloodshed at a funeral.

A military police company that dealt with warrants—the 812th MPs—sent a squad to the house to settle the dispute and disperse the crowd. An hour later, they arrived at our station with five women and eight children who were living in the Sheik's house. We searched the women and children and escorted them to safety in the back of the station until the chaos abated. The 812th MPs went back to the Sheik's house to gather the dead bodies. When they returned, my curiosity got the best of me. I walked out to the front of the station to peek at the exposed DB in the bed of the truck. The body was grotesque and mangled from a homemade grenade. Gashes tore through the flesh in his face and legs, exposing his muscles and tendons, and his right wrist was only a stump of tendon and bone. The other body was covered in shrouds. Within an hour, the bodies were taken to the morgue, and the women and children returned home. Just an hour in that crushing heat and blaring sun was too long for the corpses. I swear I could smell it decompose and see the skin bloat as the minutes passed.

In the meantime, the mob of 150 to 200 people who carried their AK-47s and other small arms marched peacefully past the PD. We could have been overtaken in a heartbeat by a group that large. My heart thumped as they moved by and for many minutes thereafter. We continued our high alert for the remainder of our shift because a few other groups had threatened the PD. Anticipating an unknown attack got old fast, and maintaining a high alert for 12 hours was exhausting. My body felt like it had been through the wringer by the time I went to sleep. The weight of the vests paled in comparison to the sore muscles caused by anxiety and stress of the unknown.

IRAQI CIVILIANS

Cultural differences arose in basic facets of everyday life. The subsequent paragraphs outline a few of the noticeable Iraqi oddities. To start, the Muslim religion forbids the use of alcohol, and since the majority of Iraqis were Muslim, they were forbidden to drink. This was not reality, however. Even though we rarely saw an Iraqi consume alcohol, we saw many drunks at the station. We even had an alcoholic IP who swayed a little too much when standing still, smelled of two-A.M. frat parties, and slurred his already unintelligible Arabic. We heard the vendors sold booze on the side streets because they were not allowed in the marketplace. These same vendors were bombed and shot at by radical Muslims during our time in Iraq.

One afternoon, an elderly drunk man staggered to our front gate. He was stumbling over his own two feet, squinting as his sentences bled into each other through his missing teeth and swollen-lipped mouth. Adnon and I watched him grab his loose-skinned left wrist with his right hand and twirl his arm around. The middle of the humerus bone moved around under the sagging skin of his upper arm. He had a compound fracture and was too drunk to feel the pain. We snagged the IP, Ra'ad, and asked him to take the drunk man to the hospital. Thankfully, he did what we asked without hesitation.

The majority of the Iraqis smoked. As a nonsmoker, I shooed the smoking Iraqis outside or away from me. In addition to Moon, the Iraqis called me the Smoking Nazi. One of the IPs said, "I can't smoke my usual four packs a day because you won't let me."

I laughed and said, "You're welcome."

In our opinion, the Iraqis did a lot of asinine things. We called them SHTs—Stupid Human Tricks. Many of the SHTs could have been our own misconceptions and cultural differences.

Regardless, we saw a lot of dangerous and unnecessary things. It was common for Iraqis to steal electricity from the city's main lines because of the daily outages. One day Verbsky said, "Hey! Check out the SHT," and gestured towards an Iraqi who was about to connect his homemade electrical wire to the main line. The precarious main line was already sagging low over a busy highway. The stupid human only had yellow dishwashing gloves to protect himself from electric shock. We watched him scale an electrical pole with his homemade wire secured between his teeth. He held fast to the pole with one hand and secured his barren wire to the main line with his lunch-lady gloved hand. While he was still stuck to the pole like a monkey to a vine, a double-decker bus antenna snagged the main wire and dragged it even lower before it bounced back into position. It was only a matter of time before the main line gave way and everyone in the area lost power.

The ice makers and peddlers had a steady job with the combination of high temps and sporadic electricity. The ice came in a hefty 3-foot-long rectangular cube. The preteen ice vendors rode up and down the streets on donkey-drawn carts yelling, "THELLAGE, THELLAGE, THELLAGE." We bought a $3 block of ice every day from a prepubescent boy with darkening peach fuzz growing on his upper lip. Without it, our water at the station was warmer than piss and tasted like it, too. If the thellage vendors didn't peddle our street during our shift, I would wet down a clean old sock and stick my water bottle inside. The evaporation off the sock did a remarkable job of cooling down the water in my bottle. It was an ingenious idea that I can't take credit for, but it allotted me thousands of satisfying drinks throughout my deployment.

Iraqis wore a plethora of American clothing. I saw Packers, UW-Madison, Bucks, Badgers, Brewers, and an embroidered Wisconsin sweatshirt. I saw men wearing shirts that read: *World's*

Best Grandmother, That's Miss Bitch to you, and *I'm not sassy, I'm a redhead*. Spotting these anomalies became our *Where's Waldo* of Iraq.

Most of the men who could grow mustaches, did have mustaches. It was peculiar to see an adult Iraqi male sans mustache. Comb-overs were another common feature among the men. Unlike the men in the U.S. who shave or buzz their balding heads, the Iraqis grew their hair out. I once saw a man's hair lift off his head in the breeze. It started at the base of his neck, proceeded around the side, and then went up and over. His hair was much longer than my own, which extended down to my shoulder blades.

Dentists and ophthalmologists must have been a rarity in Baghdad. Iraqis had terrible teeth. I didn't see more than ten perfect smiles among the adult population. Additionally, barely anyone wore glasses or sunglasses, and no one wore contacts.

According to the Muslim religion, men were allowed up to four wives. Most men only had one, but two was common as well. Regardless of the number of wives, kids were prominent. Forty percent of the population in Iraq was younger than 15 years old.

Iraqis were generous in nature. They gave anything they could: food, drink, cigarettes. That also meant they thought they could take anything that wasn't theirs. We had to eye our water bottles closely because the IPs drank out of them knowing full well they weren't theirs. Moley even ate Nada's cake right from under her nose.

The Iraqis owned a lot of weapons. According to Adnon, almost everyone owned an AK-47 and a handgun. Iraqis nonchalantly carried their weapons through the streets. Obviously, this heightened our vigilance because they could aim their muzzle at us in a heartbeat. I took many reports from Iraqis about how they shot each other haphazardly. When the Iraqis celebrated a wedding, *futbol* match, or anything, they shot into the air. The duration of the celebratory fire could last up to an hour. Within one night, four Al Sha'ab civilians were injured from falling bullets. On many other occasions, we had deaths due to falling bullets.

The celebratory fire went a little too far in November because it was rumored that Saddam had been captured. Most of the Iraqis were ecstatic with the news and shot into the air. Soldiers were pulled off the roofs and brought into the police station to avoid stray or falling bullets. Hart said he heard some ricochets while he walked around outside. In the end, we received word that Saddam had not been captured. It was only a rumor. Later that day, the IPs brought a dead body to the police station. He was hit in the head with a falling bullet. Another guy came in a little bit later with a bullet hole in his leg.

When we heard gunfire at the PD, we looked at our interpreters, hoping they knew what was being celebrated. Instead, we received *maku*—nothing—just testing the weapon, or it went off accidentally.

We witnessed many tragic stories while working at Al Sha'ab. Regardless of cultural differences, any major city has its unique occupants. To illustrate, the 812th MPs went to a house in the middle of July because a man named Omar said his son, Malik, kidnapped his wife Amara and daughter Zara. When they questioned the occupants and neighbors, they discovered that Omar beat and pimped out Amara, Zara, and two other women. To make matters worse, Zara was in the third trimester of her pregnancy and was being sold to anyone who would take her. Additionally, Amara had something wrong with her stomach but wasn't allowed to go to the hospital for assistance. He pimped out the four women for anything he could get his hands on. The only reason Omar wanted to turn in Malik was to get rid of the one person who could defend the women. The warrant squad said there was nothing they could do at the moment because they had no hard evidence of the prostitution and pimping. They were going to keep an eye on the house until they could detain the father.

An orphaned seven-year-old boy was living in a FOB—Forward Operating Base—by Al Sha'ab for ten days. The infantry helped and cared for this boy who showed up on their doorstep. They fed him and tried to find him a home, but no avail. When the FOB received RPG fire on the tenth night, the boy was too scared to stay there anymore. He begged to go somewhere safer. The infantry brought him to Al Sha'ab, hoping that someone there might be able to take the boy home. The frail thing fell asleep almost as soon as they arrived. He slept on a small brown wicker mattress at Sha'ab on the night of August 25. I wanted to pick him up and take him back to America with me. His tiny frame, wide dark eyes, and yearning expression yanked at our heart-strings. The Iraqi generosity showed through that night. When Ali, an IP, laid eyes on the boy, he offered to adopt him. Within minutes, a few other IPs offered to take the boy as well. A new IP named Yasif who had a son with special needs ended up taking the orphan home. He thought the boy would be a perfect addition to his family to befriend his ailing son.

The Iraqis thought that we, the Americans, were omnipotent. They came to the station for any problem under the sun, whether it was legal, physical, mental, or domestic. We had a variety of injured Iraqis come to the police station only to be sent to the hospital. Every once in a while, we assisted with minor injuries, but more times than not, we told the injured to go to the hospital.

To drive my point home, a well-dressed, forty-something, intellectual woman named Lanya sat down in front of me at the station with her red suit, dark hair, and bright makeup and complained, "My money was stolen."

"OK," I said, "Tell me more about that. Where was your money stolen? Do you know who took it?"

"I don't know who took it. The money was at my house. I sold my kidney and someone came to my house and stole the money. I want you to pay me back." Her lips pursed into a small heart shape and her eyes narrowed in on mine.

Taken aback, I responded, "I'm sorry, we can't just give you money. If you know who might have taken it, we can investigate the matter further."

"If I knew who took it, I would get it back," she said defiantly, "You are no help. Just give me some money." This time her chin lifted and she crossed her arms and she looked at me through her bottom eyelashes.

"Lanya, that's not how it works. I'm sorry. Unless you have anything else you would like to tell us, I'm going to have to ask you to leave."

She stood up, spat on the cement floor next to my metal chair, looked at me with hate, spun on her bright red heels, and walked out.

We went to Baghdad University for a recon mission later in our deployment. The vegetation was plentiful with tall palm trees surrounded with flower beds, beautiful pink, red, and white flowers adorning the manicured bushes, and manicured lawns with coeds sprawled out in small groups. The brick buildings reminded me of UW-Madison with their uniformity and lack of a sand-blasted hue. The students looked, acted, and dressed like typical stateside college students. The traditional Islamic dress was rare and looked out of place. The students were not carrying books or backpacks, only Trapper Keepers or folders. Some females carried purses, and a few carried handbags. For the first time, I saw male and female groups commingle. They were talking, taking photos, and even flirting. It felt like we had passed through another dimension.

The students' nasty looks and lack of salutations told us all we needed to know about their negative impression of our presence. It didn't help that our convoy blocked their popular walking paths for an hour while we waited for the commander to do his bidding with Lord knows whom. We selfishly took over their territory, causing them to walk around our gigantic metal beasts. As if this were sacred ground, the students' anger and resentment grew with every ticking second. When we drove out of the gate, almost 50 guys mobbed together to protest our occupancy and our interference at their university. They stood on both sides of the road with rage in their faces and anger in their voices. They were closing in on our convoy. Some had makeshift weapons of sticks and rocks. One of the guys was upset enough to be held back by his friends. In the end, nothing happened, but they were ready to retaliate if we made one wrong move.

Garbage littered the city. It was everywhere. The medians were dumping grounds. People carried their trash in bags, bins, and boxes by the handful and threw it in between the roadways. Every once in a while, it was burned or picked up. Nightly, we witnessed hunched old ladies, who were wearing black from head to toe, fill their sacks with unknown treasures. To limit confiscation and maintain confidentiality while at the station, we burned our garbage in a barrel behind the PD—even the plastic. It was unusually windy in Iraq, which caused the unkempt garbage to meander everywhere. The streets, playgrounds, and soccer fields that were already decrepit dirt patches were made even worse by the rogue loose trash. The IPs didn't help the situation. They threw their cigarette butts and garbage on the ground without a second thought.

Wild animals added to the city's chaos. The wild dogs barked and fought in their packs. The dirty, gangly cats hissed and screamed their meows when they got into it, roosters crowed, and rats squeaked throughout the otherwise silent nights.

The dreaded, disgusting, copious amounts of rats ran onto our boots as we walked through the station, their feces covering the floor, and their ceaseless crying getting under my skin. Two met their maker when I crushed them with rocks. I had been working at Sha'ab's front gate, and the rats were scurrying slowly—as if in a stupor—around the construction mess. This was my opportunity to take out my anger and frustrations. They were probably sick anyway with how clumsy they were. I grabbed a big piece of rubble and smashed their little gray heads in. It didn't make me feel better, though. I felt worse. What had I turned into? How had a lost so much connection with my prior self? What I did was monstrous, disgusting, and repulsive. I never would have thought of doing such a thing back home.

Rats were a problem in our compound as well. While doing laundry by hand, I discovered that rats had eaten the crotch out of four pairs of my underwear. Thereafter, I hung my laundry bag on a hook and I set a trap under my bed where I used to keep my laundry bag. A few nights later, a fat, ugly, beady-eyed rat stared at me next to the trap. He wasn't in the tipped-over-trap but was injured and unable to move. Unlike at the station, I couldn't kill this rat among my own things in my *home*, and I didn't want to feel the same sense of emptiness I had obtained at the station. I set my feminism and pride aside and asked Sgt. Hoyord to do the deed. Brutally, Sgt. Hoyord bashed the rat's black head with the trap. Blood and rat excrement littered the floor. I smelled the gore hours into the night, even after a thorough cleaning.

After a late night at the station, Kirking and I were getting ready for bed in our bathroom when we noticed a rat in the garbage bag. They must have loved women's scents, because the bag held our used toilet paper and feminine products. Without wanting to disturb the other ten sleeping females, we tried to kill the rat. Our mission was futile. We were in a floor-to-ceiling marble bathroom and used a broomstick to bash the rat. She evaded our death stick by plunging into the bidet hole. Kirking and I were reeling with laughter near the end. We knew how ridiculous we must have looked trying to silently bash the rat with wood on marble. I felt drunk with humor by the time the rat squeezed down the porcelain hole.

Five times a day, the mosques blared the call-to-prayer over their loudspeakers. The memorable chant was eeriest while I was on night shift. The men's melancholic singsong voices broke the city's silence at dawn with the first signs of the black sky transitioning into its lighter navy blue. Six surrounding mosques competed for my ear with their ominous sound when they let out the first prolonged note, one after the next. My body tensed and the hairs on my arms stood on end. I was torn from my exhausted semi-alert state after a long night of trying to stay awake. It reminded me of dangerous storms back home when the color of the sky turned green and you knew you had to take shelter from an incoming tornado. My gut always told me to hide in fear. How were we supposed to know that the chant was a call to prayer as opposed to a call to war?

The Iraqi men stared relentlessly at me and the other female soldiers. Like sirens coming out of the sea, we were alluring and tantalizing, casting spells on them. We sang the enigmatic songs that pulled them from their thoughts and forced them to ogle our every move. They couldn't look away. Like I did with the children, I tried many tactics to divert their gaze. I smiled, used the middle finger, stared back, ignored them, or made funny faces. The only way to stop the eyeballing was to get out of their line of sight. The men correlated our light hair, light eyes, and athleticism to Hollywood. They put us on pedestals like they did with movie stars. The local women were typically dark, short, and plump. Who would have believed my brother, Joe, when he said that deployed female soldiers got treated like queens?

Sfc. Phair approached me one day while I was sitting on the second-floor fighting position and said, "The IPs think you're the most beautiful thing in the world. They said you have gorgeous eyes. Ali even brought his wife to the station to look at your beauty."

Taken aback, I bashfully responded, "No, he didn't. I know I'm not ugly, but I'm certainly nothing special. Back home, I'm just a plain Jane."

He shrugged and said, "It's true. You're easy on the eyes."

I gazed at him as he stood next to my seated fighting position. His seriousness and off-the-cuff compliment brought butterflies to my unassuming stomach. *Did he just flirt with me?* "Um, thanks," I stuttered. I wasn't sure where to take the conversation next.

After a long, passionate look, he spun around and left me alone with my heated thoughts. *How can I go from detesting this man to wanting him in a split second? Another effect of war, I guess.*

Al Sha'ab was under construction during the month of August. A handful of construction workers broke down walls, put up new ones, tiled the floors, painted the walls, blared Iraqi music, raised dust, and interrupted our daily routines.

They used sledgehammers and pickaxes to knock down walls and raise tiles off the floor. They had about ten different projects going at once, on all sides of the building. Two men painted outside, three men broke down a wall inside, two more laid tiles in the front room, and two more meandered around, gabbing with the IPs and other workers. They were everywhere, like ants on a picnic.

The construction left us without a working toilet for a couple of weeks. We peed outside on the ground and pooped in a box in a vacant back room. When we were done defecating, we took our box outside and burned it. After a couple of nights, we transported the old toilets Sgt. Hoyord had built from Mustang to the station. The problem with the old toilets was that we had to burn our feces mixed with diesel fuel in 50-gallon metal drums. I can't think of a worse job than stirring a barrel full of burning shit and diesel fuel.

The IPs were not quite as discrete with their defecating. Most of them popped a squat in the back of the station next to our vehicles. During the month of August, we had more than animal feces to watch out for as we maneuvered around our Humvees.

It was 2230, the sky was dark, the streets were deserted, and I was sitting alone at my fighting position. I couldn't hold my bladder anymore. I did the only logical thing I could think of; I snatched my PUD, inserted it, maintained a low profile, and let my pee flow over the two-story edge. I stopped midstream. *Did I just hear someone in the alleyway?* I peered over the edge of the roof and to my horror, saw Verbsky standing directly below my stream. *Oops.* I swear, we made eye contact, and he had to have known I had urinated over the edge, but neither one of us mentioned what I had done.

Murray (left) and Henry (right) in front of Al Sha'ab Police Station after it was remodeled. They are standing behind sandbags for added protection. 8/30/03

DRIVING PATROLS

We modeled, trained, and then accompanied the IPs on driving patrols during the month of October. One of these patrols took us to an old Iraqi army base outside of Baghdad. Homeless Iraqis were squatting in the old single-story barracks and had taken over the abandoned establishment.

The drive from Baghdad to the old army base led us along the Tigris River. The bright sun, palm trees, papyrus, and rushes made our drive seem more like a lush Hawaiian island than the typical sandy Baghdad. We got lost along the winding roadway and tall vegetation and pulled into a civilian's dirt driveway to turn around. The owner rushed out and begged us to stop. He waved us in and mimicked drinking and eating with his hands and mouth. "He's inviting us in for something to eat and drink," I said, more to myself than anyone else. His house was a mere shack, and here he was, offering us some of his meager possessions—another shining example of Iraqi generosity. Even when they could barely support themselves, they wanted to give to others. Reluctantly, we declined. We were cautious because Iraqis had begun to poison soldiers.

When we arrived at the abandoned base, we drove around to assess the number of vagabonds and their unkempt homes. The roads were cracked, covered in rocks and dirt, and missing chunks of cement. The weeds and thistles were dancing across the landscape, infiltrating the barren lands. The formerly abandoned, gray plaster-covered buildings were sandblown, missing doors and windows, and aged from the extreme heat and blaring sun. The base had a ghost-town feel that accompanied the howling winds.

Like a bat out of hell, two cars careened out of their parking spot from a house about 20 yards away and bolted away from us. "Follow them!" Hart bellowed.

"You got it!" I said with a huge smile on my face. I pressed the gas to its max and pursued the shady-looking vehicles. *I love this!* The uneven terrain jostled our vehicle as we chased the renegades through the base. They had to have known we were following them, but they didn't stop.

"Woohoo!" Hart whooped. "This is it! We're onto something big."

"Wait, where did the first vehicle go? I lost track of it as it turned the corner." When the words left my mouth, we watched the second vehicle bottom out on a four-foot-tall sand berm about 50 yards ahead of us. It rocked back and forth on top of the berm like a teeter-totter. The first car must have been light enough to clear it, but the second car was loaded down with five occupants and continued to sway on its pivot point.

We exited our vehicles to approach theirs on foot. Not knowing if the car's occupants were insurgents or not, we edged closer with our guns raised. Using international language, we motioned to the Iraqis to get out of the vehicle. They jumped out, scared of our presence, but the process slowed down when the passengers had to assist the driver out of his seat. His left leg didn't work properly, and he couldn't stand up on his own. We frisked all five men once they were safely out of the car. Then we moved on to search the vehicle.

The five men stood in a line about 15 feet away from the vehicle. They watched as Verbsky and Hart searched their getaway mobile. When the search closed in on the trunk, the five Iraqis yelled at Verbsky and Hart and moved their arms up and down in the air. My hair stood on end. It did not feel right. Something bad was about to happen.

Verbsky and Hart's eyes darted this way and that. Their faces creased with concern. They opened the trunk slowly, watching for tripwire or a booby trap. They ordered me to look through the crack as it inched open. I edged closer to the vehicle to get a better look at the trunk. I crouched down less than ten feet away. The trunk's dark slit opened a little further, letting light in. I jumped as something moved inside. My heart leaped in my throat. *What was that? Phew, I'm still alive, must not have been a bomb.* "OK, keep going," I said as I took a deep breath.

Hart looked at me inquisitively and continued to open the trunk. The farther it opened, the louder the Iraqis grew. They made strange, high-pitched noises and flapped their arms. That's when I solved the puzzle. They were making bird noises and gestures. "There are birds in the trunk," I said almost simultaneously with Verbsky. He inched it open a little farther to reveal ten uncaged live birds in it. To contain the unpenned birds, we closed the trunk and backed away from the vehicle.

Without an interpreter and with our search revealing only live fowl, we let the Iraqis get back in their vehicle. The driver got in first to clear the berm before the four passengers squeezed into the compact car. We drove away in the opposite direction, puzzled by yet another Iraqi mystery.

Weeks later, we were back to pull security while the infantry raided the old military buildings. Their intel pointed toward stashed WMDs in this location. Unless a couple AKs and tank rounds counted as WMDs, they didn't find anything except for squatting families and their livestock. One of the squatters approached our vehicles to gift us fresh rock bread. Her bright-red dress was adorned with gold highlights. Her dirt-smudged face couldn't hide her internal beauty and the few wrinkles that had begun to etch themselves on her freckled facade. She was cooking the bread on an outdoor clay oven so rough looking, it could have been slapped together by children trying to build mud pies. But my-oh-my, was that bread tasty. Warm, slightly toasted, and deliciously chewy. We tried to decline, knowing she couldn't afford to part with the food, but she refused. In exchange, Hart gave her a half-bag of mints.

We watched as the infantry worked around us. They combed a large weedy field by driving their 20 Humvees alongside one another. Cow poop and a recent rainfall muddied the field, causing a truck to lose traction and sink into a hole. After an unsuccessful attempt to push the out Humvee, the infantry brought in the big guns—a Bradley—to pull out the Humvee. To add insult to injury, the Bradley sank as well. Thank God for the infantry and their absurd brute force. I was on the verge of tears from perpetual laughter. After two hours and an M88 recovery vehicle, they successfully cleared the field.

Sgt. McDermott, an infantry squad leader, approached my vehicle and asked Sfc. Phair, "Can a few of your females follow us around to help search the women? We're ready to search the homes now that the grounds are finished."

Without hesitation, I jumped at the opportunity. Anything beats standing around idly waiting for the seconds to tick by. I said, "I'll do it!"

Phair had the gall to say, "No, our females can't go anywhere by themselves."

I glared at him with my best death-look, thinking even worse thoughts.

Phair made eye contact with me and said, "You can only go if a male soldier accompanies you."

Sgt. Freier, a team leader in first squad, overheard the conversation and stepped up to the plate. Thank goodness. I liked Freier. His intelligence was intimidating, but we had a lot of fun together.

Again, that damn double standard. We were fighting the same war, wore the same uniform, were held to the same military expectations, but he didn't think we could take care of ourselves. *Who's going to screw with a six-foot-tall female? That's what I want to know.*

DRIVING SCARES

Driving was the most dangerous and stressful part of my deployment. The roadside bombs, thrown grenades, small-arms fire, and ambushes were constant threats. Being ever vigilant left me mentally and physically drained and my muscles sore from the never-ending tension. The longer the drive, the more worn out I became.

Our death could occur in the blink of an eye. One day, I thought I heard either Hart or Murray shoot from their spot in the Humvee. *Bang!* I scanned the vehicle to decipher which teammate had shot. Both Hart and Murray were flinching upon my glance and with wide eyes and gaping mouths, they looked back at me—frightened. It wasn't them shooting; it was someone shooting at us within close range. I slammed my foot on the pedal and drove as quickly as the mammoth beast would let me until we exited the unknown rifle's range. It could happen just like that.

On a mundane commute home from Al Sha'ab, we were coasting along the three-lane highway when we approached a slow-moving stake-bed truck jam-packed with chanting men. They were wearing black clothes and bandanas, were holding black banners with white lettering, and were unified in their chants—the sound penetrating through our Humvee walls. The bed held at least 30 men confined between metal slatted walls. Unsure of their intent, we slowed down in case they were anti-American. We did not want to engage with such a large number of men. Upon slowing down, an identical truck full of men crept up on our left side. *Oh no! There's more than one?* I moved the Humvee to the far right lane only to realize that we had more trucks on-ramping the highway on the right side. In an instant, all four sides of our vehicle were surrounded by loud, angry, protesters. *This is it. I'm going to die. We are sitting ducks.*

Then, just as quickly as they appeared, they vanished amid the highway traffic without giving us the time of day. We were not their focus. *Thank God!*

July 21st, 2003, was our first introduction to an improvised explosive device—IED. During our pre-mission briefing, Ssg. Verbsky said, "Yesterday, four soldiers and an interpreter were killed by a roadside bomb called an IED. All drivers are ordered to avoid debris and garbage along the roads in case it's a bomb." Previously, Hart mentioned that the terrorists' killing methods were evolving, and this was proof.

Two weeks later, Verbsky shared, "There were three major attacks on military personnel in Baghdad within the last twenty-four hours. Two coalition deaths and two amputations were reported. Three men from our platoon, Ssg. Caldwell, Ssg. Seifert, and Sgt. Fohey, were involved in one of the attacks and helped return fire. Two Humvees appeared parked on the side of the road but were actually disabled from an IED. When Caldwell's truck closed in on the other two Humvees, a second IED exploded.

"The blast pushed Sgt. Fohey out of the vehicle and burst his eardrums. Two soldiers from the original Humvees ran out of an Iraqi building that they were hiding in. They grabbed and dragged Sgt. Fohey into their 'safe' room. In a state of deafness, Sgt. Fohey saw another injured soldier in the room. Sgt. Fohey didn't need to hear to understand the pain and agony his fellow soldier endured as tourniquets cut off the blood supply to his missing lower legs.

"The enemy fired at the U.S. forces after the IEDs exploded. The able-bodied soldiers, including Seifert and Caldwell, returned fire until extra support came. Within minutes, a tank rolled in and leveled the enemies' building. Later, all three of our men were hospitalized for heat-related problems."

My squad was speechless. Within two weeks of the initial IED, our company had been attacked and received injuries. *This war just got real.*

Ssg. Caldwell was the squad leader in second squad. His machismo mansplaining left me feeling frustrated after almost every interaction. His overbearing self-confidence contradicted his incompetence. During our simulated-war training at Ft. McCoy, he was in charge of taking the injured soldiers to the medevac site. I happened to be one of the injured soldiers and had to tell him what to do and where to take me. I practically drove myself to the medevac site.

Ssg. Seifert was a different story. I trusted him as a soldier, but not as a civilian. He was a sleazebag with one thing on his mind, and that mind was not the one between his ears. He had been in the military for a while and knew his stuff, but was degrading toward women of any kind. His dirty jokes never ended.

Sgt. Fohey, on the other hand, was one of the best guys around. He was quiet, humble, and focused on the mission.

DAYS OFF

We rarely received a day off—about every 13 days or so. I was relaxing in the compound by my room on my first coveted day off since our Baghdad arrival. The sun was shining, as usual, and the birds were chirping. It was a quiet day in Baghdad's standards. There weren't gunshots pounding through the city streets, and the choppers were keeping their distance. I sat overlooking the lawn and watched the palm trees sway in the slight breeze as I read my book. *This might be a great vacation spot in an alternate universe where war and sexism didn't exist.*

The pool wasn't in working order yet, so after a while, I took an extra-long shower with the lukewarm water washing the smog, sweat, and stress away. *Weird.* I saw smoke wafting over the Gurkhas' side of our shared wall. I turned the water off, towel dried, and slid into my PTs. When I came out of the shower stall, I could see a fire blazing on their side. Sparks were flying into the air, and the same soft breeze grabbed a hold of a few and slammed them into our dried grass. Before I knew it, the fire was blazing on our side and was quickly spreading through our lawn. I called out a few yards away to wake first platoon, who was working the night shift at the station and got other soldiers from the compound to help fight the blaze. After an hour hauling bucket after grueling bucket, we extinguished the fire. I found myself once again taking a shower to wash off the sweat, the stress, and this time, the soot.

By the time I had my third day off, we were living in the basement of our compound, and the working pool was a perfect antidote to endless days of tiresome work. Before I dove into the crystal-clear warm water—let's face it, nothing is cool in that country—I grabbed my pampering paraphernalia and went into the pool house. I rubbed a mud mask on my face and soothed cooling gel into my callused feet. Then I sat in the quiet darkness of the tiled oasis and let the lotions do their magic. Fifteen minutes later, I dove into the refreshing pool and swam laps. Every stroke I took made my body happy. My sore back elongated with every twist of my torso, and as my arms reached overhead, I felt free of the weight of the vest and the guns. My legs kicked through the liquid and felt lighter than air, free from the dark socks and heavy combat boots. I felt naked, weightless, and unshackled. I felt human.

Eventually, I coasted down to the basement to find myself ankle-deep in cruddy water. The utility closet in the basement spewed water into third squad's room. Two-inch-deep water crept toward duffel bags and personal property. Three other soldiers were already busy trying to keep the water at bay. I joined them. We were able to save everything except for a few wet duffel bags. We then spent over an hour and a half soaking up the water and cleaning the disgusting residue. Luck was not on my side when it came to having a day off.

FAMILY

Missing my family made the deployment even more difficult and defeating. My never-ending guilt complex weighed heavily on my mind. Letters from home were amazing treats that I relished every night from the privacy of my bunk. I took the time to write every single individual back, whether it be my grandparents, an entire second-grade class, or strangers from my church. I needed each and every one of them to know how much their time meant to me. Letters from Andy, in particular, were emotionally bitter-sweet. They made me cry and laugh at the same time. They were filled with quips and jokes but remained sentimental and loving. It made me miss him that much more. It was as though a piece of me was missing. *Who knew my twin meant that much to me?*

I asked Grandma Naylor to write her life story in her letters, and every single correspondence I received was a living gem. A decade after my return, she had a stroke which left her physically untouched, but more mentally vacant. She hadn't lost touch of her sweet side, but she was often times confused. On her subse-quent birthday, I read snippets from her letters. She was present when I was reading those letters. We saw a grandma we hadn't seen for months. It was as though she found life in the words that she scribed years before. She added funny details here and there and continued to reminisce when I was done.

Phone calls were another story. My family and I waited 17 long days to reconnect once I got to Baghdad, and we did so the oddest route possible. A random Iraqi civilian brought a satellite phone to the station and charged 12 dollars for ten minutes. It was a rip-off, but worth every penny to reconnect with my loved ones. Those days stretched like years. I didn't know what my family did or didn't know. I didn't know if they were receiving the letters I sent every week, or if they were waiting to hear if I was still alive or not. They were relieved and joyful when they heard my voice, and I was renewed and rejuvenated when I heard theirs. They had received word that we were doing well through the family network, but didn't know the extent of our circumstances. Shortly after that call, our company received a satellite phone to share among the 140ish troops. Thereafter, I called every couple of weeks or so, sometimes after waiting in a long and boring line.

My birthday on August 26th started out as a nightmare. I woke up with a dark cloud over my head. It was my birthday, but the very person I have always shared the day with was not there. I had no one to tell, "Hey, it's our birthday! What should we do today?" No one gave a rip that I was turning 22. No one. My excitement was wasted in my solitude. To make matters worse, the pool was closed and the company phone was gone. I couldn't talk to my twin brother on our birthday. My TWIN Brother! I missed him more than ever. It was our first birthday apart.

By the time we arrived at the station, my eyes were red and patchy, and I moped around, depressed. The IPs and even civilians looked at me with pity in their eyes. They could feel my sadness. A few IPs asked me what was wrong. I told them that it was my birthday, and I couldn't talk to my family. Unbeknownst to me, while I was sitting on the roof, Hakim—a shy IP—found a satellite phone in the neighborhood and brought it to the station. Sgt. Hart called me on the handheld radio, "Naylor, come down to the front of the station."

"Roger."

I shuffled with leaden feet across the rooftop, down the first flight of stairs, through the hallway, down the next flight of stairs, across the entryway and out onto the foyer of the building. I lifted my gaze to look for Hart but instead saw Hakim with a wide smile and kindness in his eyes. He was extending a satellite phone out to me.

I smiled and let out a happy sob as I asked, "For real? I can call home?"

Red translated, Hakim spoke, Red translated to English, "Yes, call home. It is free. For you. For your birthday."

"Oh, my God. Thank you so much!" I patted my heart to show Hakim how much his gesture meant to me. Without wasting another second, I called home. As if the stars aligned, Andy answered the phone. I wept at the sound of his voice. I couldn't talk. It took me a couple minutes to recover from my sobbing frenzy before I could speak. Our glorious conversation lasted close to a half hour. Pity was the only reason I could stay on the phone for that long. Normally, it would have been ten minutes tops.

When I gave Hakim the phone, the rest of the IPs saw that I had been crying again and thought the phone call made things worse. I tried to tell them the last batch of tears were happy ones, but I'm not sure they understood.

Being at the station wasn't all bad. The IP's generosity fixed my birthday blues. And the night kept getting better. Nori, an older IP, brought me a cake that his wife had made. It had white frosting and a chocolate interior. The frosting between the layers was made with pistachios. Nothing tasted better in that moment than the love of newfound friends. As he handed it to me he said, "I know you miss your family, but we are your family here."

I melted. I was blown away by his kindness and selflessness. How did he make that happen so quickly?

Within an hour, Hadi brought me a dark, rich chocolate heart-shaped cake that he bought at a store. That sweet little gnome of mine with his wife and five kids. His flirting could definitely be mistaken for infidelity, but he was loyal to his wife nonetheless.

Before the night concluded, I received a third cake from my fellow soldiers who gave Hadi money to purchase from a local bakery. Their cake said *Happy Birthpay* instead of *Birthday*. *At least the baker tried!* Mmmm...that cake was the best cake I had ever had. It not only had pistachio frosting on the inside, but the cake itself was made with pistachios. The chocolate frosting was melt-in-your-mouth good and the perfect complement for the interior. I felt blessed to be surrounded by such wonderful people. The day turned out to be better than I could have ever imagined. I guess other people did care that it was my birthpay. I mean *birthday*.

The BirthPay cake that I received from my fellow troops. You can just make out the P in *birthpay*. This was right after I called Andy and my world had started to look a little more cheerful. I'm standing in the processing office right by the front entrance to the police station after it had been remodeled. 8/26/03

JOE

My older brother, Joe—the jock—was an obvious important facet to my close-knit family. His arrival in Ramadi, Iraq, on September 9th, 2003, was another devastating blow to our family of five and those close to us. He was sent on a year-long deployment as a medic in an infantry unit until September of 2004. Even though we were in the same country, the 60 miles of separation felt like an eternity. Calling him was near impossible, and snail mail took weeks, if not months, to make the round trip. *How had we both deployed to Iraq at the same time?*

On October 21st, Hart found me in my room and said, "Your older brother, Joe, is on the landline in the TOC. He's on hold. Hurry up and get over there."

I jumped out of my bunk, ecstatic that I could finally talk to Joe. Breathless, I snatched the army-green rotary phone when I arrived and said, "Joe! Is that really you?"

"Yup," he laughed, "It's me. Pretty cool that we can chat over a landline, huh?"

"Sure," I said, wondering how much I should say and how long I could talk.

"Anyways," he said, "I have a chance to come to BIAP tomorrow. You should totally meet me there."

"Oh, my gosh! That would be amazing! I'm not sure I can. We just started a new mission. Maybe I can join the mail run tomorrow."

"OK. You need to make it happen. It would be awesome to see you."

"I have to find out. How do I call you back?"

After explaining the steps, we hung up, and I raced to Hart.

"Sgt. Hart, Joe's coming to BIAP tomorrow. Can I take the day off and go on the mail run?" I asked.

Without empathy and a second thought, Hart responded, "There's no way. You're conducting business as usual." He paused as my mouth dropped open. Then he continued, "No one else gets to see their family. Why should you?"

I wanted to yell back at him, "Because no one else has family here. That's why!" But I kept my mouth shut, climbed the stairs, walked to the TOC, and called Joe to let him know that we couldn't see each other. I felt crushed and defeated. Hart's uncharacteristic lack of empathy hit hard.

Like any soldier in Iraq, Joe has a lot of war stories. He, too, could write his own memoir. My favorite story was when he resuscitated his platoon sergeant after their convoy hit an IED. He brought nonbreathing and pulseless Ssg. Jeremy Craig back to life. A week later, my dad was on a business trip in Washington, D.C. He visited Ssg. Craig because Craig had been transferred to the Walter Reed Hospital. When my dad introduced himself, Ssg. Craig's first words were, "Your son saved my life." Can you imagine the pride my father must have felt, to know that his son saved a man's life? Chills. Serious chills.

ROVER DUTY

My company ended our official 12-hour shifts at the police stations on September 1st. We were attempting a partial transfer of power over to the IPs. My team was put on rover duty. Our mission was to take over for the various teams in our platoon to give them a shift off—which meant that my team worked three days on night shift, then three days on day shift. Our various substitute jobs included commander escort, gate guard, and station check-in team.

COMMANDER ESCORT

Our first day as the commander's escort did not go as planned. Whose plan, you ask? Well, my plan as a lowly specialist, and we all know that doesn't carry much weight. Glenn requested that we were ready by 0900. I was up and ready to go by 0800. I ate, conducted personal hygiene, and PMCSed the vehicle. In the middle of my PMCS, our standby time moved to 1030. I finished the job at hand, grabbed a crossword puzzle book, and sat next to my Humvee, waiting for 1030 to arrive. It was a beautiful September day. The temperature had subsided to the 90s, the breeze felt somewhat cool, instead of like a blow-dryer, and the sun wasn't quite as scorching as it had been. It was a great day to soak it all in. The minutes passed, and so did 1030 with no commander insight. *Are we ever going to hit the road?* "Hey Hart," I said. "What are the chances we're going to do anything today?"

"Not sure," he quipped. "Let me check." And off he ran to the TOC to find the commander. He returned a few minutes later and said, "Mount up. It's just us. We're staying in the green zone. The brass wants us to look for the pool-table guy 'cause we're getting pool tables for the basement."

"Wait, what?" I questioned. "Where are we going to find this guy?"

"He gave me the coordinates and said the guy'll be waiting outside for us when we drive past. Let's go."

"Roger." Hart, Murray, and I scampered into the Humvee, happy to be doing something with our time.

Hart plugged the address into the GPS and we hit the road. We drove a few miles until we reached our destination. There was no one in sight. We circled around a few times, driving down side roads, scanning the sidewalks for a man, any man, and found no one.

We cut our wild-goose chase short and drove to the famous Cross Swords and the tomb of the Unknown Soldier, which were safely located in the Green Zone. *Might as well see some history while we can.* The Cross Swords were two gargantuan pairs of swords that act as the gates on both sides of Saddam's parade grounds. The hands that held all four swords were replicas of Saddam's hands—said the security guard at the site. He also said that the helmets embedded in the cement across the threshold of the gates were the Iranians' helmets from the Iraq-Iran war from 1980-1988. The Iraqis took the slain Iranians' helmets and put them on their parade grounds so that they could march over them with their robust military whenever they wanted.

The Crossed Swords Victory Arch that bookended Saddam's parade grounds, the stadium lights, and the building where he gave many famous speeches. 9/3/03

The tomb of the Unknown Soldier was a somber yet slightly less significant monument. It rested on a man-made hill. On top of the hill was an open clam-looking structure with a 15-by-15-foot cube sitting where a pearl would be. In front of the clam stood a spiral-shaped tower maybe 20-30 feet tall, adorned with the colors of the Iraqi flag.

We drove slowly through the area in awe of the magnitude and the historical context of the sites. While we were creeping along, Mustang called and requested our presence at noon to escort Cpt. Glenn outside the city limits to the Al Radea police station.

Our taste of tourism ended just that quickly, and we meandered back to Mustang. We joined two other vehicles that were prepped and idling and then we headed for Al Radea. We were the last vehicle and didn't know the exact route or coordinates, but figured we were in good hands.

That was a bad idea in a safe location, but in a war zone, our decision could have cost us our lives. Our gap in common sense became even more apparent when we realized we had just driven in a circle, not once, but twice. Circles pose a serious hazard, because they give the enemy an ambush opportunity. Hart and I couldn't believe our luck. First, we failed Army Basic 101, and then we put ourselves in harm's way because we couldn't help with navigating.

A few minutes later, we pulled up to a small tan building with a gravel-covered driveway and parking lot. The commander jumped out of his vehicle, followed by his security guy—Spc. Ilgooth—and hustled into the station. My team and I disembarked and waited by the vehicles for three hours while the Commander did what he had to do in the police station. Glenn claimed he discovered a stash of important documents that included details of every IP officer in Iraq and all the cases since the 1970s.

After Glenn made his miraculous discovery, we headed back to the compound. He said, "Stand by, we'll be leaving again shortly."

"Roger," Hart replied.

We took our gear off and grabbed something to do. Hart and I read books and Murray grabbed a magazine. We waited. I switched to crossword puzzles. And waited. We grabbed MREs to eat for supper. And waited. Hart and I played cards. And waited...

Frustrated, we called it quits at 2130. Hart said, "All right. I think it's safe to say we can stand down and hit the hay."

My day didn't officially end until 2200 because I had to unload the vehicle and prep my gear for our 0430 mission the next morning.

The two vehicles permanently attached to Glenn's entourage joined us for the next mission as well. The vehicles included the commander's vehicle with a gunner—Spc. Koll—and Spc. Ilgooth, who drove. They were both in the admin platoon. The other vehicle included the team leader—Sgt. Rodriguez—and any other soldiers they could find from the company who weren't currently on missions. Rodriguez was curt, arrogant, and unfriendly to my team. Beyond working in our Tactical Operations Center, I had no idea what his job consisted of. He looked like a rat with his pointy nose and graying mustache. Being the complete opposite of Sgt. Hart, they butted heads often. On our second escort mission, Rodriguez wouldn't give us our destination's grid coordinates or tell us where we were going when Hart was adamant that we get them. Hart let him have it. He said, "What would happen if your Humvee hit a roadside bomb, or for some reason, we lost your vehicle in the middle of traffic? It's dangerous and idiotic not to tell us our destination and to hold back grid coordinates. This is essential mission information."

The rat Rodriguez—who had no sense of humor—grinned arrogantly and said, "Cool down. You'll be fine."

Hart stormed away. Rodriguez put our lives on the line for his pathetic ego.

As mentioned previously, Glenn's motives weren't always clear throughout our deployment, and I questioned the philosophical reasoning behind his priorities. Winning the hearts and minds appeared to be Glenn's primary mission for the duration of our escort month. For example, he visited a Mother Teresa orphanage twice a week. I knew helping the orphans was a noble and selfless thing. It also brought us much joy to be doing positive work in the middle of the dire war. Yet, Glenn was putting nine soldiers' lives on the line twice a week to visit orphans outside the wire. Worse yet, he put the orphans' lives in danger by associating with them. Within a year of our return to the states, the orphanage was bombed by insurgents for this very reason. I do not know what the casualty rate was or if the orphans made it out OK.

Twenty orphans with varying disabilities occupied the orphanage. The kids could have had wonderful futures but were hindered due to the orphanage's and the country's lack of resources. The orphanage was nestled amid two-to-three-story buildings that shared walls. The building was nondescript and blended in with the rest of the off-white, sandblasted facades. We walked up three steps, through a gated doorway and then a wooden one, and into a narrow hallway. I was hit with sour milk and dirty kid smell with a hint of cleaning solvent that reminded me of the chemicals used to clean up puke in my grade school. The tan hallway brought us to a large room with two-toned walls—glossy tan on top and glossy green on the bottom. There were cribs on both sides with thin wooden rails. Some cribs held orphans, others did not. The floor had an oval-shaped woven rug with a few kids crawling around on it, playing with wooden

toys and scrappy dolls. The next room held a small white kitch-
enette and a short wooden dining table and chairs. The yard's
door was on the far side of the dining room. Outside held mostly
sand and cement with a few outdoor plastic toys and rubber
balls. The children had benevolent nuns who took care of them,
but no therapy—physical or otherwise. Even though the nuns
loved and cared for them, the women were stretched thin.

The orphans were elated to see us when we arrived. Starved
of adequate attention, their eyes lit up knowing they would be
the center of attention, even for a brief moment. We assisted
during supper time by spoon-feeding the children. They were
fed watered-down and mashed peanut-butter crackers. None of
them could feed themselves or knew how to.

My favorite was a nine-month-old girl named Nora. Her
nonstop laughter illustrated her palpable love of life. Born
without limbs—only one- to two-inch stubs—didn't slow her
down. She kept up with the rest of the orphans by rolling on the
ground and was able to sit up on her own. I fell in love with Nora
the second I saw her.

Nora and I at the orphanage. 9/12/03

Zara, a 12-year-old in a two-year-old's body, stole a piece of my heart as well. Her stature was small, but her muscles were not. She stood about two feet off the ground and was able to pull herself into her crib. She reached up, grabbed the top horizontal bar on her crib, flipped her whole body over like a gymnast, and stood in her crib, proud as a peacock. She was like a baby on steroids. Sadness presented itself in Malna, a blind orphan, who acquired a boxy cranium due to lying in her crib for an exorbitant amount of time. So much heartache and joy wrapped into an hour-long visit.

Our next commander escort mission was the antithesis of the orphanage visit. It took us to an abandoned city council building to evict four squatting families. The white building was stately with pillars that extended to the second-story roof line. At one time, this building could have rivaled a historic colonial home with a twist of middle-eastern flair. Palm trees decorated its overgrown flower beds, and the once-rich exterior was starting to show some wear and tear. It was yellowing from the smoggy and sandy air, some of the windows were broken or missing, and the stone was crumbling from the intense climate.

A week previously, IPs informed the four families to move out or the coalition forces would help them. Having no other options, the families refused to leave. Our mission was to support the IPs as they evicted the squatters. Ten IPs were present, but only two or three did the dirty work. They banged on the door, telling the Iraqis to grab their stuff and get out. The women and children could be seen peeking through the windows and tattered shades. A few men were yelling from the doorway, while another two were posturing and yelling loudly at the IPs. An IP had enough and wrestled the two men to the ground, trying to arrest and cuff them. Five IPs watched him struggle, laughing. Unfortunately, we, too, were laughing. Our callous joy repulses me as I write this.

After an hour of resistance, the enraged families reluctantly agreed to move out. The women and children gathered in a huddle about 20 yards away. They were wailing and yelling in Arabic. A distraught teenage boy called Achmed walked back and forth in front of our trucks, yelling, "Fuck you! Fuck you! Fuck you!" while the rest of the men dragged their belongings onto the curb. Again, we laughed at the absurdity of the situation. Internally, guilt and empathy tore at my heartstrings, but from the outside, I was tough as nails.

Achmed's mom, Ana, stepped out of the huddle and joined him. She screeched incoherently at us between her sobs. Then she knelt in front of us, begging us to let them stay. We stood by our trucks and watched the chaos unfold around us. The wailing, the screaming, the swearing, the yelling. Ana must have been too much for Hart. He ordered, "Naylor, calm down that woman or arrest her. Whatever you do, shut her up and get her the hell away from us."

"Yes, Sergeant."

I stepped toward the woman, reached down to console her, and attempted to move her away from our trucks. Another woman named Lina was on the periphery of the huddle. She gasped and fainted when she saw me approach Ana. She must have thought I was going to hurt Ana. The racket intensified as Lina's limp body met the pavement. The other squatting women and children screamed and yelled even louder—they were hysterical. The wailing reverberated through my bones, and I shivered in spite of the heat. Ana left her knees and ran back to the huddle to make sure Lina was OK.

The commander announced that our mission was accomplished a few minutes later. The squatters were out, the IPs had secured the city council building, and we were causing more harm than good.

This day still haunts me. We set ourselves up for the retaliation and hatred that we were about to endure.

Other escort missions brought us to many beautiful parts of Baghdad. The most memorable was the Presidential Palace within the Green Zone. It was known as the Office of Coalition Provisional Authority—CPA—and for a brief time, it was the U.S. Embassy. It was about a two-mile drive from our compound and housed most of the international civilians affiliated with the war. The building was beyond secure. It was surrounded by barricades and included a checkpoint where we had to present our CPA badges before entering.

The first visit took a bit longer because we had to get our badges made. The building's magnificence was converse to the PD squalor and the mud-hut squatters. Marble covered the floors, walls, and ceilings. Detailed mosaics gave the palace a sense of wealth and prosperity. People were starving a stone's throw away, yet the palace doors were plated in gold. After the vast entryway, I looked up in the great hall and couldn't tell which portion of the ceiling was higher or lower—it played tricks on our eyes, like an optical illusion. Saddam had a mosque inside the palace with an oversized, gold-plated throne. Behind it, a horrific mural on the wall depicted seven missiles flying through the air—in his place of worship. And now we know the true sanity of the mad-man Saddam.

After our short tour, we entered the dining hall, the huge, elaborate, anything-you-could-ever-want-to-eat dining hall. Any food imaginable was at our disposal, such as fruits, vegetables, ice cream, cakes, lobsters, steaks, and corn on the cob. I ate too much. I closed my eyes when I bit down on the grilled burger and thought of tailgating. The corn on the cob reminded me of warm summers in my parents' backyard. The ice cream brought me to my favorite childhood establishment—Scoopers. Our experience got even better when we were allowed to use the

CPA's phones to call home. It was during these special occasions that I called my best friends, Sam and Hannah.

One day, while washing my hands in the CPA bathroom, a ritzy lady—who no doubt had a prestigious job in the U.S. Embassy—sashayed in. Since the solid stall doors made it difficult to decipher occupancy, I kindly mentioned that the first stall was open. She glared at me with a disgusted look on her face and said, "Are you kidding me? I would never use the first stall. That's the most disgusting stall of them all. Everyone uses that one."

Really? Really!? *I pooped in a box and had to burn it. I watched a rat crawl out from a hole two feet away. I had to stir diesel fuel in a barrel of burning human excrement. And you're complaining to me?!? About a stall in an elaborately decorated marble bathroom with a stand-in-maid who wipes it down after every use?* By the time I had collected myself, she had disappeared into the last stall.

I am sitting on Saddam's golden throne in his mosque. Its grandeur is accentuated by the height of the throne. He was only one inch taller than me, and my feet were a few inches off the ground. His would have been as well. Notice the rockets—in his place of worship—in the mural behind me. 9/6/03

MORE TIME AT AL SHA'AB

I found myself on the Al Sha'ab roof in physical discomfort on September 8th. For the first time since we landed in Kuwait, I was cold. Not just cool from a nice breeze. I was goosebump, grinding teeth, freezing-extremities cold. I'm not sure what the temperature was—it could have been 75 degrees for all I knew, but 75 degrees felt significantly colder after living in 120 degrees for four months.

Al Sha'ab was going down the tubes after we handed over partial control to the security guards and IPs. The security guards slept, leaving the gate unattended. The IPs detained prisoners for no reason. Papers were strewn over the flat surfaces, cigarette butts were piled in the corners like paper cobwebs, the bathroom was smeared in gore, the toilets were missing all of their seats, and the new white-tiled floors were coated in a dark film of cigarette soot and dirt. Adnon overheard the IPs saying that they wanted us to leave because they wanted things to return to normal—including the torturing of inmates.

Our next monitoring shift at Al Sha'ab included three foot-patrols. It was our first venture on foot outside of the police station walls. I welcomed the street perspective after spending countless hours in the fighting position looking down. Our first patrol left the station at 1900. It took us an hour and 45 minutes to walk a three-block radius. The second we stepped past our Hescos, the city caught wind and raced out of their homes and shops to get a closer look. The curious children surrounded us—putting themselves in potential danger. Their curiosity got the best of them. They even reached out for our weapons and gear. I gripped my pistol tightly and held onto my ammo, not wanting it to run away with their little fingers. Most of the women kept their eyes downcast, not making eye contact. Every once in a while, I would find an inquisitive side glance. Their eyes would either widen in surprise that I, too, was a female or dart away out of embarrassment for getting caught. Most of the Iraqis we came across wanted to share their hopes, dreams, fears, and concerns about their country. The common themes were too much gunfire, more IP presence in the neighborhood, more foot and driving patrols, and more safety.

Exhausted, we pushed through the crowd to get back to the station to take a break. By the time we got back, my feet felt laden and blistered, my upper back and neck felt like someone just tied 33 bowline knots into my muscles, my eyes hurt from scanning the crowd and buildings for enemies, my lower back was sore from schlepping 70 pounds of gear, and my brain was exhausted from being on edge for 105 minutes.

Our second foot patrol was set for 2300. At 2250, the IPs bustled around, shouting in Arabic with worried expressions and short, clipped, sentences—the station went from its sleepy nighttime routine to anarchy in a split second. They gestured emphatically when they ran past us. Unsure of what was going on, Verbsky called out to Red, "What's all the fuss about?"

Red explained, "They say we're about to get attacked by fifteen terrorists who are marching to the station right now."

My squad reacted by putting the majority of the soldiers on the roof for the best vantage point. We waited close to a half hour, but no one showed up. Another false alarm. Delayed by thirty minutes, our second patrol only lasted 45 minutes. The 2300 city-wide curfew turned our neighborhood into a ghost town. Even though the streets were empty and the chaos had subsided, I couldn't shake the feeling that something bad was about to happen. When our boots crushed a rock, it sounded like someone was pulling the hammer back on their pistol; when someone cleared their throats, it was as though they were giving me a signal to get down; when metal scraped on metal, it sounded like a cocked shotgun. I tiptoed through the empty streets to make sure I could hear any sign of encroaching death.

My apprehension subsided as we entered our PD's gates.

Then, at 0130, a deafening explosion interrupted the still night. A third platoon squad, who was on a driving patrol, radioed our TOC and said, "We were just hit by an IED three blocks from Al Sha'ab. We're en route there for security and to check for possible injuries." From the roof, I watched as their dust, headlights, and then Humvees approached our gate. *Please let everyone be OK. I cannot believe our company endured that thunderous explosion.* The soldiers exited their vehicles, checking one another for injuries. They were visibly shaken but appeared injury-free. The explosion was most likely a percussion grenade instead of an IED.

We left the station at 0200 with third platoon in tow. We dropped them off at the 28th Combat Support Hospital—CSH—located in the Green Zone—to check for hearing damage. Then we headed home and hit the sack.

The excitement intensified the next time we monitored the station. Our first foot patrol, at 1930, was smooth sailing until we stumbled upon a wedding party two blocks from the station. Twenty or so Iraqis flowed into the narrow streets, singing and dancing. Like cracks of lightning, the celebratory gunfire jerked us out of our walking trance. I jumped through my skin when the first bullet echoed between the three-story buildings. *Damn celebratory fire.* We ducked into our vests, aware of how easily the muzzle could orient itself in our direction. At least ten deafening rounds erupted around us. My squad, wide-eyed and worried, scanned each other to verify if we were unscathed or not.

The blessing and curse of a war zone was that we quickly became acquainted with how to decipher between a bullet aimed at us or away from us. An accompanying whistling noise meant we were the bullet's target. Luckily, none of the shots from our foot patrol were aimed at us. After our scare at the soirée, we headed back to the station. We had enough excitement and scares for one foot patrol.

As we were taking off our gear in the rear room, the TOC called to inform us that a first platoon element was hit by two different IEDs.

Apparently, they saw a suspicious-looking box on the roadside. Instead of calling explosive ordnance division—EOD— they pulled over and investigated the situation themselves. Spc. Ryan stepped out of her vehicle to investigate the box. The bomb detonated when Ryan peered inside and covered her with shrapnel. They flew her to Germany for immediate eye surgery. The explosion hit a couple other soldiers in their ankles as well.

The second IED wasn't quite as serious. The bomb exploded next to one of their moving vehicles. It hit Sgt. Bloechl—a team leader—on his left arm, causing minor damage. He was able to resume missions immediately.

Roadside bombs became increasingly prevalent as the war dragged on. We had no means of identifying them before they exploded. We didn't know if a piece of garbage or bump on the side of the road was a bomb. We didn't know who detonated the explosions, who set up the bombs, who they were aiming for, or who *they* even were.

Due to the recent IEDs, we weren't allowed to go on our second foot patrol and were sent home an hour early. I was *not* upset about that decision.

The next day I called my parents. When my mom picked up, she sounded frazzled. "Oh, it's so good to hear your voice! Are you OK?" she asked.

"Yes, I'm fine. Why are you worried?"

She let out a sigh of relief and explained, "Family Support had called and said that three soldiers were injured, but they couldn't release names yet."

"What? Why would they do that?" I asked angrily. "Why the hell would anyone think it was a good idea to call you and tell you that with no further information? At least identify the fact that I'm not one of the injured soldiers! For Christ's sake! I can't believe you waited a day without knowing if I was one of the injured soldiers! I can't imagine what you must have been going through."

"Well, at least now we can get some sleep tonight knowing that you're all right."

GATE GUARD

Guarding our gate was the third job we had as the roving team. The ease of gate guard or, as it was more eloquently called, Force Protection, was a welcome respite from the chaos of leaving the Green Zone. Every two hours, one of our teammates rotated out, which meant we had four hours on and two hours off for 12 hours. While working, we checked IDs, searched Iraqis and their vehicles, and patrolled the immediate area. Every vehicle that came through our gate had already been searched and questioned at the Green Zone entrances. The chance of a hostile situation was minimal, being that we were the second checkpoint.

SOCCER

I played soccer in a Battalion soccer jersey and my black PT shorts a handful of times throughout my deployment. Glenn approved the bizarre endeavor, to once again win the hearts and minds. Having played goalie my junior and senior years in high school, I fit the bill and was offered a position on the battalion's soccer team. The carefree nature of the event transformed me into my civilian life, if only for a brief hour or so. It was freeing and joyful. Due to my prior experience, I played goalie—until a male came forward. He became the goalie and I had to take a midfielder position, the worst position for me. My kicking ability pales in comparison to my guarding abilities. I am not afraid of the soccer ball coming my way and will sacrifice my body to block a goal. I cannot, however, kick the ball well. My feet lack aim and strength. On most days, I could throw the ball farther than I could kick it because athleticism resides in the upper half of my body.

The culminating soccer event came when we played against the Iraqi Traffic Police in early November. I joined the 60-minute game as a mid-right fielder 15 minutes into the second half. The Iraqis didn't waste an opportunity to brush against my privates. Disgruntled, they found my protruding knees and elbows instead. If they wanted to play dirty, I would too. Miraculously, we tied the soccer enthusiasts two to two. Ramadan—the holy holiday that forbids eating, drinking, and smoking during daylight—saved us from complete annihilation.

We enjoyed an Iraqi dessert that the Iraqi Traffic Police provided after the game. When I was sinking my teeth into the delicious baklava-like pastry, an Iraqi came over and said in broken English, "You too pretty to play. You news reporter. You no work so hard."

Another opponent joined the conversation and said, "You prettiest girl on field. You put on field to make it hard to play. A distraction."

I laughed, "Thanks, guys, but I'm not *that* pretty." I walked away, shaking my head.

THE HUMAN SIDE

> Because so few in America have served, they [veterans] can
> no longer relate to their peers, friends, and family for fear of
> being viewed as some type of monster, or lauded as a hero
> when they feel the things they did were morally ambiguous or
> wrong given the nature of the situations they were involved in.
> ~Benjamin Sledge

The life of a GI often left us feeling used and inhuman. We were cogs in a wheel, insignificant, disposable beings, pawns in a giant chess game. We had no control over our fate. Our humanity was being chiseled away as the days passed. A war zone will make anyone do things they aren't proud of. We searched for avenues to feel human, to obtain a semblance of control of our fate and destiny.

The fact that our company was coed opened the doors to the world of romances, some of which resulted in adultery. Intimacy's powerful force outmatched morals and values. War turned us into different people. Because of this, I vowed to never marry a military man, no matter how strong our bond and faith in each other. I could never trust a war zone's power to change a person. Imagine the thrill of finding a time and secret place amid the palm trees, dark corners, and empty rooms for a sexual rendezvous. The ability to set the fear and stress of war aside, while passion and sexual urges rise to the surface.

Few of us were innocent, and the majority of the soldiers—male and female alike—took advantage of each other to subside our deep biological urges. Why not? We didn't know if we would make it home or not. Here's some historical fiction for you because there are things I'm not going to incriminate myself about, and it's not my place to tell other people's secrets. Ssg. Stud made Spc. Sexy feel like a woman—a sexy, wanted woman—with his buzzed brown hair, broad shoulders, tanned complexion, and beautiful hands and feet. He told Pfc. Sexy that she was his type. Her long blond hair waterfalled across her shoulders, her penetrating almond-shaped eyes, her athletic build, her narrow waist, her young and smooth skin. They met in the shower stall on their first forbidden rendezvous. He dared her. After weeks of flirting, he said, "Sexy, tonight's the night."

"Oh, yeah?" she hummed in response, thinking this was another one of his attempts to flirt.

"Yup, 2300, shower stall. See you then."

"Ha! Yup, see you then." She smiled and winked and the butterflies jumped about in her anticipatory belly. *Did we seriously just make a plan? Is this really going to happen?*

"I'm serious. 2300," he whispered under his breath when he walked passed her later that day. Their arms brushed against each other. Electricity hummed through her body from his touch. Her body yearned for more. She lost her voice for a split second. *Jeez, girl, get your composure. Pull yourself together.*

"I'm serious, too," she whispered back after he was already five paces away.

Once night fell, she lay down on her cot. Her head was swimming with steamy thoughts: Stud's image, his smell, his tall, broad stature, his caramelly voice, his forbidden touch.

"I bet you won't show up." His voice broke through her thoughts. He was bending over her mosquito net, undressing her with his eyes.

"Whoa, you scared me. I didn't even see you approach."

"So much for your battle skills. Might want to work on that, Sexy."

"Excuse me for being deep in thought from the safety of my own bed. And you can bet all you want. I'll be there."

"We'll see." He smirked as he walked away. She would lie if she told you she wasn't checking him out from behind.

An hour later, she crept out of her bunk, maintained a low profile, snuck past the third squad male's room, turned the corner, then snuck past the first squad male's room, slid through the ponchoed shower stall doorway, and stepped into the 5-by-5-foot shower stall. *Hey, my military training comes in handy for this as well.* He was there. Waiting. Breathing. Waiting. Pausing. "You came," he said, barely audible.

"I wouldn't miss it."

He took a giant step toward her, wrapped his warm, tender, muscular arms around her, and pressed his lips against hers. She melted. She turned to human mush. This one insignificant act meant lust and joy and humanity. She was a woman and nothing more in that moment. His wide hands covered the span of her back. He continued to kiss her supple lips, her neck, her ears. She was in heaven. They continued their steamy affair with only the thin ponchos protecting them from scandal.

At times she felt that rush of femininity and exhilaration, and at other times she felt used by him. Word spread that he was doing the same thing with other women. He was, after all, Ssg. Stud—the best looking guy in the platoon. Although Pfc. Sexy enjoyed the intimacy, the escape, and the thrill. She knew she had to maintain her own self-respect and dignity—what little she had left in Iraq. After months of almost getting caught, of loving and hating herself, she knew she had to end things. The next time he pursued her, she shook her head and cast her eyes to the ground. "We're done. I can't continue to be used like this. I'm not one of your playthings. This isn't fun anymore. It's hurting my self-esteem and my self-worth."

"Got it. I'm here, though—if you ever change your mind," Stud responded.

Rumors ran amok as soldiers paired up. Some were true, some were not. A few couples were found guilty of having affairs, and some couples were demoted and fined for crossing the different levels of rank. For example, specialists could not fornicate with those who were ranked above or below them. We could, however, date within our own rank.

In August, Phair confronted me as I was getting out of the pool. He said, "We are accused of having sexual relations."

"What?!" I exclaimed. "By whom?"

"I don't know, but we have to sign a sworn statement claiming that we didn't have sexual contact, relations, or intercourse. So do Kirking and I."

"Kirking?" I asked. "What does she have to do with it?"

"Nothing," he responded. "Let's just get this over with and move on."

Did Phair's flirtatious mannerisms spur the allegation? Why hone in on him when dozens of other affairs were occurring? The three of us signed our papers, stood in front of a panel, and swore our innocence. Then, as Phair stated, we moved on.

Affairs didn't only occur on our end. A few bad apples back home fell under the pressure. Second Platoon's medic, Alicia Smith, left her infant twin daughters at home with her husband. She took a leave of absence from Iraq for a while because her husband—Tom—had moved in with a neighbor named Melissa. The girls called Melissa "Mom" instead of Alicia. *As if leaving your children behind isn't painful enough.*

A gunner in my squad named Tasha Saunders gave her fiancé—Brad—power of attorney after the 21-year-old proposed weeks before our deployment. Around Christmas, Saunders discovered that Brad had stolen $10,000 out of her checking account and bailed on her. Legally, there was nothing she could do about it.

I was thankful that I did not have a significant other back home waiting for me. I didn't have to worry about infidelity happening on either end. One less thing to stress over during my deployment.

While relaxing in the pool one night, Hart and I jokingly deduced that we were part of a lovers' triangle. The battalion chef had the hots for me. He flirted, winked, and gave me long, passionate looks. He also gave me extra food, which I didn't complain about. One day, Chef saw Sgt. Hart and me in the pool together. I didn't say hi to Chef because Hart and I were busy laughing about the albino-hermaphrodite-mini-donkey that I hit. It was actually a dog, but we changed the story because neither one of us wanted to laugh about hitting a dog, regardless if it was a stray or not. Thereafter, Chef gave me sad puppy-dog eyes whenever he saw Hart and me together. He must have thought that Hart and I were in a relationship. Hart jumped at the opportunity and concocted a plan.

"Naylor, you have to ask Chef to serve biscuits and gravy for breakfast."

"Ew. I don't even like biscuits and gravy," I responded.

"I don't care. Imagine how happy it would make me. It's been forever since we've had any. I'm craving them like crazy."

"All right, all right. I'll see what I can do."

The following morning after our night shift, we went to the chow hall for breakfast and I asked, "Chef, any chance we could have biscuits and gravy for breakfast sometime soon?" Then I locked eyes with him and gave him a seductive smile.

He grinned from ear to ear, and with a wink said, "I'll see what I can do."

Our plan worked; steaming hot biscuits and gravy arrived a few days later. Hart was in heaven and I was indifferent.

Romance also crossed cultural lines. The Rat Rodriguez acquired an Iraqi girlfriend. He stopped to see her during a mission, putting everyone in his convoy at risk. He offered to sponsor her so that she could move to the United States and stay with him in his house until she could stand on her own two feet.

Everyone assumed they were having an affair, but no one could prove it.

FUN DAY

Our battalion organized a Fun Day on October 3rd. All battalion soldiers had the day off and could sign up for tug of war, volleyball, basketball, and swimming competitions. We started with a battalion formation at 0745. It was a relatively hot morning. The air felt heavy and stagnant. Bugs were buzzing around our heads and the breeze had taken the day off. We could hear the distant sounds of war echoing through the vast city while we stood in perfect rows, trying to stay focused on the CSM who droned on about pride, hard work, tough missions, more to come, huge strides so far, and on and on. I could tell it was more humid than normal because the longer we stood there, the more I could smell the acrid stench of body odor rise among the ranks.

The formation lasted an agonizing hour. Our entertainment came when soldiers started passing out. Under my breath, I said to Murray, "Check it out. 0200. Swaying soldier." His eyes scanned the crowd until he locked in on the female who looked like she just took 20 shots. A few seconds later, the soldier crumpled to the ground. Her comrades' quick reflexes prohibited her from hitting the ground too hard. Almost simultaneously, someone from First Platoon did the same thing. Then another. And another. And another. And another. They were dropping like flies, and we were losing our cool. Every subsequent faint caused the rows of soldiers to laugh a little louder and longer. Our somber formation turned into a circus. By the time the CSM had finished, he had lost everyone's focus. It didn't help that we all thought formations were fool-headed in a war zone. A mortar or rocket attack could wipe out dozens of soldiers at one time.

That exact thing happened to my older brother's company in Ramadi. The bloodshed haunts him to this very day.

My Fun Day activities started with a raucous game of basketball and then volleyball. After my two intense sporting endeavors, my teammates and I walked back to our compound to cool off in the pool and prepare for the swim event.

Halfway there, we crossed paths with disheveled looking Boutilier and Taylor. I smiled at them and said, "Cheer up. It's a good day!"

They looked at me as if I were a cold-hearted quack and retorted, "Haven't you heard?"

"Heard what?"

"Someone just drowned in our pool," Boutilier responded.

"What the hell? How in the world did that happen? Who was it?" I sputtered.

"Someone from the battalion. He was in a breath-holding contest and never came up. He choked on a sucker while he was at the bottom of the pool and drowned. Our medics tried CPR, but it didn't work. He was taken away by chopper to a Med Unit."

"Holy shit! Does this mean that the Fun Day is canceled?" I was repulsed by the insensitive words that left my mouth. *Have I become that shallow? Does someone else's life mean so little to me?*

This 18-year-old kid—he was simply trying to have fun on our first Fun Day. I can't imagine what his family went through when they received the news. "I'm sorry, Ma'am. Your son died in Iraq. Don't worry. It wasn't from war; he simply drowned in the battalion's pool."

I was numb and—as much as I hate to admit it—I was angry. Fun Day was one of the first times I could let loose among my comrades and assume an equal playing field among the ranks. In the blink of an eye, my joy shattered because the Fun Day did indeed get canceled.

Glenn claimed our day wasn't canceled because of the death, but rather because the infantry had conducted a raid nearby and the primary suspect escaped. The rest of my company rolled out in search of the thug without my platoon. Four hours later, my platoon left to continue the search when everyone else returned. They consumed the delicious Fun Day feast as my platoon nibbled on MREs while chasing a shadow. Our Fun Day was never rescheduled.

DRIVING PATROLS

The beginning of October meant the end of our roving duties. Instead, my platoon switched to Driving Patrols. And. They. Were. The. Worst. All those boring hours standing guard at Al Sha'ab was like a cakewalk compared to driving around Al Sha'ab and Sadr City for eight hours straight. It quickly made me realize I better be careful about what I wish for. The stress was almost too much to bear. Every muscle ached after only one day on the road. Even my eye muscles throbbed by the day's end from scanning the road for possible IEDs, pedestrians, crazy drivers, stray animals, animal-led carts, and flying garbage. My eyes were too sore to read, write letters, or sit in front of our mini-TV. My back felt bruised from the vest's steel plate. I either hunched to contour to the vest's concave shape or sat straight up only to have the top and bottom edges dig into my lower and upper back. My right calf throbbed from pressing onto the gas and brake. My ever-vigilant brain felt like mush. And my shoulders felt like I had just played in a weekend-long volleyball tournament. There were knots everywhere.

The purpose of our driving patrols was to train the IPs on proper driving patrol procedures and report anything out of the ordinary to our TOC. It was imperative that the IPs assumed a stronger presence to deter insurgent activity, and we were the driving force behind that—pun intended.

Aimless driving wasn't our only mission in October. We were also tasked in assisting the Iraqis in their currency exchange initiative. In October of 2003, the Iraqi currency—dinar—became obsolete because it contained images of Saddam and his regime. The new money's images reflected Iraq's culture, architecture, and landscapes. Iraqis arrived at the banks in droves to exchange their life savings, which they had separated into 6-inch-thick wads that were placed in duffel bags. The prior regime had left them with little trust in government-sponsored systems, which is why they held onto their money instead of keeping it in the bank. The long lines—one for women and one for men—stretched for three city blocks.

We helped pull security and reconned other banks to assess their level of security. Because of the millions of dinar exchanged daily, it was imperative for the security to deter would-be thieves. For once, I felt like the Iraqis did something right. Their security was robust. One bank had three IPs, one driving patrol, 16 security guards, and 20 bank staff standing guard.

The days we spent checking in on the banks brought in cooler temps and the first clouds during our time overseas. When the small puffy clouds first covered the sun's rays, I knew something was different but couldn't figure out what. By the third or fourth cloud, it finally dawned on me. I said, "Hey Kirking! Check it out! Clouds!"

Her eyes reached to the heavens and she laughed. "Holy cow; would you look at that. How long has it been?"

"Since we left home. What is that, five months? These are our first clouds of the Middle East. Crazy to think about, huh?"

"You got that right. I thought something was different but couldn't figure it out."

"Me, too!"

The other difference was that we didn't sweat anymore. The temps had subsided to 70s and 80s during the day, and it got downright chilly at night. We had to unpack our thermal clothing and coats, which was nuts after months of continuous sweat and unimaginable heat.

One of our driving patrols brought us to an arid dirt road north of Baghdad. The endless tan sand began to sparkle under the bright sun. It reminded me of bright winter days when the snow had an icy sheen on its top crust. The ground contained its own light that mesmerized the onlooker. "What is that?" I murmured to Hart.

"I'm not sure."

"Is that metal under the sand?" I asked.

"Whoa, whoa, whoa. Maybe we should slow down and investigate," Hart cautioned.

The radio interrupted our dialogue. "Stop driving. We need to find out what this is," said Verbsky.

We slowed the three-vehicle convoy down to a stop. Hart and Verbsky got out and crept to the edge of the road. "Yup; they're metal pieces," Hart yelled towards my Humvee.

Verbsky joined in. "Holy shit! They look like small rockets." There were dozens, maybe even hundreds, of two-foot-long rockets.

What? All of these shiny reflections are rockets? We would be annihilated if they detonated. I pictured one rocket igniting, causing the ones around it to ignite until the acres around us were filled with black holes in the ground, like a room full of readied mousetraps. Once one goes, they all go.

We called EOD, gave them our coordinates, put our Humvees in reverse, and got the heck out of there.

An hour after our discovery, we received orders to go back to the site. Our TOC said the EOD operation had an uncontrolled explosion, they needed assistance, and we should bring a fire truck with us. *A fire truck? Where the hell are we going to find a fire truck?* We scooped up an interpreter from Al Sha'ab, who conveyed the message to the IPs.

Six Humvees, two Iraqi patrol cars, an interpreter, and a never-before-seen fire truck hauled ass to the site within an hour of the order. It was rush hour, and traffic jams clogged the city streets. We opted to drive on the outskirts of the city through the ghetto. The slum's obstacle course included donkey carts, ghetto-fabulous-mobiles with a top speed of 20 miles per hour, a plethora of pedestrians, potholes too large for Humvees to navigate, and livestock herds. The squalor paid no heed to our blaring horns and the fire truck sirens. The humans and animals didn't flinch, move, or even acknowledge our presence.

When we finally arrived, we drove directly to the first vehicle we saw—a five-ton—which held all the explosives. In haste, the EOD soldiers raced toward us in their Humvee to cut us off from potential harm. We didn't have direct communication with them, and this was the only way they could get our attention. The rough terrain was pockmarked with holes and jagged embankments. The EOD troops didn't care. Their mission was to save our lives, and in the process, they totaled their EOD Humvee. Regardless, they accomplished their mission, and we diverted our trajectory away from the five-ton.

When we safely dismounted, the EOD's platoon sergeant, Sfc. Hauck, briefed us by saying, "When we were clearing the rockets, we discovered a mortar cache close by. As we put the mortars and rockets into our five-ton vehicle, a rocket sparked and caught the five-ton tarp on fire. We couldn't extinguish the fire, so we ran as fast as we could. We left a non-running Humvee and our weapons behind because more explosives began to detonate. We lost the five-ton along with a 50 cal., M16, a Kevlar, and three of our soldiers' belongings. The fire's out, but we're going to hang tight for a while longer to make sure nothing else happens. Y'all showed up a little too late. You can head out as we're all set here. Thanks for coming."

The next day, a car bomb exploded outside of the Turkish Embassy. The TOC called our patrol. "Mustang Seven. What's your location?"

Phair responded, "Just north of the Green Zone."

"Did you hear that explosion near you? That was the Turkish Embassy. They need immediate security. Go there now."

"Roger," Phair responded. "And yes, we heard the explosion. We wondered what that was. We're en route now. Over and out."

We were within a mile of their location and the first ones on the scene. The destruction was maddening. The entrance was caved in, people were walking around in the haze of dust, bloodied, shouting, lying on the ground. Bystanders were supporting the victims and shouting out orders to onlookers. People were flooding out of alternative exits to offer their support. Ambulances and IPs showed up shortly after we did. It was chaos. I wanted to help the wounded, to get a closer look at ground zero, but we were ordered a block away to secure the driveway. In a split second, media vans, trucks, SUVs, and sedans from a multitude of countries arrived. Helicopters buzzed overhead. They were like fruit flies to ripe fruit. They came out of nowhere and tried to sneak past our makeshift security line. Verbsky, Phair, and Hart were each conversing with a different media organization, forbidding their entrance. They would interfere with the recovery efforts and prohibit swift evacuation of the wounded. Within a turn of the hat, our mission changed into a fight against the media instead of the insurgents. We were yelling at them; they were yelling at us. More troops joined our fight against sensationalizing the catastrophe. It escalated. We had to physically push them away from us to get through to them. We had enough things to worry about. The media should not have been one of them.

A few days later, our TOC received intel that insurgents were stripping wires and metal out of the vacant Ministry of Trade building to construct their IEDs. One of our driving patrols was cut short because Glenn wanted us to search the building. *Sweet! I love MOUT—Military Operations in Urban Terrain!* The four-story Ministry of Trade building used to be a shopping mall with escalators, artistic ceiling decorations, and many stalls and shops dedicated to Iraqi treasures. Our liberation forced the grand sand-hued cement building to close. The gated parking lot had multiple potholes. The blue marble sign that read *Ministry of Trade hopping Center* was missing tiles—like the obvious capital S—and had begun to fade. The deserted building looked post-apocalyptic with busted windows, hanging light fixtures, and a ghost-like feel. The vacant building obtained the faint smell of char, static electricity, cologne, perfume, and incense. I could still feel the presence of shoppers and the hustle and bustle of the Haji Bazaars.

Our two squads entered together. We kept a hushed low profile and scanned the open floor plan. A shuffling noise, louder than that of rats, echoed through the empty chambers. Either there were animals larger than rodents in the building, or people were lurking about. Verbsky threw up an open hand—*Halt!* We froze with anticipation. Through arm and hand signals, we planned our next move. Verbsky split the group into two to clear the building quickly. He ordered the incompetent Ssg. Caldwell to lead my group.

I couldn't have been in worse hands. Caldwell couldn't remember his arm and hand signals, didn't follow our MP procedures to search the rooms, and he lacked confidence to take initiative. I could have led the troops better than he did, and I was two ranks below him.

In the end, the arm and hand signals didn't matter. The cement ground was littered with debris: soda cans, plastic bags, hangers, wires, metal scraps, newspapers, boxes, broken glass, and more. We couldn't help but walk on the rubbish, which caused a racket and ruined any chance of surprise. From a distance, we heard yelling echo through the empty building. We raced towards the shouting while watching our every move. Verbsky's group had found a teenage boy collecting wires. When we found them, they had him lying on the ground with his hands zip-tied behind his back. We put him in a Humvee and drove him to Sha'ab to sit in the putrid jail.

PART III
OCCUPATION

The gap between the citizen and the soldier is growing
ever wider. Whereas in WWII the entire nation's focus was
on purchasing war bonds and defeating the Nazis, today's
populace is quickly amused by the latest Kardashian scandal
on TV. Because the populace is more concerned about
enjoying their freedoms and going about their day to day lives,
the veteran can feel like an outcast. As though nothing they
did mattered for a country that asked them to go.

~Benjamin Sledge

Our deployment changed radically within the first six months.
We went from liberating the Iraqis to occupying their cities. And
with that occupation came more animosity and bloodshed. For
me, that defining moment when our deployment transitioned
from liberation to occupation was when Al Sha'ab was destroyed
by a vehicle-born bomb.

The side of the PD most affected by the bomb. You can see the crumbling security wall in the
background, the cracks through the PD, the wall on the side of the explosion almost entirely
blown in, and the soldier sitting guard on the rooftop. 10/27/03

THE CAR BOMB

We were lounging by the carport of our hooch on a beautiful October 27th morning, waiting for our mission to start. The birds were chirping, the sun was shining, the sky was dotted with a few fluffy clouds, the temperature was comfortable at about 75 degrees, and we all woke up in a relatively good mood. I was sitting on the second step, leaning up against the stairs behind me. I had just finished my Power Bar and PMSCing the Humvee. Our gear was waiting for us on our vehicle seats. Two earth-moving explosions boomed in the city. One of the bombs was close, causing us to mumble *holy shit* and *wonder what that was* under our breaths as we scanned the distant buildings across the Tigris. We didn't pay it too much heed, because we had become accustomed to explosions. The birds knew something was up. They screeched loudly and many took to the skies.

Within moments, second platoon said over the radio, "We just received an RPG attack at the Al Sha'ab police station. Our squad is headed to the closest CSH because we received multiple injuries from the blast. Al Sha'ab needs immediate assistance. There are multiple fatalities."

Without an audible order, we threw on our gear, mounted up, and drove like hell to the station. We accomplished the 45-minute drive in 25 minutes. I scraped the side of an Iraqi car that took too long to give us the right-of-way, drove down the wrong side of the road, jumped over medians, and tore through intersections.

Hart and I gasped as we turned onto Al Sha'ab's main road. Within a half hour of the blast, hundreds, if not thousands, of curious men and boys had poured onto the streets. The thick crowd covered every square inch of the major roadway up to the station, like a mob in Times Square on New Year's Eve. *How are we going to get through this crowd?* The mob flowed to either side like the parting of the Red Sea, as if we had a siren on our vehicle. I honked the puny horn, Hart screamed *Ishta* out the window, and Murray stood up in the turret, waving his hands. The parting bystanders slowly revealed the ruined station. The air was still clouded with explosive particulates. *The bomb must have been more than an RPG.* One side of the station and our ten-foot security wall were gone, along with two houses and at least ten shops across the street. Homes and businesses within a four-block radius had blown-out windows, and shrapnel had torn through their walls. The destruction was mind-numbing. I could smell burning buildings, garbage, flesh, and bomb residue.

The crowd was still massive the next day. You can see them held back by concertina wire, the soldiers on guard in their Humvees and the Iraqi Force Protector on the ground. All the windows were blown out from the bomb in the visible buildings. 10/28/03

We vacated our Humvees and pushed the crowd away from us, our vehicles, and what was left of Al Sha'ab. Then we went to the explosion site—ground zero—where a ten-foot-deep and 20-foot-wide crater yawned from the depths of the earth. Four unidentifiable vehicles looked more like heaps of melted metal than cars. We pushed the crowd back again, away from the blast site, to secure the area. Recovery men dug bodies out of the rubble. While we maintained crowd control, I watched three girls get unearthed and dragged from the rubble of their former homes. Their fathers sobbed over their charred and mutilated bodies as they cradled them like babies onto the street behind us. These were the same little girls I watched every day while I sat in the fighting positions at the station. It took two hours to move the swarming crowd one block. Once we had the block quarantined, we encircled it with concertina wire.

This is the location of the car bomb. The water entered the hole due to a water line bursting. Notice the soldier standing by the crater. All of the buildings behind him were two stories prior to the explosion. The ground was cement, but in this picture, it looks like dirt. 10/27/03

I surveyed the damage throughout the station when I went to the roof to pull security. It reeked of blood and burning flesh. A lone hand lay on the ground, palm up, in the front entryway. Blood and dirt smudged the lifeless phalanges. The walls along the length of the police station were snaked with cracks. Blood splatter and smears caked the walls and floor. Pieces of shrapnel stuck out of the walls and corners. Almost all the doors on the second floor were blown off their hinges. The prison door was ajar with a six-by-two-inch gaping hole in the middle of it. All 60 prisoners had escaped. Clothes littered the floor among the debris. Most were torn to shreds to gain easier access to various wounds. The individual tiles were indecipherable because the floor was covered with debris, rubble, and a thick layer of dust that was still settling. There were blood puddles in every room on the side of the explosion. Our MP office was annihilated with two or three feet of rubble and upturned desks. Four IPs had flown through a wall and into our office, killing them instantly. *What would have happened to us, the MPs, if we were in our office at the time of the explosion?*

Our MP office within the station. The blast was on the right side of this picture and tore through two cinder block walls. We would not have survived if we had MPs in our office at the time of the explosion. 10/27/03

Simpson, a mechanic who was a big country boy in his late 20s, Hart, and I were sent across the street to stand on a rooftop to watch for more vehicle-born bombs. We attempted three different staircases before we found the right vantage point. We sat idly for four hours and watched as Al Sha'ab picked up the pieces. Distant wailing, Arabic yelling, swept glass, and sounds of building debris being thrown around resonated through the destroyed streets.

At 1915, we left Al Sha'ab and headed back to Mustang. Once back, Sgt. Hart shook my hand and said, "You're one hell of a soldier. Good job today."

His formal praise caught me off guard. I responded, "Wow, thanks. Just doing my job. You did great as well. It's nice having you as a leader."

He chuckled. "Normally, I would have been scared out of my mind having someone else drive as you did on the way to the station, but I wasn't."

"I'm glad you trust me. That's all I ask," I responded.

I maintained a military façade throughout the long and arduous day, because I was in shock.

When we debriefed that night, we exchanged stories. A White Nissan SUV had torn through the concertina wire at the end of the block behind the station. The Iraqi Force Protectors who worked at the Community Center, the building directly behind the police station, had seen the vehicle approach the side of the PD and had shouted at the driver to stop. The shouts caused our MPs to dive for cover, saving their lives. As they ducked into their Humvees, the vehicle-borne bomb exploded on the side of the station, blowing it to pieces. Three MPs were in the station and received the worst of the blast. Lt. Zick, second platoon's leader, was seriously wounded with deep lacerations to his head and a partially severed ear. The other MPs had ringing ears, blown eardrums, concussions, and minor scrapes. Six IPs and 21 civilians had died. Over 120 injuries were reported. Phair estimated the crowd to be close to 2,000 people when we arrived. Four choreographed explosions tore through the city that morning. The attacks included three police stations and the Red Cross.

The following day, we went back to Al Sha'ab and pulled security on what was left of our fighting positions, conducted crowd control, moved more c-wire, and loaded three truckloads of salvageable items. The bomb left little intact.

Once again, various media outlets arrived in droves, including the BBC, CBS, and NBC. We remained civil throughout the day, but the Turkish Embassy debacle was still fresh in my mind. I would have accidentally shot a few photographers if the ROE weren't in place. While I was sitting on the rooftop pulling guard, I watched with caution while three different men meandered onto a roof directly across the street and pointed something black in my direction. The glare of the sun, my scratched sunglasses, and the distance between our rooftops made it difficult to decipher what they were pointing. I put my finger on the trigger and turned my weapon to fire in case the shit hit the fan. After a short time, they left without incident. I found out later that day they were photographers who took my picture because I saw myself sitting on the roof when I logged onto Yahoo.com later that evening.

Our despair didn't end with the destruction of Sha'ab, the ruined lives, the destroyed infrastructure, or the loss of the Iraqis' trust in us to keep them safe. We also lost two of our trusted interpreters and friends. Red and Adnon quit. Red was present during the explosion and was hit in the head with shrapnel and was left behind. Neither man wanted to continue to risk his life.

By the third day, my shock had worn off and I felt like crying all day. Tears slipped out of my eyes without warning, and I choked on my own sobs, filled with stress, fear, loss, and devastation. Thankfully, the work day was relatively short, a mere eight hours. We were back to our bunks by 1530. I untied my boots, hung up my weapons, and crashed into my pillows, fully dressed. I sobbed into the softness of my bed and blankets, shaking my bunk. By 1600, I rose out of bed with reddened, swollen eyes and a slightly lighter heart. I put on my PT gear and running shoes and went for a run. The sweat and excursion helped clear my mind and release leftover toxins. By the time I got home, my emotions had leveled out, and I was feeling more like myself.

After the last series of attacks and injuries, our company opted to get steel plates put on our Humvees. We weren't any closer to getting the much safer up-armored versions, and we had to do something before we lost a soldier. Within two weeks, we hired Iraqis to put on our quarter-inch diamond plates. The Humvees were heavier and less agile on the road, but we felt safer.

The building and houses across the street from the PD. These are the same buildings from the prior picture, but just panned to the left. There are cars lining the road that have been blown into unrecognizable metal pieces. 10/27/03

TRAINING SQUAD

A few days before Al Sha'ab was destroyed, we had switched missions from Driving Patrol to Training Squad. We drove to several different IP stations around the northeast part of Baghdad, some of which hadn't had MP contact yet. The training included proper personnel and building searches, weapons and pepper spray usage, and other policing tactics.

Our first mission took us to Bab al Sham, a decrepit station on the northern outskirts of Baghdad. We pulled into a pockmarked dirt frontage road and turned right through a rusted white hinged gate that was broken and stuck in the open position. If it weren't for the IPs standing around and the lone lit light bulb in a building the size of a chicken coop, I would have thought the station was abandoned. It was a single-story building with the same sandblasted cement wall that most of the Iraqi buildings possessed. I caught a glimpse of a lone metal table, two chairs, and a few stacks of paper on an ivory-colored tile floor through the opened PD door. The white and blue paint was flaking off the walls, and there were shards of glass poking out of the window sills. Curid—an interpreter—Verbsky, and Hart conducted classes with the five IPs on duty on how to apprehend subjects while the rest of us sat in our Humvees and waited. I read a book and did crossword puzzles.

We returned to Bab al Sham a few weeks later to train the IPs on how to search personnel. In jest, Hart inappropriately searched me for the demonstration. He made sure to wipe his hand across my chest a few times to offend the IPs. Disgust and horror showed on their faces when his palms swiped the metal plates on the exterior of my vest. Neither one of us could feel a thing through the inches of gear. Although it was unethical, we laughed about it for days. Gallows humor at its best.

The next time we walked through Bab al Sham's gates, we were welcomed by a dead man sprawled on a plastic lawn chair. His splayed arms and legs made him look like he was in post-crucifixion rigor mortis. He was covered in bruises and blood smears. His clothes barely hung onto his skinny frame. What? *Who? Why? How?* I walked up to Lawn Chair Larry, as we affectionately called him, to determine how he died.

This is Lawn Chair Larry, moments after we discovered he was still alive. Notice the decrepit establishment. You can even see the lone light bulb lit in the IP office. 11/13/03

"Holy shit!" I yelled. "He's not dead!" Lawn Chair Larry was breathing heavily through a broken nose. His nose was tilted to one side and his face was covered in dirt and blood. One of his eyes was swollen shut, and the other one had a cut across the eyebrow. Hart and Verbsky stomped over. Their expressions turned from curiosity into anger.

"Are you serious?" Verbsky inquired.

"One hundred percent," I answered.

Verbsky spun on his heels and viciously approached the two IPs sitting outside. "What the hell is going on? Why is this man out here? What did he do?"

Through Cudis, the IPs explained that they shot and beat Lawn Chair Larry because he was a bad guy. They left him in that chair all night, hoping he would die.

Once again, we could tell the extent of Verbsky's anger based on his face's shade of red. "You will take this man to the hospital at once. We will stop by every week to make sure he's still alive. If he dies on your watch, you're fired."

The IPs gathered their things, gently placed the man in the bed of their truck, and drove him to the hospital. Sticking to our word, we checked on Lawn Chair Larry for weeks afterward. They tucked him away in their jail, which was a loose term. The construction looked more like a large animal pen. Its black metal bars extended from floor to ceiling on one side. The other three sides were bare cinder blocks, and the slanted roof was corrugated steel. The prisoners sat on the floor gazing out at us with soulless expressions. Even in the decrepit conditions, Lawn Chair Larry recovered and thanked us every time we checked on him.

The days passed by as we trained hundreds of IPs in the various stations. I mostly stayed by the Humvee and read, chatted, or pulled security. Thankfully, I could help with the Glock training, which included how to clear, clean, hold, and assemble the weapon. I also recorded the IP's name, rank, badge number, and weapon's serial number. Within a few days, some of the issued Glocks showed up on the black market—and there was nothing we could do about it.

On the way to one of our training sessions, we received an urgent call from another company. They had hit an IED close to our location and received small-arms fire. They needed our assistance to establish a security perimeter because their Humvee was disabled, and they had to wait to evacuate.

We pulled onto the edge of the northbound Canal Highway—a major six-lane highway with a canal going through the median.

We walked a few hundred feet to their location. Their squad leader, Ssg. Rusch, said, "Thanks for coming. We need you to search the local houses to find out who was shooting at us. If you find the assholes, take them into custody. We'll be fine here as long as you can keep the small-arms fire at bay." There was only one house and a couple shacks that could have hidden a shooter, and they were located in the median. That's where we headed.

I led the 11 soldiers on foot to hunt down the shooters. Hart was right behind me with directions and motivation. I walked at a moderate pace to ensure the other soldiers could maintain their three-step interval. We moved in a single-file line past the disabled Humvee. Its front end was crushed to a quarter of its usual size, pushing the engine into the driver's seat. It's a miracle the driver had survived. There was barely room for a piece of paper to fit between the steering wheel and the seat. *Will she ever walk again?* We walked onto the bridge that crossed over the highway and then marched down the southbound exit ramp.

A small bunker came into view on our right side. I held up the *halt* hand signal. We silently crept to a kneeling position covering the 360 degrees around us. Hart tapped my shoulder and motioned his head in the direction of the bunker. I nodded and did my job. Because I was the lead soldier, I had to crawl inside to verify that the small area was clear. Like Demi Moore in *G.I. Jane,* I turned on my ass-kicking mentality. With my pistol in one hand and my flashlight in the other, I scrambled down the embankment, took a deep breath to calm my racing heart, and whipped around the corner, ready to pull the trigger. The bunker was empty. I hopped out and said, "All clear." The soldiers stood up and resumed their positions in the line. I let out a large sigh, shook off the adrenaline, and kept on going.

Two small straw huts with dirt floors came next. We followed the same procedure. Once again, I conducted a quick and thorough search of the one-room huts and found nothing. We walked another 200 hundred yards to the largest dwelling, a small adobe house.

Before we entered, Red—who had re-joined our company—yelled to the inhabitants to come out with their hands on their heads. With apprehension, the family of five emerged from the house. There was a boy around ten, a girl in her upper teens, their parents, and grandmother. We made them stand side-by-side with their fingers interlaced behind their heads and posted a few guards to make sure they didn't try anything. I entered the house with Hart close behind, followed by Verbsky and Taylor. I kicked open the front door and searched the entryway. "Clear!" I yelled, and the rest of the soldiers entered the small entryway.

I moved to the kitchen. It was clear as well. I peered into the hallway. Two open doors extended off the hall. Hart and I saw a man in the bedroom and yelled in unison, "There's a man in the house! Not clear! Not clear!!" *Is he a suicide bomber? Does he have a gun?*

In a split second, Hart pounced on him and secured his arms behind his back. I scanned the room and noticed piles of needles. *What is this, a drug house? What the hell is going on?* We handcuffed him and dragged the man outside. He was too weak to stand. We were irate that he didn't follow the rest of the occupants. The exasperated father—still standing with his hands behind his head—explained to Red that Needle Man was diabetic and couldn't walk. Verbsky, who had been taking up the rear, demanded, "Red, find out if there are any more surprises inside. If so, they better tell us now."

Red inquired and the man adamantly shook his head.

We reentered and wrapped up our search. We found two AKs, ten pistol magazines, and a water cooler full of anti-aircraft ammo sitting in a five-gallon pail in the kitchen.

Verbsky looked at the man and asked, "What are these for?" as he pointed to the pile of weapons.

Red translated; the man responded. Red said to Verbsky, "For self-defense."

Regardless of what they told us, we couldn't trust a soul in that god-forsaken country. We confiscated the AKs and anti-aircraft ammo but left the small-arms ammo.

We kept the family outside with their hands on their heads while we searched the surrounding area. A three-foot-tall metal drum overflowing with junk stood next to the family. *Jackpot!* It was the perfect size to hide weapons. I sauntered over, confident that this is what we were looking for. I rummaged through it. *Wait, did something just move inside the drum?* I shoved the notion aside, thinking it must have been a coat sleeve. Then a giant rat, the size of a small cat, jumped out of the barrel. It scampered onto my chest and shoulder and pushed off my upper back before it landed on the ground. I put my hands up by my face and let out a high-pitched wavering scream. The same kind of scream my friend Jill would make when a fish or seaweed brushed her leg while swimming. The Iraqis, who were watching my every move, burst into laughter. They even mimicked the way I screamed. My GI Jane toughness went down the tubes because of an oversized rat.

MORTAR ATTACKS

Back at the compound, mortars breached our wall for the first time in October. I was watching *Punch-Drunk Love* on a relaxing evening when the lights flickered and the windows vibrated. Explosions erupted above. Insurgents were shooting mortars from across the Tigris River into the Green Zone, into our safe haven.

My fellow troops and I couldn't believe what was happening. "What's going on?" I asked Hart after walking into his room.

"I'm not sure," he responded. "Seems like they're bombing us."

"I know! But how?"

"Most likely mortars or rockets."

"Oh. Great; our safest place in Baghdad is in jeopardy. Just great."

"Everyone, get your gear on. TOC just called. We're going to the roof to pull security," bellowed Phair through all three chambers—the 3rd squad male's room, the entryway, and the female's room. After donning our uniforms, gear, and loading our weapons, we flew to the roof. Sgt. Hart, who had been getting the lowdown from Phair, pointed to a spot across the roof and said, "Go over there."

He didn't give me my line of fire, he didn't tell me how long we were supposed to stand there, or if we had received intel on who might have shot the mortars. I was done with my insignificant specialist rank. I was sick and tired of never knowing, only doing what I was told. Doing it over and over and over to no avail. No retribution, no redemption, no salvation, no end to the madness, for nothing. I stood at my post directly behind the five-foot wall—alone. I listened to the three amigos—Hart, Phair, and Verbsky—laugh and joke behind the rest of us while we stood on the front line. We surveyed the Tigris River and beyond, looking for something in the dark. Something suspicious, something moving, something sparking, something, anything. From 300 yards away, it was fruitless and ridiculous. We were a free gift to an enemy sniper. We were sitting ducks, waiting to attack an unknown enemy, yet at the same time unveiling ourselves to get attacked. After 45 minutes with nothing but a few distant pings of gunfire, we were told to stand down and go to bed.

A few nights later, a deep, hollow sound interrupted our peace—the mortar attacks had begun. We counted the thud of the launches to know how many incoming explosions to expect. A whistle would resonate through the air, followed by earth-shattering compressions. The insurgents walked the mortars toward their target by adjusting the tubes a couple of degrees. We could hear and feel the mortars getting closer. Again, my squad was ordered to pull security on the roof. With less haste, we gathered our things and stood guard on the roof for 30 minutes. We were bored. *What is the point?* We knew the insurgents didn't stand around after shooting the mortars. They ignited the bombs and ran. If our own American bombs couldn't penetrate our compound's basement, the insurgents' weaker bombs wouldn't be able to either. We were putting ourselves in more danger by exposing ourselves on the rooftop. It was stupid and dangerous.

Mortar attacks continued for the remainder of our deployment. A handful of times, my squad was ordered to cross the Tigris River and search for the mortar launch sites. We rolled out at 2200 on November 6th for this reason. The problem with these missions was that mortars were launched from inside buildings, on top of truck beds, and in fields, which were cleared within a second, as if nothing had happened.

We maneuvered over a bridge to cross the Tigris and took our first right into an alley with five- and six-story buildings looming overhead. It was perfect for snipers. I squeezed the steering wheel with one hand and the pistol with my other. My trigger finger was at the ready as I scanned the deserted streets. The civilians had gone underground, sensing danger. We convoyed through the dark alley, unscathed, and took another right, which brought us closer to the river and the alleged launch site. Once all three vehicles had rounded the bend, two rounds of small-arms fire zinged at us. I could see the muzzle flash.

That is it! We had enough of taking fire and not returning it. We slammed on the brakes, parked the truck, and got out. With split-second decision-making, Phair, Verbsky, Hart, Mattingly, a specialist in my platoon, and I attempted to flank the enemy.

The rest of the soldiers stayed with the vehicles and pulled security.

Hart shot two star clusters to light up the area. The five of us descended the sloping road to the river's edge. When we got past the point of the muzzle flashes, we scaled back up the bank, staying prone. We split up at the crest of the hill. Phair and Verbsky crept along the river's edge while Hart, Mattingly, and I spread 30 feet apart with our night-vision goggles secured to our Kevlars. With our rifles raised and our senses peaked, we combed the field that stretched for half a city block. We assumed the field was the launch site, but we never found mortar remnants or the culprit who shot at us. We cleared an old conex shipping container when we reached the far side.

"Shhh." Hart beckoned us to halt. "Do you hear that?" he whispered.

We heard Iraqi voices. With our muzzles leading, we edged around the corner of a three-story brick building. Four Iraqis stood outside a hidden tavern, drinking their booze under the lone light illuminating the dark alley. This was the one and only time I witnessed the Iraqis consuming alcohol. Hart forced them against the wall and searched them one at a time. We tried to intimidate and scare them by barking orders at them, pointing our guns at them, and posturing with gusto, but they were drunk and made light of the situation. The drunkest of the four had the gall to leave his position against the wall, grab his bottle, and chug its contents. He drunkenly staggered toward his buddy, said something in Arabic, and then they laughed. Hart ordered him to get back to the wall, but without an interpreter, we couldn't blame the men for disobeying our orders, and their jovial attitudes and apathetic nature were kind of catchy. As far as we knew, they weren't threats. To my surprise, Hart and Mattingly both laughed at our ridiculous predicament and we let the men continue to get hammered.

The three of us retraced our steps, calmer than we were ten minutes earlier. Distant shots rang through the night but were too far away to be a threat. Once again, we didn't see any mortar remnants when we combed the field for a second time on the way back to our trucks. Hoping to find something, we walked down to the river bank and under a bridge. An Iraqi, who was on force protection somewhere nearby, joined us. We welcomed his skilled investigatory work. He looked under piles of debris, searched every crevice, and somehow knew what we were doing without guidance from us. A dog that Hart called Lassie joined our crew. When I flipped over a suspicious-looking box with my rifle's muzzle, the dog gave it a glance and then peed on it. I laughed and said, "I guess it wasn't harmful after all, huh, Lassie?"

With another fruitless adventure in the books, we called it quits and headed home.

We were pounded by mortars and rockets a few nights later. Glenn told us to put on our Kevlar and vests at around 2130. I was drained and cranky—sleeping would be impossible with curved plates digging into my back. I jumped out of bed and joined the rest of my platoon. Korb, who's always up for a good time, put on some dance music and yelled, "Let's see your moves, Naylor!"

Since I love a challenge, I shook my hips to Sysco's "Thong Song." My gear banged around while I tried to ooze sexy. Laughter filled the room and the other females joined me. The joy in the room lasted even after we got the all-clear. Outkast's "Ms. Jackson" brought down the house. By the end, everyone had stripped down to PT shorts and sports bras.

It was 2300 before we turned off the music. I hadn't had that much fun since we got deployed. When I get asked, "How did you deal with being on edge all the time?" I bring up this night and the many nights the other females and I went to the rooftop to talk, laugh, and play the bongo drums. The many nights we cleaned our weapons and watched *The Sopranos*. The nights we swam and skinny-dipped. The many runs and workouts, and the fact that we had each other to lean on and cry with.

Because the attacks weren't ceasing and our enemy was elusive, the Air Force joined the fight and retaliated with their gunships—helicopters designed to annihilate the enemy. Their thunderous staccato rhythm lulled us to sleep. *How can this show of force not scare the insurgents away? Why aren't we beating them?* Often we would hear mortars and gunships simultaneously. The gunships didn't stop or even slow down the mortar attacks. The mortar prevalence only intensified, and at times, their aim drew too close for comfort.

SECOND SQUAD SWITCH

I switched to second squad on November 22nd while Hart was on leave. I was excited to work with Korb—one of my favorite girls—but her team leader, Sgt. Spooner, rubbed me the wrong way. His ego inflated after losing 50 pounds at the beginning of our deployment, but somehow, he still seemed to be compensating for his low self-esteem. He was six feet tall with a long thin face and a slight underbite. Sometimes Spooner was a great guy: easy to talk to, light-hearted, passionate, and intelligent. Over time, though, I realized how much he complained. It was exhausting to be barraged with negativity for hours on end.

I felt bittersweet about Hart's absence. We needed a break from each other, but I missed his humor, intelligence, and most of all, his impeccable leadership.

One of the first missions with my new team was a raid at a housing complex. The infantry requested our MP company's investigatory skills to help in the search for notorious criminals. Additionally, they needed our females to search the Iraqi women.

We drove into the dark, impoverished neighborhood at 2100 and pulled security while the infantry knocked on doors. Within a half-hour, they had found a house that had over $400,000 worth of receipts. A different MP team that was present was tasked with the investigation.

I was beckoned to search Iraqi females at 0100. I searched 11 women from two different households. A couple of the women tried to hide wads of cash under their clothes and crevices. I counted at least 300 to 400 U.S. dollars and found a five-inch-thick stack of 10,000 Dinar bills and a few other smaller note stacks. *I hope there will be a day when the Iraqis can store their money in banks and trust the police force.*

I looked up from searching a woman to watch the infantry engage with the neighboring house. Initially, the inhabitants refused to open the door. I could see their shining eyes from behind the wrought-iron door. The infantry couldn't and *wouldn't* take the blatant refusal. They drove their Humvee an inch from the gate and revved the engine. The fear worked. The Iraqis opened their gates and evacuated the house. The infantry moved seamlessly through the building, clearing it in methodical movements.

I marveled at the U.S. military at that moment. *It is an amazing well-oiled machine. Soldiers from every walk of life act as one unit and speak the same language. We turned a clumsy act of running through a house with 60 pounds of gear into a silent, well-choreographed art form.*

Without incident, the raid ended at 0230 and we returned to our compound a little before 0400. I went straight to bed—exhausted.

THANKSGIVING

Thanksgiving was our first major holiday overseas. Cpt. Glenn rounded up our company at 1230 to pat us on the back and wish

us a Happy Thanksgiving. Afterward, my fellow troops left for
chow while my team stayed behind. We were chosen to go to
BIAP to greet and eat chow with an unidentified special guest. I
was *not* looking forward to spending more time with the misog-
ynistic Sgt. Spooner. Plus, the mission didn't feel right. There
were too many unanswered questions to seem factual. *Who is the
guest? How and why were we chosen?*

My team and nine other troops from our battalion left for
BIAP at 1430.

The lieutenant in charge, Lt. Buenning, put the 12 of us into
two different groups after our BIAP arrival. My group of six ate
and then relieved the second set of six that were securing the
vehicles.

I needed to use the bathroom before I went into the chow hall.
Spooner made Korb go with me because female soldiers couldn't
go anywhere alone. *Another cringe-worthy double-standard our
platoon upholds. Another way the women are not treated equally
to men.* Korb and I walked around the exterior of the chow hall
to the back side and down a short road to the porta-potties. On
our hike, we noticed the back side of our chow hall was split
into two different sections. Soldiers entering the other side were
being searched. Really searched—with metal detectors. *Did our
company go into the wrong side of the chow hall?* We didn't know
what the hell was going on. We thought Lt. Buenning knew what
he was doing, and that the special guest was coming into our side
of the chow hall. We headed back to our group and mentioned
what we saw to deaf ears. We ate a delicious—but not quite as
good as home—Thanksgiving meal on the non-searched side of
the chow hall.

We relieved the second group of soldiers once our bellies
were full. While we waited, BIAP officials approached our group
and said, "You need to move your vehicles to the PX parking lot.

We need all vehicles at BIAP in one location." *Who is this guest person?*

Korb and I grew bored from the long wait and asked to check out the PX. With the go-ahead from Spooner, we walked over. It was closed. Being curious delinquents, we snuck over to the other side of the chow hall. We went through the security line—having to leave our guns and knives behind—and entered the secure side. That was the side we were *supposed* to go to. Our hunches were correct and Buenning was wrong. Our brigade had an assigned table for 12 troops. Come to find out, all six of the soldiers who ate on the second rotation had gone into this side of the chow hall. They figured it out once they rounded the back side of the chow hall.

Spooner grew concerned when our absence took too long and called us on our handheld radios. "Naylor and Korb, it's time to report to the trucks."

"Sgt. Spooner, we found out that we're supposed to be on the other side of the chow hall, so we went in. Lt. Buenning is here and we have a table set up for our battalion. Get your butt in here!" Korb said.

"Are you pulling my leg?"

"No, it's awesome! There are tons of brass and civilians and the special guest hasn't arrived yet."

"OK. I'm on my way," he clipped.

He attempted to join us, but the security had tightened further. They were no longer letting soldiers into the vicinity of the chow hall. He was irate and took it out on us.

"Korb and Naylor, they won't let me in, and you weren't allowed to go over there in the first place. I order you to get back to the truck, immediately."

"What?" Korb responded. "Are you serious?"

"Absolutely. If you don't do what I say, it'll be an Article Fifteen for both of you," he spat into the handhelds.

"What the hell is his problem?" I asked Korb.

"He's always like this," she said, "He's jealous. He's probably pissed that we're here and he's not. He pulls this shit all the time."

"I can't believe we can't see the special guest because of this jerk!" I was pissed.

Korb and I moped back to the trucks. Security said that there was no re-entry upon leaving. Didn't matter to us. Spooner wasn't letting us out of his sight. The six of us waited by the trucks. We waited...and waited...and waited for *four* hours.

Lt. Buenning claimed that he tried to get us once he found out who the special guest was, but it was too late. They wouldn't even let him *leave* the chow hall. Who was the special guest, you ask? None other than the President of the United States—George W. Bush. We missed him by less than ten minutes.

MORE GATE GUARD STORIES

You know those people in life who bring out the joy in you. They make you laugh uncontrollably, give you a sense of adventure, and make you want to spend as much time with them as you can. Korb is one of those people. I loved working with her on the gate. It was even more enjoyable when Spooner took his break.

"Naylor, get down here and play baseball with me."

"OK," I responded, even though one of us was supposed to be manning the SAW at all times. She picked up a stick and tossed a stone in my direction.

"Here, pitch."

I lobbed the stone in her direction and she swung and missed. We laughed at her error, so I found another rock and threw it in her direction. She cracked the stick against the stone. It bounced out of sight. We switched positions and played for a while until we heard Humvees approaching our position. I jumped into the gunner's seat and she checked their IDs. Although insignificant in hindsight, our simple rule-breaking gave us the thrills and excitement we had been longing for.

One night, the TOC had us watching for submarines. "Korb, do you believe this stuff? Submarines? Who the in the hell has a submarine? And why would it be in the Tigris? Sometimes I feel like we're the only ones with brains in this place."

"I hear ya, Naylor. Hey, should we shoot off some flares and tell them that we thought we saw a submarine?"

"Yes!" I responded, having always wanted to shoot off my own flair.

"One flair, coming right up." She grabbed Spooner's weapon and flair from their ammo box and then *zoom* the rocket shot into the sky and illuminated the world around us. We geeked out over the experience. It left us in hysterics the rest of the night. Spooner returned after his break and was none the wiser about what had happened.

Another one of our favorite pastimes was flirting with the guys who ran and drove past our checkpoint. The special forces and infantry laid the schmoozing on thick because they didn't have females in their companies. Two infantrymen, Zeamer and Zube, talked with us the most. Their compound was three down from our own with the Gurkhas and the rest of our battalion—the 233rd MPs—in between. Two battalion guys, Trantow and Lang, also stopped by often. They were kind enough to bring us hot cocoa on chilly nights. Trantow was my favorite with his wide smile, light-brown hair, a dusting of freckles, six-feet-one physically-fit stature, and a courteous demeanor.

Sgt. Zeamer was a nice guy, born for the military. He wasn't well educated, was short, and it was obvious he was trying to get into our pants. Regardless, when he offered Korb and me a ride in his Bradley—an armored personnel carrier—we couldn't resist. We planned to sneak out and meet them a quarter-mile down the road at 2300. Korb and I were determined to pull it off.

We plotted, schemed, and analyzed various situations but realized that confidence was key. There was no way to steal past the bright lights at our gate, so we acted like we owned the place. We strolled out of our building at 1055 and through the gates of our compound. Sgt. Bloechl was working the gate at the time and couldn't have cared less as long as we weren't putting ourselves in danger. Darkness enveloped Korb and me once we left the spotlights of our gate. Like a bear out of his den, the Bradley popped out of the shadows and rolled to a stop a few feet away. The back hatch released and Korb and I jumped in. My claustrophobia set in after the hatch closed. I got dizzy and felt a shortness of breath. My body wanted to explode out of the metal beast. *How did the infantry stuff eight soldiers into the tiny compartment?* I coaxed myself into a calmer state and tried to enjoy the experience.

The Bradley stopped after a short distance and the hatch opened. Korb and I climbed out. Zeamer gave me a tour of the turret and taught me how it traversed. Korb was sweet-talking the driver into giving her a chance at the helm. Her flirtatious magic worked. I stayed in the turret while Korb drove. We secured headsets with the rest of the crew before she took off. Korb had no idea what she was doing. She accidentally turned the hazard lights on and couldn't figure out how to turn them off. After the hazards shut off, the tank lurched forward. My upper half was like a rag doll being thrown in every direction. Korb couldn't perfect steering or accelerating smoothly. It was a miracle I didn't have whiplash afterward. Everyone was trying to tell her what to do. I couldn't help but laugh hysterically throughout the ride. When we parked, Korb got out and stormed over to me. "I couldn't hear what anyone was saying, because you were laughing so hard. Thanks a lot!" she said in a sarcastic tone as she punched me in the arm.

I laughed some more and was finally able to say, "I'm sorry." I had a case of the giggles.

After a group photo, Korb and I climbed into the back hatch.

The driver yelled out to us, "Hold on!"

The Bradley jolted forward and I slammed against the back hatch, causing my head to bang into the metal door. Thank God I was wearing my Kevlar. It was Korb's turn to laugh. The fact that we couldn't hear each other in the confines of the Bradley made our situation even more comical. We used facial expressions and hand gestures to talk while we were being whisked away. The bumpy ride and raucous laughter left me having to pee and wondering if I could hold it until they let us out. Luckily, we were released a few minutes later.

We invited the guys into our compound to give them a tour. It was the least we could do after the entertaining night. We crawled into our beds at 0100 after a good laugh. The night was a success! Sgt. Zeamer tried to touch me a few too many times, and my bladder prohibited me from attempting to drive, but other than that, it was a night of a lifetime.

Me inside the belly of the Bradley. I am trying to maintain my composure and smile at the same time. 12/6/03

BACK TO THIRD SQUAD

My fun times with Korb came to an end too soon. Sfc. Phair wanted me to switch over to my original squad to continue training the IPs. He became my team leader until Hart got back.

Phair's antics were at an all-time high when I came back. He gave me crap the first morning for being away from third squad, being a pussy driver, and hanging out with Trantow. Not quite the welcome I was hoping for—or the welcome that I deserved.

A kid was waving at us from the side of the Canal Highway on our drive to the Shleck PD later that day. He was holding onto an anti-aircraft round and was next to the house I had searched with the giant rat. We pulled over on the side of the busy highway to investigate the scene. We found hundreds of munitions in the swampy ground and stopped the traffic going in both directions on the six-lane highway. Three IP vehicles, an EOD squad from the U.S. and from Iraq, five tanks, two Kiowa helicopters, and a Black Hawk helicopter buzzed overhead to assist. Three hours and an EOD vehicle full of munitions later, we were done.

EXTENSIONS

On December 11th, my company received orders stating that we would leave Baghdad on April 4th. Extended tours, back door drafts, call it what you want, it happened and it happened often. Our six-month tour moved to an eight-month tour. They said, "You'll be home by Thanksgiving. You won't miss major holidays."

Then they said, "You'll be home by Christmas."

Christmas came and went. Next, it was, "You'll be home by January 29th."

Sure, uh-huh. I lost faith in "their" word.

They then said, "All deployments will last a year."

That meant we would be home in March.

Within a blink of an eye, their tune changed to "You need to have boots on the ground for 365 days. That's right, a year in the country, and then you can go home."

Bull! When will it end? Our cynical inside joke was that we had already died and gone to hell. Our hell was being teased with the hope of going home and then getting extended. My dreams of home turned into nightmares when I woke up and realized I was still in Iraq. I felt like I got kicked in the stomach every time I woke up from a fanciful dream of home.

CAPTURED SADDAM

On December 14th, Fox News declared, "Saddam Hussein has been captured." We were hesitant to believe it because we heard it before: Saddam dies of blood disease, Saddam found dead in a top-secret location. Both preceding news reports appeared credible, and the latter report even caused some gunfire to ring through the city. But this time when the streets grew crowded with celebrations and upset Saddam followers, we knew it was true. The celebratory gunfire sounded like the Fourth of July, and bullets rained from the sky. Our company was ordered to return to Mustang with the turrets closed. We loaded into the MWR room and watched the news. Red joined us and roughly translated Arabic.

Of all the days to return from leave, Hart was lucky enough to return on this chaotic day. I was ecstatic to see him. Not that I hated Phair, but I was done with his mind games and welcomed Hart's consistency.

We braced for retaliation from Saddam's followers on the next day. I woke up at 0415 to get ready and was standing by the truck at 0515 waiting for our orders, which resulted in going to the Shleck PD. Hart had the day off to acclimate to the time change. So once again, Phair was my team leader. The day started out like any other—quiet and boring. When I transitioned to the

190 • LAURA NAYLOR COLBERT

front gate, I found a homemade grenade on the ground on the opposite side of the three-foot barricade. I told Phair and he told the IPs to put it in their unexploded-ordinance pit. Instead of putting it directly in the pit, they played with it. They threw it around like a hot potato, and then one of the IPs stuck it in his shirt pocket and walked around with it for a while. The volatility of homemade explosives didn't faze the IPs. I, on the other hand, gave them a wide berth. I wasn't about to die from their SHTs.

We left for Sadr City at 1400 to check on a launch apparatus that the civilians had found. We followed IPs to the poverty-stricken Al Sadr neighborhood. The launch apparatus was a two-feet high and one-foot wide cylinder bomb that was sticking halfway out of the ground. Instead of approaching the potentially dangerous weapon, we took pictures, then went back to Shleck. The mission took no more than an hour.

Around 1600, a pro-Saddam demonstration marched through the Adhamiyah district—Shleck PD was located in the aforementioned district. The gunfire intensified enough to cause the birds to take flight. Like Alfred Hitchcock's movie *The Birds*, they flew from their perches, filled the sky with squawks, chirps, and cheeps, and flew around in angry choreographed mobs. There wasn't a passing second without bangs echoing through the streets. We couldn't take cover from the falling bullets because the threat of attack was imminent. The bullets pinged off the roof and fell through the leaves. Sgt. Henry's voice came over the handheld, "Palmer just got hit in the nuts." Then Henry laughed. *Did he laugh?*

What? Why is he laughing? "Is Palmer OK?" I asked into my handheld radio.

More laughing. "Yeah, he's fine."

I yelled at Kirking across the roof. "What the hell? Why are they laughing?"

She looked over the edge, where Henry was, and yelled down, "What's going on?"

Henry responded, "A bullet bounced off the ground and hit Palmer in the balls. Don't worry, the bullet didn't penetrate his clothing. He's fine."

We received our third order of the day at 1700: report to Adhamiya Police Headquarters with a squad from second platoon. The drive was pure chaos. Pedestrians clogged sidewalks and streets, cars were flooding the roadways, gunfire and explosions were booming from every direction. The quickest route to Adhamiya brought us to Antar Square where the citizens were holding a protest. Cars and people obstructed the lanes of the traffic circle. The Iraqis hung off balconies and covered the rooftops. Everyone was shouting, screaming, jumping, holding their rifles and pistols, and waving the Iraqi flag. Bursts of gunfire erupted around us. I ducked into my seat as bullets whizzed past our Humvee. Ssg. Verbsky stuttered something into the radio about people and AKs, but the attack took him by surprise and he couldn't get out a full sentence. I was leading the convoy with Phair in the team-leader seat. He yelled, "Gun it!"

I slammed my foot on the gas pedal and got the hell out of there. We jumped over curbs, drove down the wrong side of the street—and on the sidewalk—forcing civilians to jump out of our way. I heard myself say, "I fucking hate this shit!" but didn't know I said it until it was out of my mouth. My whole body was trembling.

The second we got to Adhamiya, a gunfight erupted a block away. It involved IPs from Adhamiya, who returned moments later, unscathed. Next, a vehicle-borne bomb blasted through Gunner Main's walls, six blocks away. I could feel the percussion of the bomb in my soul. *It is going to be a long night. We are in the middle of a full-fledged battle.* For optimal protection, we assumed a position behind the cement jersey barriers that surrounded Adhamiya PD's parking lot.

In the meantime, our battalion was ten blocks away and had gotten into a firefight by the Adhamiya mosque. No one was hurt, but their vehicles sustained damage. With no more than ten minutes of rest, my squad left to help. We were going to hoof it, but with Adhamiya's tumultuous state, it was safer to drive.

The shortest route was blocked by tanks and APCs—armored personnel carriers. When Phair reported the situation over the radio, TOC scrapped the recovery mission and told us to set up a checkpoint on a bridge to prohibit more insurgents from entering the area. Lt. Zick took charge. Without thinking, he led us across the nearest bridge to a dead end. His ill-informed decision put my squad in the worst predicament—a possible ambush. We sat idle at the dead end for 15 minutes while the leadership fought over Zick's mistake. They pulled out the maps, found the right bridge, and planned our next move. We retraced our steps with caution, knowing we had given the insurgents ample time to set up an assault. Before we even crossed the bridge, TOC aborted our checkpoint mission and sent us to the mosque to assist the battalion once again.

The second we pulled up to the side of the Mosque, a Bradley shot its massive gun a block away. The deafening noise and earth-shattering vibrations shook my Humvee. *What is going on?* We couldn't see around the mosque and didn't know why the Bradley was shooting. *If I still have my hearing after this, it'll be a miracle.*

I stood outside of my Humvee and pulled security while we waited to receive our next order. Phair had meandered away without a word, leaving Murray and me to fend for ourselves. Murray was as good as deaf with the anarchy erupting around us. I felt abandoned during one of the scariest moments of my life. I choked up in desperation. *Am I going to die? What if an insurgent is hiding in one of these houses right in front of me? My God, please take care of me.* I repeated my mantra: "I'm in God's hands. I'm in God's hands. I'm in God's hands." *I can't die. I can't let these Iraqi monsters take me away from my family. I am young and have a lot more to achieve.*

The TOC called, "Move to the other side of the Mosque."

I radioed Phair on the handhelds. We mounted up and drove through a few alleys before we reached the rear of the mosque. I discreetly choked down sobs and wiped my tears away. I didn't want Phair to see how weak I felt.

Four Iraqi men sauntered around the corner after we dismounted. "Stop! Get up against the wall!" Phair yelled at the men. They obliged, and we searched them to eliminate them as a threat. We forced them to sit against the wall, and I was put on guard duty for the next hour or so. We didn't want them to add to the night's chaos.

I couldn't hear the radio, and my fellow troops were too far away for conversation. To fight boredom and exhaustion, I sang "Amazing Grace" to myself and the Iraqis got a kick out of it. We struck up a conversation without an interpreter. One of them gestured to me that he had to pee. I let him face the wall and pee. The three other men couldn't believe he urinated in front of me. One of them was intrigued by my nonchalance and proposed to me. Again, I had to turn down the poor fellow.

After an eternity, Phair hurried over. "Murray and Naylor, grab your flashlights and a manpack. We're going to hoof it through this area to clear the fields and tunnels." Another MP company joined us and moved out in a wedge formation. We followed. I was the point person for our wedge.

The foot march took us through one of the mosque's large yards. I managed to cake my boot in muddy filth by stepping in a mud pit perfectly sized to smother my entire boot. Large two-foot-tall cement steps brought us to the riverbank. We inched down the Goliath-sized steps, under a bridge, and back up the riverbank steps. Another large yard loomed ahead. We waited in the prone position for over an hour while the first wedge searched the field ahead of us. I was tired, crabby, cold, and sore. *What the hell are we doing here?*

We descended down the riverbank steps toward our trucks after the other company came back. After the first step, I slipped, rolled my ankle, and tumbled down the other three. I lay there for a brief moment to make sure I didn't break anything. My body and ego hurt from head to toe.

We headed home after we reached our trucks—almost 22 hours after we started our mission. Per protocol, I needed to fill my Humvee with fuel before I went to bed. Phair said, "Go ahead and use your fuel cans instead of driving over to Viper. It's been a long day."

"Thanks," I muttered with exhaustion. I hobbled over to my fuel cans and found each one of them empty. Someone had used my fuel previously and had not refilled the cans. *You've got to be fucking kidding me!* All of my anger, stress, hatred toward humankind, pain, fear of dying, questioning what we were doing there, and utter exhaustion had finally caused me to snap. I yelled at my fellow squad, stopping them dead in their tracks. "Why the hell are you so lazy? You can't fill up fuel cans when you're done? What is your problem? How can you be so irresponsible? I'm so fucking sick of this shit! Fill up my fuel cans when you're done and do your job!"

Murray walked over, put his arms around my shoulder, and said, "Come on. I'll go with you to Viper to fill up the Humvee and the cans."

When we were done, I limped to my bunk and fell fast asleep.

Four IPs and several civilians died that day. Yahoo! News and CNN.com said there were no injuries and only wrote a few brief paragraphs about one of the scariest days of my life.

The following day, we loaded and cleaned the trucks and left for Adhamiya at 1500. Our eight-hour shift changed to eleven the moment we arrived. A squad from second platoon joined us to help with security.

All was quiet until 1800. A deafening explosion rocked the west side of the station next to second platoon's Humvees. A military convoy was passing by, and we assumed it had hit an IED. Shouts from Sgt. Diener's truck told us otherwise. A grenade, shot from an AK-47, had wounded Diener. Blood was pouring out of the back of her leg. Shrapnel had lacerated her calf. Per Hart's orders, I retrieved the medic and then ran upstairs for the ammo case. Hart wanted to shoot star clusters into the air. The ammo case was supposed to be with Murray, but he told me it was downstairs. I rushed downstairs and over to Mondello, a second-squad soldier from my platoon. He had the case. I handed the ammo case to Hart and he filled the sky with light. He shot 15 star clusters throughout our shift.

Gunner Main rushed over to retrieve Diener and took her to the 28th CSH. Her injury was worse than we had thought. They flew her to the States to have immediate surgery because the shrapnel had severed one of her nerves and she couldn't walk.

The night was never going to end. Moments after Diener was hit, a firefight erupted at a gas station a block away. Two civilians pulled their guns on each other. Sgt. Hart jumped behind the Humvee in fear. He was edgy on his first day back on duty after leave. The rest of us shared his fear but knew how to control it. We even laughed at Hart and called him green. Two more firefights occurred during our shift. I was crushed by stress. My stomach was tight and achy, and I thought I was going to throw up. After our replacements arrived—late—I hit the sack at 0300. That ended our tenure in Adhamiya—for now.

CHRISTMAS

The Army did what they could to increase our morale for Christmas. With Glenn's guidance, the 32nd organized and hosted a Christmas party on December 19th for the orphans we had been working with and other children who lived in the Green Zone. We played pin the tail on the donkey, Duck Duck Goose, magical chairs, had coloring areas, and listened to Christmas music. The children's faces glowed with bright white smiles, and laughter could be heard all evening long. We gave the children presents that our families and friends had donated from back home. Sgt. Adams put on a Santa costume and presented the gifts and stuffed animals to the children. We had a dance party with the kids once Santa was done distributing the gifts. We held the orphans in our arms and danced with them since most of them couldn't walk. My fun came to a screeching halt when Salah pooped on me. The smell mirrored that of the jail at Al Sha'ab. I gagged from the putrid odor. I had my uniform top off stat and sealed it in a plastic bag to enclose the scent. Salah was fully changed by the nuns because the poop had seeped into her clothes as well.

This is the snowman my parents sent over. We inflated it for the children's Christmas party. I'm on the left and Taylor is on the right. 12/19/03

As the night came to an end, a few of my fellow soldiers and I were hanging around by our Humvees. An angelic baritone voice rose from the low murmurs. In the black of night, our conversations stopped to listen to Spc. Ruehmling sing a haunting rendition of "O Holy Night." The beauty of his Elvis-like voice, the starry night sky, and thoughts of home crashed into me. It's one of those memories that are as vivid as the day it happened.

The World Wrestling Federation performed at Camp Victory—a base adjoining BIAP—the following day. The sky was cloudy, but the temperature was comfortable in our uniform. No need for long johns or extra coats. When we were walking toward the outdoor wrestling ring, I felt like I was going to a concert back home. Hoards of people were grouped together, sharing inside jokes, laughing about life, and carrying on in a cheerful manner. I would have forgotten that I was in a war zone if it weren't for the uniforms and guns we were toting around.

John Cena's soldier-honoring rap bolstered our pride and set the tone for the raucous performance. He said, "Saddam never had a chance with troops like you around.

"You should have buried that bastard in the same hole you found him in.

"I want to say thanks for protecting me and my children's children.

"You're fighting for the people who lost their lives in the day of the fallen building.

"You all are the real heroes. I place nobody ahead of you.

"This is coming from my heart. Peace, Y'all. I love you."

Steve Austin followed with his scantily clad women dressed as elves. The wrestlers fed off the thousands of hollering troops. The two-hour performance helped to revive our spirits.

Our battalion held a Christmas service in our theater on Christmas Eve. Troops performed with a live nativity scene, sang

Christmas carols, and a chaplain preached about the good news of Jesus's birth. My soul was at peace inside that tiny theater.

David Letterman and Paul Shaffer surprised the troops with an impromptu visit to the Cross Swords that afternoon. I drove over with a small group from my company. He gathered the 50-or-so troops into a huddle. Our BN commander said a few words, gave David Letterman a battalion patch, a boonie cap, and his coin, and then read David Letterman *The Top Ten Things We're Looking for Now that Saddam Hussein Has Been Captured*:

10. Saddam's hairstylist
9. The socks and underwear the laundry has lost over the past few months
8. The bath, not a Baathist
7. Toilet paper in the porta-potties
6. Paris Hilton video
5. The Cubs winning season
4. French soldiers
3. MPs who aren't on the front line
2. Baghdad's Hard Rock Cafe
1. Jimmy Hoffa

Behm, David Letterman, Cooper, and I. David Letterman was down to earth and thankful for our service. We were thankful for him. 12/24/03

David Letterman responded, "God bless you. Thank you very much. I feel silly accepting this, because before I came over here, I have a lot of friends who work in the national media, and I know what a risky proposition you are up against. But by God, I will cherish this for the rest of my life. I feel unworthy of this presentation. Thank you for having me here. How's everybody? Are we all right? When you get back, come to New York, and we'll treat you like big shots. Tickets are free." We applauded and then stood in line for autographs and a photo. I left with a picture with David Letterman and a signed MP brassard.

That evening, the girls and I put on our one and only Christmas CD—Destiny's Child—opened a non-alcoholic bottle of wine, and sat around our three-foot-high Christmas tree with presents from our family and friends piled underneath.

Laugher, smiles, tears, and hugs filled the room while we opened our presents with our new brothers and sisters. A photographer from the Milwaukee *Journal Sentinel*, who was embedded with our company for a few weeks, visited us during the party and took pictures while we opened our presents. When the unwrapping was done and the sparkling grape juice was gone, we cuddled together to watch *National Lampoon's Christmas Vacation*.

Back in the states, my parents opened the Milwaukee *Journal Sentinel* on Christmas morning to find my picture on the colorful front page, fashioning the hat they had gifted me. My Christmas cheer had grown enough that it didn't matter that I was in Iraq; I was genuinely happy.

I called my parents from the TOC in the morning to wish them a Merry Christmas. In mid-conversation, mortars flew across the Tigris. The explosions erupted within 100 yards of my location. I yelled on the phone, "Holy shit! That was close. I have to go, I'll call you back later."

I slammed down the phone and ran from the TOC to the safe basement for cover. After the explosions stopped, I went back to call my parents to alleviate their worries. "Hello?" my mom asked.

I could tell she was shaken. I didn't hear her smiling voice that usually answered the phone. "Hi, Mom. Sorry about that. It wasn't actually that close. I'm fine."

"Thanks for calling back, honey..."

Boom! Boom! I yelled, "Holy fucking shit; that's even closer!" *Boom!* "OK. I'm going to go get cover. I'll email you when I'm safe to let you know that all is well." *Boom!* They were walking the mortars toward my direction. By the time I hung up, the mortars were impacting less than 50 yards away. I was shaking and flinching with every impact while running for cover. *Boom!* I couldn't believe I did that to my parents on Christmas, of all days. I emailed right away as promised.

Around noon, the TOC ordered me to report to their location. They requested Joe's contact information. *What is going on?* As I was eating lunch at the BN, they called and ordered me to go to the BN TOC. Joe was on the phone. "Laura," he said. "Can I come and visit tomorrow? If so, I'm going to get the ball rolling with my company."

"Really? Oh, my God! That would be amazing. Let me go find out."

I ran over to our compound, asked Hart, who passed it through the chain of command and received the go-ahead.

At 1830, Joe called the BN back and told me that he was coming to Baghdad the next day. I ran back to my company and arranged as many logistics as I could. Back in the states, my parents must have moved mountains from Wisconsin to get our companies to accommodate a visit. I still don't know exactly what happened but am thankful that it did.

The next day, I drove in our company's mail run to pick up Joe at BIAP. We pulled into our meeting place, which was the PX parking lot at 1245. There was Joe. He swears that his commander let him hitch a ride with whatever companies he could find headed to BIAP. It was a miracle he made it there in one piece and on time. I ran over to him and hugged him so hard we almost fell over. Family. There wasn't anything quite as sweet as seeing a loved one after everything I had been through.

When we got back to Mustang, I gave him a tour of our building. We shared photos, worked out, played pool, and went on the Internet to talk to our family. Joe's visit was the best Christmas present I could have gotten.

I worked almost every day when Joe was visiting, but we found time to walk to the infantry compound a mile away to see Uday and Qusay's lions. We witnessed the adult male spray his urine— to protect his cubs—on a bystander who was ten feet away. We also watched ESPN, played games, and worked out during the five days we had together. Joe went on only one mission with me. We didn't want to push our luck. It would have destroyed our family if something had happened to both of us at the same time. Joe was impressed by how tough my fellow females and I were. He witnessed us watching *The Sopranos* and cleaning our weapons. We sat in front of the TV and pulled out our knives, then our pistols, then rifles, then SAWs, and then our MK-19s. Our badass-ness far exceeded that of *The Sopranos*.

On January 2nd, I returned from working the night shift to find him packed and ready to go. We gave each other long heartfelt hugs, shared "I love you's," and then he was off on his way to BIAP. We had a new bond—a brother and sister at war. Knowing I might never see my brother again made me appreciate him more than ever.

Joe and I are standing along the Tigris. This is the mile-long running route that we used.
12/31/03

MY LEAVE

Jan 3, 2004: The day I left on leave. It was an arduous journey. Wake-up was at 0430, followed by a convoy to BIAP at 0700, and a long wait until we loaded a C130 at 1630 to fly down to Kuwait. The C130 was an uncomfortable way to fly. It was rough, loud, and tightly packed. The guy sitting next to me—Ssg. Seefeldt—helped make the horrific experience tolerable. Once again, my height was the topic of conversation.

"Wow, how tall *are* you?" he asked.

"Six feet. Well, actually, five-feet-eleven and three-quarters, but who's counting?"

"Haha. True. I've always wondered what it would be like to date someone so tall. I think it's sexy."

"Thanks. My high-school self would have loved to hear that—back in the days when I couldn't find a guy to save my life. That, and jeans."

"So did you play basketball? I bet you're a pretty good athlete. I mean, you look athletic."

"No, not basketball. I'm a volleyball player. Still play competitively."

On and on our conversation went. I could write a script for these kinds of guys and their conversations.

We arrived in Kuwait at 1800 and slept in destitute conditions. Our packed items were limited, and mine only included a thin blanket and no pillow. We slept in a non-heated tent with cots that let the bitter cold creep in from the top and the bottom. The night left me quaking and teeth chattering. Peeing was the worst. I put my boots on, walked 100 meters out of the tent, into the dark and cold porta-potty, then back into my frigid bed.

We were briefed and searched for contraband at 1430 and then put into a sanitary tent. After many briefings and hours of waiting, we boarded a commuter jet at 2130 for our long-awaited venture home. After five hours, we refueled in Germany. Then we flew nine more hours to Baltimore. I strutted in my uniform through the Baltimore airport to my Chicago connection. I was a veteran soldier who had put my life on the line for our country, and I was damn proud of it.

By the time my last plane touched down in Chicago, my body and mind were exhausted and weary. Then I found out that every flight to Wisconsin had been canceled. On the verge of tears and so tired I felt like throwing up, I went from counter to counter, begging for a flight to Wisconsin. Another soldier, Spc. Cuff, was doing the same thing. When we found each other, we opted to rent a car and drive the two and a half hours to Madison.

When I ventured through Madison's airport, I spotted my dad first, and the exhausted tears started again. My mom ran to me and wouldn't let me go. We stopped at my Grandpa and Grandma Shanks' house a half-hour away, took pictures, and headed the last two hours home.

A crowd of 20 people was waiting for us outside our driveway. It was beautiful. Friends and relatives were there to welcome me home. My tiny, fragile Grandma Naylor jumped out of her seat at the kitchen table and ran to me when I went inside my parents' house. She hadn't been able to run in over 25 years.

Waves of fatigue hit me while I conversed, sipped wine, and soaked in my surprise welcome. Forty-eight hours with little sleep and the surreal feeling of being home hit me as I lay down to sleep—in *my* bed. A normal bed. Heaven on earth.

My leave was a whirlwind. Obligatory visits to friends and family who supported my deployment through letters, gifts, and donations left me with little time to do what I needed and wanted to do. I wanted to be by myself. To hit the open road. To be in nature. To process the previous nine months. I was happy to see everyone, but when it was time to leave on January 20th, I felt hollow. I hadn't taken time to heal, reflect, and prepare for the hell to come.

My parents received permission to come to the gate and wait with me before I boarded the plane out of Madison. This goodbye was tearful, but I was prepared for the departure. I put my civilian identity aside, faced the horizon, and turned the soldier persona back on before the plane took off.

The journey to Baghdad mirrored that of my departure. Same cold night, same boring briefings, same C130, same Baghdad.

RETURN TO WAR

Cpt. Glenn gathered the 32nd together a few days after I returned from leave. He said, "We'll be done with missions by 27 February. Our battalion is convoying south on 15 February, and we've been asked to escort a convoy to Kuwait."

What? That's awesome! I'll be home soon! Wait, should I get excited? Should I prepare for another inevitable extension and letdown? Should I tell my friends and family back home? Should I pretend like I never heard the news? It was safer for my mental health to pretend I never heard about going home. The danger of high hopes cut like a dagger whenever we received news of an extension. My intuition was right. February came and went and we were still stuck in the desert hellhole.

On February 4th, Sgt. Hart told Murray and me, "You're moving to Camp Victory tomorrow to become the brigade's new escort. Sgt. Hoyord will be your team leader instead of me. I'm going to stay here and lead a squad in first platoon."

Saddam's hunting and fishing grounds were known as Camp Victory—the same place we saw the WWF show. The beautiful marble buildings, pools, lakes, wildlife, and vegetation created an oasis in the deserts of Iraq.

After processing for a second, I said, "OK; first things first. Hoyord? *Hoyord*?!? Are you kidding me? There is no way I'm going to be able to handle Hoyord as my team leader. Second, why do we have to move? Why can't we escort the Brigade by driving over to Camp Victory every morning and hanging out? I know I don't have a lot of stuff, but it's still a pain in the ass to move."

Hart looked at me like a disappointed father. "Laura, quit bellyaching. There's nothing you or I can do about it. Keep your head down, do what I taught you, and you'll be fine."

"How long will it last? Will you ever be our team leader again?"

"I don't have the answer for either of those questions."

"That sucks. We'll miss you," chimed Murray.

I nodded, emphatically. I needed someone good to take Hart's place—to keep me laughing.

BRIGADE ESCORT

We moved into a grand marble building. Its magnificence was diminished by the plywood and two-by-fours that divided the open space into several small rooms with curtains for doors. The dividers did nothing to soften the noises—including snores—that reverberated off the hard surfaces.

Our new brigade was made up of green Fifth Cavalry soldiers. They were the fresh fish that we were tasked to escort.

Their pressed uniforms, clean boots, and sweatless Kevlars set them apart from our grunge, as did their lack of efficiency and mission wherewithal. It took the brass 45 minutes to get their heads on straight before we left for our first mission—the mission from hell. The mission I would have rejected had I known what they were up to. Their giddy dispositions and lack of preparation set off warning sirens. We didn't have communication with anyone, because their coms hadn't been set up yet. Only one person on the convoy knew our route. *Yikes.* My E-4 rank left me unable to speak my mind.

Even though Hoyord was my acting team leader, he let me choose if I wanted to drive or be the gunner. I chose the driver's position without hesitation—I hated the turret.

Murray was able to stay behind because we didn't have enough room for him. The rest of my non-up-armored Humvee was filled with brigade captains who wanted to go on a joyride to see the city.

Our first destination was the dreaded Freedom Market, one of the most volatile areas in Baghdad. My company had been banned from the Freedom Market for the last six months because there had been too many coalition casualties. The insurgents' preferred killing method was to drop grenades into turrets as the convoys went under a bridge. The captains knew and had chosen this location intentionally, along with our two unnecessary passes under the death bridge.

It got worse.

The nine newbies exited their vehicles to walk through the Freedom Market while we—the drivers and gunners—rode alongside them. We provided protection from the massive crowd and towering five-to-ten story buildings. For an hour, the newbies clumped together and meandered through the market.

Do they have a death wish? Are they not trained properly? Please spread out, please spread out. If one grenade blows, they're all toast. They were sitting ducks, prime for the picking, begging for an ambush, sniper fodder, grenade-toss targets.

While we crept along, an Iraqi pedestrian reached inside my open Humvee window and dropped something into my lap. *Oh shit, a grenade! Get it off! Get It Off!!! Oh God, oh God, oh God, please let me get this grenade out of here before it explodes.* I reached down to throw the grenade out the window. It took a second to register that my hand found a pile of lollipops instead of a grenade. My heart was lodged in my throat, beating so fast I thought I was going to have a heart attack. I yelled up to Hoyord, "Sergeant, can you face left? I just had an Iraqi throw candy into my lap. I'll watch right since I have to watch the brass anyway."

"Roger."

From that point on, my left hand steered and my right hand held steadfast to my pistol, which was pointed outside my window. That *would not* happen again.

Our death march took us to Antar Square next—the same crazy traffic circle where we were attacked the day after Saddam was captured. The newbies acted like cowboys. I overheard Captain Newbie say to Major Newbie, "I should have stayed back. You promised me some action today!" *What? My life is expendable because you want to see some action?* That was the moment a tiny seed of hatred for the military and for my country was planted within my soul. I had stopped fighting for the greater good; I was fighting to stay alive. My faith in IOF—Operation *Iraqi Freedom*—was dwindling. *Why does our military turn a blind eye to faulty leadership? Isn't it the most important aspect to the success of a mission? Shouldn't there be a more intense promotional code besides time-in-service? How can my life be so insignificant to these assholes who see me in the flesh and blood?* It was one thing to be a pawn in the larger military machine, but the complete disregard for my well-being by the Fifth Cav soldiers sent me over the edge.

After Antar Square and a brief drive through Adhamiya, we hit a traffic jam on a large bridge. I had been downing water during the escapade. It was almost noon, and I hadn't had a single pee break. I was about to go in my pants. I rocked myself against the steering wheel, trying to overcome the urge. *What am I going to do?*

It came to me. I said, "Captains, I have to pee. I'm going to use this funnel. Please try not to look." I scanned their three faces to find astonished and questioning looks. They were too surprised to respond.

With my right foot still working the speed, I kept our Humvee creeping across the bridge. I stuck the PUD in my pants and connected the empty water bottle to the other end of the funnel. Without even trying, my bladder released a waterfall into the funnel. *Shit!* The PUD head was tilted back too far and the pee was filling my pants and my seat. After resituating the funnel, I filled the 1.5-liter bottle in no time and still had to go. I stopped midstream and kept on driving in a puddle of my own urine. Humiliating.

Our next stop was an Iraqi Police Station that I hadn't been to. We waited at the station while the newbies stood around and chatted. I found a porta-potty immediately and finished what I had started in the Humvee and then I put an old towel on my seat and discretely air-dried my uniform by walking around and fanning my uniform top. I also avoided eye contact out of embarrassment.

Relief washed over me when the newbies gave us the go-ahead to drive back to Camp Victory. *I will live to see another day.* After arriving safely, I hoped the brigade would give us a pat on the back and send us on our way. Nope. After a short deliberation, the newbies decided to see more of the city. I braced myself for my first defiant military moment. *I am not going to drive for them anymore. They will not use me for their own stupidity.* Captain Newbie said to me, "Specialist, you can stay behind with the other driver. We'll be taking your vehicle, though."

"Yes, Sir," I said. My stomach unknotted, and the ringing in my ears subsided. *I won't have to defy their orders after all.*

My embarrassment and humility, however, increased. *How am I going to explain the pee-filled seat?* I walked over to the captain who was looking at the darkened fabric and mumbled, "Uh, the turret was open during last night's rainfall." I hurried away, hoping to never deal with them again. And no, it hadn't rained the night before. That's karma, Captain.

A few nights later, mortars screamed into Camp Victory and landed within yards of the computer building that I was in. The windows shook—on the verge of breaking. Just when we thought they were done, more explosions erupted even closer. My familiarity with mortars left me mostly unfazed once the explosions ceased. They were done; I was alive—it was time to move on. The newbies' reactions left me laughing. Sgt. Newbie was sitting next to me and looked like he saw a ghost. His gaping mouth, wide eyes, and translucent skin couldn't hide his fear. I was about to tell him to relax, the explosions were done, carry on. But Captain Newbie came screaming through the building, "Get your gear on and report to your leadership! Get your gear on and report to your leadership!"

This time, I laughed out loud and shook my head. Kirking and I nonchalantly meandered back to our building.

"Can you believe this shit? What a waste of our time," Kirking murmured.

"I was thinking the same thing. You should have seen the guy sitting next to me. Talk about fresh fish."

A flash of camo raced past us as Sgt. Newbie sprinted to the safety of his building. Once again, Kirking and I had a good laugh. We hung out at our hooch, waiting for the chaos to subside. After the "all clear," we walked back to the computers to continue emailing. We didn't see Sergeant or Captain Newbie for the rest of the night.

Our brigade escort missions mellowed after our death convoy. Colonel Richards became one of our primary principals. He was an on-call surgeon with barely any calls. Standing at around five feet tall, with mannerisms similar to my deceased grandpa, I loved spending time with him. His strong east-coast accent made him even more likable. He enjoyed touring the Green Zone, which allowed us to view the historic sites we would have otherwise missed.

We also escorted the military personnel in charge of paying the IPs and Iraqi contractors who received a weekly crisp $100 U.S. bill. One day, we went to BIAP to pick up $528,000 fresh off the presses in $100-dollar bills. The wads were shrink-wrapped in a large stack in the middle of my Humvee. The temptation to steal was there, but both my integrity and the shrink-wrap held tight.

This is the $528,000 in $100 bills in my Humvee. I was so excited to take this picture. 2/11/04

A first-platoon squad from our company was also living at Victory and escorted General Sanchez—the general in charge of Iraq. It was a prestigious and dangerous job.

They became our close friends during our stint at Victory and beyond. Olinger, a gallant, good-looking guy with a deep voice, dark eyebrows, and constant five-o'clock-shadow became a much-needed distraction. I didn't know him before Victory, but he often hung out with Kirking and me after our arrival. We had our fair share of visits to their hooch as well. I enjoyed Olinger's company, his humor, intelligence, empathy, and flirtatious nature. Our platonic relationship toed the line—and sometimes eked across—with nothing more than hand-holding and the act of sitting tightly next to each other to exchange body heat and intimacy that we so lacked from months of physical neglect. The nights he came over made my stomach flutter with anticipation. For months I had no idea if our friendship would blossom into more, but the excitement of wonder made me feel feminine, and his interest in me as a person gave me some of my humanity back.

When I visited his platoon, we sat next to each other and played *Halo* on the Xbox. Electricity coursed through my veins when our skin touched. I knew he felt it, too, through his penetrating brown eyes. We had a strange nonverbal connection that gave me the comfort I was pining for. Those dark round eyes and long lashes told me that I was special and worth getting to know, that he cared about my well-being.

Rumors ran amok about our relationship. We left them guessing and laughed about it when we were alone. Sometimes we draped our arms around each other in a weird embrace as we talked for hours about life, our future, our past, war, and theology. Olinger asked time and time again, "I don't understand why we're here. It seems pointless. I can't keep doing the same shit for no reason."

I responded, "I'm glad I have God on my side. I know that we're here for a reason. I don't know what it is, but I firmly believe that it's for a higher purpose."

I could see how my morale—even though it was low—was nowhere near as dark as his was. My beliefs helped me to overcome the hate and anger that had enveloped our existence. I was starting to lose faith in the mission, but not in God.

Sometimes he would ask, "Can I just hold you?" or "I need to hold your hand tonight."

I would reciprocate the requests when I had my own bad days. We found solace in each other in our solitude, whether it was on the roof, in a bunker, or on our bunks. Olinger never replaced Kirking, but he certainly filled a void as one of my closest confidants during the deployment.

The long nights with Olinger helped to make my living nightmare more bearable, especially since I had been working under Hoyord. We got lost on multiple missions because Hoyord didn't know how to read a map and lacked navigational skills. I would ask him for our destinations and pore over maps before our departure. I could get us there based on memory alone on most days.

Additionally, he was indecisive during some of the most crucial times. When we were receiving small-arms fire, I asked, "Do you want me to gun it?"

He stuttered, "Uh... I don't know... um, yes. I mean no. Wait. Yes, get us out of here."

Worse yet, sometimes he would call over the SINCGARS for advice. His hesitations could have cost us our lives. His inability to lead and the number of times he inadvertently put my life in danger made my seed of hatred grow. It was too much.

After 20 days of torturous missions, Hart came to the rescue as our temporary team leader. Word must have gotten out.

A few nights later, we were returning to Victory from a mission. There was a continuous flashing light from the BIAP checkpoint—something was not right. We could vaguely make out the shape of a flipped special-forces vehicle—an APC—with its turret detached, lying a dozen feet away from the vehicle. Creeping forward, we saw the outline of four bodies sprawled on the pavement with oil and diesel fuel covering the ground— reflecting the overhead light. "Are they dead?" I whispered.

The gate guard, who was flashing the light, pleaded, "Please help! Seconds before you got here, the APC approached way too fast. It must not have seen the barricades that ran along the left side of the entrance. The side of their vehicle drove up the barricade, causing it to flip."

Ssg. Verbsky and Sgt. Hart were in my vehicle. We exited with Sgt. Watlin, a soldier from first platoon, on our heels. No one had been helping the four injured soldiers lying in the debris. We were combat-lifesaver certified and knew how to triage the injured.

After a quick scan of the victims, Verbsky told me to tend to the least injured soldier. Hesitating, I walked over to him. I did not feel prepared to be the link between life and death for another human being. Knowing that my brother was faced with this responsibility every day as a medic made me respect him tenfold.

My guy was conscious. I talked with him to calm him—and to calm myself. "Hey, you. Help is here. I'm going to start by supporting your head, OK? What's your name?"

"Holy shit. Thanks, dude. My name's John."

"How old are you, John? Tell me about yourself."

"I'm twenty years old, from Pennsylvania, and have a serious girlfriend of two years," he responded.

"Oh, yeah? What's she like?"

"She's amazing. Brown hair, brown eyes—she's my brown-eyed girl—ha! Ouch."

"Tell me what hurts."

"My head, my neck, and my right arm and leg."

"I can see that you're bleeding from your temporal and parietal lobes. It's not too bad, but I'm going to support your head in case you have a neck injury, OK?

"Sounds good. I think I broke my arm and leg. How do they look?"

"Well, your leg might be broken, but I'm not sure about your arm. Just lie still and help will come soon."

"Roger."

"Tell me about the other soldiers you're with." I winced as the words left my mouth. I shouldn't have brought up his dying comrades.

He groaned, knowing that they might not make it. "Are they going to be OK?"

I looked through the darkness. The gunner was unconscious, with blood pooling around his head. Hart, Verbsky, and Watlin were trying to save his life. He must have sustained life-threatening injuries when the vehicle flipped and the turret flew. Another soldier was in and out of consciousness, but it looked like he was going to make it. I couldn't see the fourth soldier but figured he was OK. No one was attending to him, and I knew he hadn't died yet.

I responded softly, "John, I'm pretty sure they're all going to make it."

Finding the courage, he told me about the soldiers and their lives. When describing the gunner, he said, "Mac is expecting his first child and couldn't be more excited."

The minutes ticked by without a medevac in sight. "They'll be here any minute, John. We called them the second we got here. Both Victory and BIAP said they would send someone."

"OK, thanks," he groaned.

Twenty minutes passed before a chopper flew over the treeline, right above the electrical wires. "What? A chopper?" I looked around, "Where are they going to land with all the barricades, wires, and vehicles? Why the hell couldn't they have driven to our location? It would have taken them five minutes tops!"

A scream came out of Kirking while she waved her flashlight towards the sky. The helicopter was ten feet over her, about to land on her and her vehicle.

In the meantime, two Humvees holding QRF soldiers came to secure the area. I laughed out loud and said, "John, I wish you could see these naive QRF soldiers. They're acting like they're in Vietnam with their arm and hand signals. What the hell are they doing? It's so funny to watch. The thing is, our gunners and the other soldiers in my squad already had the perimeter taken care of. These new soldiers are only adding to the chaos."

John tried to laugh, but his pain was intensifying and he was too worried about his comrades to join in the fun.

A whopping hour after our arrival, the medevac found a spot to land and we were relieved from our duties. *One hour!* The medics that replaced me pushed me out of the way without a word. I couldn't even muster a goodbye to John.

That incident woke me up. I had been walking around on autopilot, numb and thinking only of how soon I could go home. Home was a mirage that moved farther and farther away. Being a civilian again—free to do what I chose—hardly seemed possible. Seeing how fleeting our lives really were jolted me out of my depression, and forced me to realize that the numbness only put me—and those around me—in more danger.

On March 5th, my squad moved back to Mustang. Before we left, the Brigade Colonel and the Command Sergeant Major had a ceremony for our squad to thank us for our service. We stood in a row while they walked down the line, shaking our hands, and giving us their military coin. When the Colonel reached me, he said, "You're the soldier that's always smiling. Keep it up, and thanks for all your help."

When the CSM got to me, he looked me over, and when he saw my boonie cap hanging from my pistol's hammer, he scowled. "Your weapon is not a hat rack," he said, and then kept moving down the line. *Eh. You win some; you lose some.*

Our new team leader from third platoon—Sgt. Gregory—moved into Hart's vacant spot upon our return. Months earlier, he had said to me, "You fill out your uniform nicely. You can always tell how hot a female is by how well she fills out her uniform."

I had muttered, "Thank you," with a mixture of flattery and disgust. I was not comfortable with him as my new leader, but I was willing to give him a try and start fresh.

Gregory was six feet tall with dark hair and a large nose. He was a smoker, which I detested. On our first day together, his stupid jokes were already driving me crazy. Nothing, however, was as bad as his continued objectification. He treated me like it was my first day in a war zone. He was only a year older than me.

He took his newfound leadership role too far. For example, when soldiers from our company were caught drinking at Camp Viper, Sgt. Gregory made me sit down in front of him while he stood with his hands on his hips and asked, "Did you sneak out last night and go to Viper?"

Really? You need to tower over me? "Are you seriously asking me that? Of course not. I would never put myself in that situation. I'm not a boozehound just because I've hung out at Viper a couple of times."

"You better be telling me the truth."

I looked at him incredulously and shook my head. *What was I, a toddler? Did he want to create a larger divide between us? What is his problem? We should be leaning on each other, not pushing each other away.*

Later in the deployment, Gregory pulled me aside and said, "I'm concerned that you're not eating enough. It's very important to eat when it's hot outside, and your Power Bars and fruit are not a well-balanced meal."

I wanted to punch him in his big nose. He ate fried and processed foods, smoked, and didn't work out. My kinesiology major and lifelong athleticism gave me enough prior knowledge to know that my eating habits blew his out of the water.

I missed Hart.

CPA ESCORT

Our next gig was my favorite. We escorted UN personnel, United States Diplomats, Senators, and other prestigious VIPs who stayed at the CPA. On one occasion, we escorted six U.S. Senators to the house of Paul Bremmer, the U.S. civilian in charge of Iraq. We were also Colin Powell's designated ground escort, but he opted to fly in a helicopter instead of drive. He chose wisely since it was safer to fly than to risk hitting an IED.

We called the person we escorted our principal. Our job was to surround the principal's bulletproof SUV while driving on the road with our Humvees. We used two lanes to execute the missions. The order of vehicles in the far right lane was: Humvee, principal vehicle, Humvee. The middle or left lane, depending if it was a two- or three-lane road, had two Humvees to protect the principal's left flank. My primary placement was the first vehicle to the left of the principal. I was called The Plow because I guided the civilian vehicles out of the two right lanes to create the greatest distance from civilians to the principal as possible. If an Iraqi vehicle didn't move over, I pulled ahead of our convoy, moved to the right of the civilian vehicle, and gently shoved them to the left until they were in the far-left lane.

The bulletproof SUV contained six civilian security personnel—Blackwater—or military security personnel who surrounded the principal within the SUV for added protection.

The security folks became some of our closest friends for the remainder of our deployment. Phil, the Australian UN Ambassador's security head, was one of the many wonderful personalities we encountered. He spent enough time with us to fall madly in love with Cooper—and to eventually propose. They were engaged for about six months before they realized their military soiree wasn't going to cut it in the real world.

It was during our CPA escort missions that we finally received up-armored Humvees—a *year* into our deployment. I wondered if our principals had anything to do with it.

Our deployment was coming to an end. We were scheduled to drive to Kuwait on April 21st and then head home from there. *It's happening! We're getting out of this hellhole.* We meticulously cleaned our gear during our spare time because we couldn't take home specimens that might be detrimental to the American environment. Murray and I cleaned the truck well enough to eat off of it. Of course, by then I'd eat off of most anything, including my grimy, unwashed knife that I had used to spread peanut butter, cut fruit, cut wire, open boxes, and any other knife-worthy task. Other redeployment duties occurred, such as moving and stacking totes, packing old tents, night-vision-goggles, and other useless items, and then—par for the Army—we loaded and unloaded the conex shipping containers three times before we had it right. We also had to practice packing our personal boxes, which was nonsensical. After we had our non-essential army-issued items packed just right, U.S. Customs inspected the conexes and shipped them home.

We had an influx of soldiers arrive in Baghdad from the First Cavalry Unit at the beginning of April. Our compound's future occupants stopped by to scout it out. Entering the war at this point was brutal. The level of danger had increased with every passing day. *At least we're scheduled to go home within a few weeks.*

The 233rd MPs, an MP company that we had befriended in Viper, left on 3 April. Saunders was dating a guy from the 233rd named Michael Whited, and he had given her a small water bottle full of lemon vodka as a goodbye present. She drank it in one sitting. Cooper and Lewis found Saunders on the roof at 2200—wasted. They ushered her downstairs.

Lewis said, "Saunders, you head straight to bed. Don't talk to anyone, don't even brush your teeth, just get in bed. We'll be down in a little bit."

Cooper and Lewis went to bed a few hours later. Lewis, who slept above Saunders, said, "Cooper, Saunders isn't in bed. Where is she?"

Cooper shrugged. "I don't know. Do you think she's in the shower? It's running."

"What? Two hours later? No way! But who else would be in there?"

Lewis tapped on the door with no answer. "I hope she's OK! Should we go in?"

"Yes! We can't leave her in there all night if something is wrong." Cooper opened the door. Their hearts lurched when they saw Saunders on the floor. Her legs were curled up underneath her with her shins, shoulders, and forehead plastered to the ground. The roundness of her naked back and butt looked like a turtle shell. "Is she alive?" Cooper asked. "Go check her."

Lewis walked over. Saunders was warm and breathing. "Let's wrap her up in a towel and carry her back to her bunk."

"Sounds good. Here's a towel," Cooper grabbed a towel off the hook. Lewis grabbed Saunders under the armpits, and Cooper grabbed her legs. They lifted her off the ground. They heard a loud thud and a subsequent vibrating sound. "What was that?" asked Cooper.

They set Saunders on the ground to investigate the noise. "Oh, my gosh! It's a vibrator!" Lewis gasped, trying to stifle her robust laughter.

"That's disgusting!" Cooper whispered. "Quick, get it! It's so loud!"

Laughing, Lewis reached for another towel, picked up the vibrator, and encased it in the folds of the towel. She ran into their room and stuffed the towel and vibrator under Saunders' bed. They picked up Saunders again, shuffled into the room, dropped her into her bed, and covered up her naked body. Lewis' muffled hearty laugh filled the room. The two girls ran out into the hallway to avoid waking anyone up. "She looked like a turtle," Lewis said.

"I know! I was thinking the same thing! Maybe we should call her Humping Turtle from now on."

"I love it!"

Saunders woke up the next morning in her birthday suit with a pounding a headache. She reached under her bunk, grabbed some clothes, and slipped them on under the covers. When Cooper and Lewis woke up, they told Saunders about her antics the night before. Pretty soon the rest of us heard the Humping Turtle story, and we laughed for days.

FIRST FEMALE KIA IN THE NATIONAL GUARD'S HISTORY

It was 2200 on 4 April. I was watching *Finding Nemo* to decompress before I went to bed. Phair barged into our room. "Gear up! Insurgents are overtaking the police stations around Sadr City. We need to go pull security at Al Sha'ab."

We got ready and raced to Sha'ab. "Naylor, put your Humvee in this spot," Phair barked.

I had a heck of a time parallel parking in the designated spot, and it wasn't because I'm a bad parallel parker. My years of living in downtown Madison made me a pro. It was because my up-armored Humvee's power steering cut out at ten miles-per-hour or less. My arms felt like Jell-O from packing the beast in like a sardine. I then sat idle for two hours because my door was against the blast wall.

An infantry unit joined us and took my Humvee's position at the gate. Like Austin Powers on steroids, I inched out of my spot and then pulled security on the roof for over an hour. My goose-bumps and teeth chattering were a constant reminder that I did not prepare well enough for the night's cool weather. Thank goodness the infantry grew bored after two hours, which meant I could warm up by moving my vehicle back into the nook. I fought off sleep in my snug Humvee until third platoon relieved us at 0430. We managed a couple of hours of shut-eye once we got back to Mustang. We had CPA escort missions the next day.

My platoon had one more week of CPA missions before our convoy to Kuwait. The other platoons had wrapped up their primary missions and had been preparing for our return home. Because they had free time, they were tasked to man Sha'ab and Adhamiya for a 96-hour operation to keep the insurgents at bay. My platoon offered the soldiers at Adhamiya respite after our CPA missions. The least we could do was help pull security for six hours or so each day.

Sgt. Hart's new squad was at Adhamiya for the full duration. Mortars, RPGs, and small-arms fire had become a constant cacophony. There were rarely silent moments. I fixated on Hart's well-being. Even though he wasn't my team leader anymore, I cherished our friendship and his mentorship. We saw each other on a regular basis, and I enjoyed the time we spent together, even more than when he was my team leader.

On April 8th, we relieved the Adhamiya soldiers at 1830. They relaxed in the safety of the station's inner rooms while my squad manned the guns and fighting positions outside. First Sergeant Daniels came with my squad and drove the lead Humvee. My aggressive driving was tame compared to his. Our roller-coaster drive almost made me car sick even though I was driving.

Initially, Murray and I were sent to Adamiya's rooftop, but within a couple of minutes, Sfc. Phair told me to join Kirking in front of the station. I sat on the Humvee roof with her while she manned the MK19. Talking to Kirking about nothing and everything helped make our long nights and days and the anxiety of the unknown bearable. Aside from a few explosions and gunfire in the distance, the night was uneventful.

At 0200, we were driving back to Mustang and were two miles from a Green Zone entrance called Assassin's Gate. We were the sole vehicles on a four-lane road with apartment buildings rising 30 stories above us. The pulsing rhythm of the heavy tires on the pavement was interrupted by what sounded like popcorn popping or clapping. From my side mirror, I saw the gunners crouch into their turrets. We were receiving small-arms fire from the dark windows in the surrounding buildings. The shots sounded muffled inside the up-armored Humvee.

Boom! A Humvee-shaking explosion detonated behind our convoy, followed by more gunfire. My toenails curled in my boots, and my knuckles whitened around the steering wheel. "Go! Go! Go!" shouted Phair next to me.

I stepped on the gas pedal hard and hauled ass into our checkpoint. The Assassin gate guards leaped out of our way. The serpentine did nothing to slow our speed. I needed to get our whole convoy through safely before I dared to press on the brake.

We pulled over to assess the damage. To our surprise, all the soldiers and our Humvees were unharmed.

By 1430 the next day, Kirking and I were hunkered down in the same positions as the night before. Our TOC shared intel that the station was going to be heavily attacked and the mosques were blaring a warning for IPs and MPs to get out of the station within 12 hours, or else. Insurgents were handing out pamphlets that read:

I want everyone to put his hand
Into our hand.
To push them out of Baghdad.
Time is today
I don't want one today
And a lot in a few months
I want everyone today.

1400 turned to 1800 and nothing happened. Then 1800 turned to 2100 and still nothing happened. We decided to leave at 2200 if it was still a quiet night. Since our luck was running thin, it was no surprise that we did not leave by 2200. Six mortar explosions about two kilometers away and subsequent gunfire sounded from the south-southeast at 2100. The soldiers on the roof shot in the direction of the incoming gunfire. Kirking and I watched the tracers light up the night sky. "Do you think anyone is dying right now?" she asked.

"God, I hope not."

"I'm so sick of fighting this war."

"You're preaching to the choir."

"Would we even know if someone on the roof was shot? Would they tell us?" she asked.

"Probably not. We're little peons down here. They've probably forgotten that we're down here. What good are we going to do with your MK19 when the walls are taller than your gun?"

"Hey, at least we're not sitting ducks on the roof."

"You got that right. And at least we have each other. Seriously, though. I don't know what I would do without you on this deployment as a bunk mate, squad mate, and best friend. Thanks for being there."

"You're telling me! Naylor, you helped me quit smoking in the most stressful time of my life. You know what else?" "What?"

"My sister told me that I'm like a different person. That I'm more positive and optimist. I told her it was your fault. Ha!"

"Kirking, that's the nicest thing you could have told me! Gosh, I'm honored."

"Well, it's true. You've rubbed off on me after all these months."

"I've learned a lot from you too, ya know. Your strength and intelligence blow me away almost every day.

A frightening silence filled the air, followed by rapid gunfire from the northeast side of the station.

"What the hell is going on out there?" Kirking asked. She got on her radio. "Anyone on the roof want to let us know what's going on?"

Silence. "Hey!" she yelled up to them. "What the hell's going on?"

Silence.

We were alone to fend for ourselves. Thank God we had each other.

Gunner Main called on the SINCGARS to fill us in. The first barrage of gunfire happened when two cars drove past Gunner Main and shot through their gates. They shot back and blew up one of the cars. Then soldiers from Gunner Main chased and caught up with the second car and annihilated them, causing the second string of gunfire.

That concluded Adhamiya's havoc. All was silent except for distant explosions and gunfire. We left at midnight.

Lt. Zick's incoherent screams broke the SINCGAR silence during our quiet ride home. The TOC begged him to slow down. Zick said, "An IED...exploded...near... received small-arms... Witmer...bleeding...the Humvee..."

"Lt. Zick, please take a breath, slow down, and repeat what's going on."

"Witmer's been hit. We're still getting shot at. An IED just exploded. There could be more casualties."

I looked at Gregory, who had started to grow on me. Our eyes were huge with worry. They had taken the same route home that we had taken the night before. *Who dropped the ball?* They should never have taken that route after we were ambushed on it less than 24 hours ago.

Lt. Zick came back over the airwaves. "There's so much blood. We pulled her into the Humvee from the turret. She's unconscious and bleeding through the nose, but she still has a pulse. We're rushing to the Green Zone CSH."

"Roger that," the TOC responded. "Keep us up to date."

I had a lump in my throat and a heavy heart for the rest of the drive home. "What do you think is going to happen?" I asked Gregory.

"Not sure. I hope she makes it. Sure doesn't sound good."

"I'm going to stay up until I know if she's OK or not."

"The hell you are."

I looked at him, not sure if I heard correctly. "Did you just say I can't stay awake?"

"Yes. You need to go to sleep."

"You've got to be kidding me. We might lose Witmer and you're telling me I have to go to bed? How the hell am I supposed to sleep?"

"Naylor, I order you to go directly to bed when we get back. No questions."

That seed of hate; it grew a foot. I hated him for that statement. For his inflated ego. For my inability to debate my case.

I dragged myself into my room, exhausted from emotions and the intense last couple of days. My plan was to hunker down until it was safe, then find out what I could about Witmer.

However, the moment I closed my eyes, I fell into a deep sleep and didn't wake up until the sun was shining into our room. I put on my sandals, combed my hair with my fingers and put it into a tight bun at the base of my neck, went to the bathroom, and dragged my weary body into the MWR room to find out what happened with Witmer.

I knew she hadn't made it the second I entered the room. The red eyes, sallow complexions, mournful expressions, silence, and the thick grief-stricken air told me all I had to know. My fellow soldiers looked like they hadn't slept in days, their shoulders slumped, their heads down—my company had turned into lamenting zombies.

Two rumors surfaced about how Witmer died. Rumor one was that she received multiple shots and shrapnel to her back and head. The second rumor was that she received one bullet through the shoulder, and it penetrated her lung and heart.

We lost a soldier. It was Witmer, of all people. The sweet, smiling, kind, soft-spoken, joyful, gentle Witmer. In the months we had been deployed, no one had any negative thoughts about her.

Witmer had an older sister in our company—in first platoon. Her twin sister was in the 118th CSH, which was deployed to Baghdad when Witmer was killed. My heart broke for her family.

Glenn pulled the rest of our company out of the stations. He claimed, "We're not going to suffer another casualty before we go home."

My platoon was still plugging away at the CPA. I was glad to have a job to do because I didn't want to face my grief.

The Brigade Colonel and the Command Sergeant Major came to our compound to give their forced and rehearsed sympathies and read us bible passages.

Ten days. That's all we had left until we were scheduled to go home. Michelle Witmer was the first female soldier in the history of the National Guard to be killed in action. Her face was plastered on CNN and FOX news. Ten days. *We couldn't have left ten days earlier? We couldn't have had one less extension? Someone couldn't have informed her squad to avoid that route after we were attacked the night before?*

EASTER

Easter Sunday was two days after Witmer's death. I called my parents to wish them a Happy Easter during our break between escort missions in the early afternoon. My mom and I talked about all the wonderful things we would do when I got home: our planned family trip to D.C. in May, watching the birds on their deck while drinking coffee, enjoying the lakes once it got nice, and finally being together as a family. After I got off the phone, we found out that our second mission had been canceled. Before rushing back to Mustang, we went inside to eat a delectable meal. In the middle of eating, Reynolds walked in from outside—he always ate on the second shift—and said, "Hurry up. Glenn wants us back at Mustang for an important meeting."

Bile rose in my throat. *Oh shit...no, no, no! We're getting extended; I know it.* Dread was plastered on everyone's expression. Our faces lost their color. Our conversations ceased. We were frozen. Like shadows of ourselves, we put down our utensils, shuffled to the tray deposit, then to outside, and mounted up. I whispered to Kirking, "Shit. I guess it's our turn to get extended, huh?"

She looked up at me. Her eyes were welling with moisture. She looked away. She was too stunned to respond. We drove the short two miles to the compound. We tried to think of other reasons for the immediate meeting and could think of none. Instead of having a company formation, Cpt. Glenn called the platoon sergeants and LTs into his office. Our platoon was called into the theater at 1915. Lt. Gray and Sfc. Phair walked down the narrow aisle and loomed in the front of the theater. My gut kept sinking. No one said a word. The air was still. Gray broke the silence. Without a bit of sugar coating, she said, "We're extended for 120 more days. Our mission will continue to be dangerous. We're going to either conduct escort missions throughout Iraq or work in EPW Camps. We have no idea where we're going to live or what our living conditions will be. We'll likely be living in the middle of the desert—in tents. We have to move by next Sunday to somewhere south of Baghdad because the company moving into this compound needs to get settled as soon as possible. "

I heard what she said, but the news wouldn't register. *120 days. Move. Tents. EPW. Next Sunday.* It was an out-of-body experience. *Moving to a new place? After it took months to build up our current compound? Do we have to go through the same thing all over again? Just as we're getting ready to resume our lives back home. All that gear we sent home. Now we have to get it sent back? Unpack it?* I couldn't get out of my seat. The weight of the extension was too crushing to overcome. I could feel my body press into the cushion, my limbs turned to lead. I don't know how long I sat there. How long we sat there.

I found myself outside by the carport. Some of our civilian security friends had received the news of our extension and came over to visit us within the hour. They brought a pile of satellite phones from the CPA. I called my parents.

"Hi, Mom and Dad. You might want to sit down."

"Hey, Laura. What's going on? Is something wrong?"

"Umm..." I paused, trying to hold back tears, and took a deep breath. "We just got extended."

"Oh, honey, are you serious? Are you OK? What can we do? How long?"

I was bawling as I said, "It's God's will, right? What the hell did I ever do to him? How can I possibly deserve this?"

"Shhh, shhh."

"We have to move, and we'll get all-new missions. No one knows a whole lot yet, but we have to stay in this hellhole for four more months. That means I'll miss even more school, all the trips I had planned, another summer, and you. I'm going to miss *you*! Damn it! I'm so pissed! What the hell am I supposed to do? I can't take it anymore!"

"Honey, we're so sorry. We wish there was something we could do."

"Call your Congressman, call the Governor, and call the President. For Christ's sake! Get us the hell out of here."

"We'll do what we can, honey. We'll start writing letters right away. We love you so much and hate to see you like this."

"OK. I have to go. I'll email you later. I love you and miss you. Oh, and can you cancel my flight to New York City and see if you can reschedule the trip to D.C.?"

"Sure, sweetie. We love you so much. We'll keep you in our prayers. We love you. Don't ever forget that."

"I know. I love you too. Goodbye."

"Bye, sweetie."

Olinger came over to commiserate. We found a dark corner on the roof, held each other, and let the tears run down our cheeks. "Will we ever go home?" I asked.

He laughed, "I don't know Naylor. It sure as hell doesn't seem like it, does it? We'll get through this. Just like we've gotten through all the rest."

Then he did the best thing he could do. He started to make me laugh. "Remember when you told me how Saunders rubbed her cigarette butt on the freshly painted Al Sha'ab wall and you asked, 'What are you doing? They just painted that,' and she honestly had no idea painters had just spent the last three days turning the tan exterior into a bright white?"

"Oh, my gosh! You're right! That was the perfect Saunders-ism. I love her, but she's not always the brightest bulb, huh?"

"Nope, but at least she's helping to cheer you up right now."

We continued on in the same manner. We talked about Palmer getting a bullet to the balls and the crazy rumors we had heard about our relationship. His touch, his voice, and even his cleft chin brought back my spirits out of the depths of hell.

After he left, I stayed up into the wee hours of the night with the security guys and my fellow females who also made the extension a bit more bearable. I sent a mass email to the rest of my family and friends before I went to bed and then I cried myself to sleep.

POST EXTENSION

I woke up with puffy eyes and a sick feeling in my belly. I spent the majority of the day packing and getting ready to move to an unknown military base. The security guys came over and shared their phones again. I called my best friend Sam. She went crazy with anger when she found out what had happened.

The next few days were clouded with sadness and resentment. We were in limbo—waiting for our next destination and our new jobs.

As if it couldn't get any worse, we had to turn in our up-armored Humvees and put the steel plates back on our non-up armored Humvee doors. We spent hours taking them off only a few weeks prior. It appeared as though the Army were going to leave us for dead in the death traps.

If I thought I was depressed at Fort McCoy before this mess turned into an actual war, I was wrong. The subsequent weeks after our extension, were some of the roughest in my life. I sent this email to my family and friends:

Another week of missing home more than I can say. It's been a rough one—a lot of emotions and not many of them good. This place is taking a toll on me. Hope and morale have been drained from my system. I'm a pile of skin and bones that does what I'm told. It's hard to think for myself anymore. I don't care. I don't care when mortars hit. I don't care when an IED goes off. I'm numb. That's why they need to get us out of here. We have nothing left—mentally or physically. It is completely inhumane what they have done to us. We have tortured souls.

I didn't have a death wish, and in no way did I intend to commit suicide, but I was secretly hoping to get hurt—to be wounded enough to go home. I didn't care if I lost a limb or suffered a disability; I wanted to be freed from the shackles of war. I couldn't see any other way to get out of Iraq.

The four-person female smoking crew doubled for awhile. Our lieutenant, medic, and a few other females went in for a puff. I think Kirking was even pondering her decision to quit, but in the end, she hung out with me while the rest of the girls did what they had to do to get through. If I were to start smoking, it would have been in those weeks following the extension or the first day my brother and his friend were begging me to do it back in 8th grade. Thank God my values won.

I wrote another essay as therapy. I never intended to publish it. Gone were my loyalties and patriotism. My life was worth more than brass joy rides and poorly planned missions. I had begun to lose faith in humankind.

A USED SOLDIER'S THOUGHTS

Have you ever been to jail? I haven't, but I might know what it's like. I have been banished to a place with excruciating heat, climbing up to 140 degrees. Our phones have been taken, and our communication is limited to letters that may not even get to the receiver. We are forced to dress and look exactly like everyone else. We are no longer a name but a pawn in this fight for someone else's freedom. We can't eat or sleep until told to do so. We are instructed exactly what our job will entail, and we perform our duties without question or resistance. Our lives are put in harm's way every second of the day. Worst of all, we have no maximum sentence, no parole, and no date to return home. Our time is indefinite. Yet we did nothing wrong. We didn't break the law. All we did was sign on the line.

The Army has a thing they call morale. It prides itself on keeping the soldiers positive and motivated. Morale has found its way into our company via the internet, satellite TV, a swimming pool, and various billiard games. Until our extension orders, these things proved useful. Not only has our unit been extended for a minimum of 120 days, but also our morale-builders have been stripped from our existence. We have to pick up and move to a place that is unknown and unfamiliar. We have built our current location and learned to call it home for the past ten months only to move and start over. I ask you, would you have morale left?

I used to trust our government. Isn't it composed of the most intellectual and influential people in our country? After hearing no less than five redeployment dates, and getting our extension orders ten days prior to our departure, I am not so sure. I don't think our government or leaders took into account what this extension has done to our company. They did not take into consideration the soldier, the person. We are not robots. We cannot keep up this immortality forever. Eventually, we are going to break down and falter. Our bodies cannot endure the heat under 60 pounds of gear much longer. The 14-hour shifts, for endless days in a row, strip us of energy. Our bodies have not seen a dentist or a doctor for over a year, and our nerves are shot.

The decision-makers do not realize that National Guard Soldiers have another life besides the military. We have obligations to those we love, work for, and to ourselves. There are three brides left without grooms this summer because the grooms are still at war. Siblings and best friends are left without best men and maids of honor. Children are growing up without a parent. Numerous plans for the summer are squelched. Birthdays pass without celebrations. Anniversaries deem useless without the other half. Divorce and separations are finalized.

Jobs start filling their vacancies. Schools start a new semester. The world moves on while we are banished to the desert.

I am a witness and a victim. Our lives have been taken from us. We are like zombies now. Our emotions have deteriorated to half-smiles and suppressed laughter. We no longer cry for ourselves, but for our family and friends who worry endlessly over our well-being. We have been overtaken by grief, exhaustion, and repetition. Hope has ceased to exist in our dreary lives. We've forgotten what it feels like to hug someone we love, to talk endlessly with a best friend, to grab a beer and watch ESPN, to dress up for special occasions, to mow the lawn, to go to church, and to be ourselves and live the life we have chosen.

In the words of Coco Chanel, "I am no longer what I was. I will remain what I have become."

WITMER'S MEMORIAL SERVICE

A Bagpiper's mournful version of "Amazing Grace" resonated across the blue water while my company converged on the pool deck on 15 April for Witmer's memorial service. Her closest friends gave eulogies, two brave female soldiers from my company sang the hymn, and the Commander, CSM, and Brigade Colonel shared their condolences. I held myself together as the majority of my fellow soldiers cried around me, but when taps played and the guns saluted, the emotions were too much to hold back. I couldn't believe what had happened to our company within days of leaving the battlefields. I was angry, grief-stricken, and hopeless. I felt like a victim without any choices and freedom. We were supposedly fighting for freedom but had lost all of ours while deployed. The contradictions were asinine. The compassionless military continued to screw with us. We should have been home by now, but because the military couldn't get their crap straight, we lost a soldier. Worse yet, Witmer's squad should never have taken that route. To this day, I'm clouded in guilt because I feel like I could have done something to better communicate to her squad to avoid those towering buildings and the IED.

A few of our security friends stood in the shadows at the edge of the pool—in solitude. After the service, we filed past Witmer's gear to offer a salute, kiss her ID tags, and say our final goodbye. Daniels and Glenn gave hugs and condolences as we went past.

This picture was taken from the diving board. It shows Witmer's helmet propped on her weapon. Her ID tags were hanging off the weapon, and her boots were below. This is one of the hundreds of soldiers who lined up to salute and say goodbye after the Memorial Service.

Each of us felt awkward and uneasy, not knowing what to say or how to act. We were trained to act tough, to never break down—and there we were—crying and hugging. Hart turned toward me. His paternal nature melted my rough façade, and I broke down in his strong arms.

"Naylor, it's going to be OK. I'm not going to let anything happen to you," he said, holding me close. "Even though you're not in my team anymore, that doesn't mean that I don't keep an eye on you. We'll get through this. We'll be home before you know it."

"Thanks," I said. "That means the world to me. I hate not having you as a team leader. I trust you and need your humor to get me through."

"I know. You still have Verbsky and Phair to go to if you need something."

Later that night, the girls and I let loose. Cooper had purchased bongo drums from the Iraqis. We brought them onto the roof and jammed out. I don't have a lot of rhythm, but it didn't matter. We rocked the roof. I danced to release emotions, I danced to release the demons that haunted my dreams, I danced to release my crippling anxiety. We talked, laughed, and cried until 0015.

The following morning, Glenn shared our next steps. "We are moving to Camp Falcon, an established base with all the amenities—except for a pool. It's on the southern edge of Baghdad. Our missions will include convoy escorts, mainte- nance, and gate guard. But before we get down to business, we're going to have a pool party today. You're all invited down for a cookout, swimming, and fun." Glenn finished his briefing. "You are dismissed."

Once the festivities began, Olinger and Siefert ran halfway across the pool deck toward me and pushed me into the pool like bulls after a rodeo clown. I tried to grab Olinger's wrist as I went down, but he slipped from my grasp.

Our security guys brought the U.S. diplomat who was in charge of the country's finances. Even though we escorted him dozens of times, we had never seen him before because on our missions, he was surrounded by security the second he stepped out of the SUV. That didn't mean he hadn't seen us—he was intrigued by the 12 females who had been his escort and asked for a picture with us. We obliged. All 12 strong, tanned young women surrounding a white-haired businessman in his 50s.

The 12 of us females with our principal. From left to right: Paulus, Cooper, Korb, Kirking, Schultz, Boutilier, Ludwig, Behm, Grey, Me, Saunders, and Taylor. We are standing on the pool deck during this photo. 4/16/04

We celebrated well into the night. We had a mouth-watering cookout of deliciously thick grilled burgers, buttered corn, and huge chunks of watermelon. It tasted like home and happiness—both things I desperately wanted but were far out of reach. Afterward, we partied on the roof with the security guys. Mike Brown, an Irishman, and an Englishman named Jack Parnell—who both worked for the UN—were the life of the party. Their witty jokes and accents left our bellies and facial muscles sore from laughter. The guys, who were civilians, were allowed to drink in Iraq and brought enough booze for us to join in the festivities. Ever the rule-follower, I bowed out to avoid getting into trouble. I felt like I was back in high school as others drank around me.

The next day, we dropped off our up-armored Humvees at Camp Cuervo. We regressed to our makeshift Humvees that were half as safe and still parked at Mustang, waiting for us. Then we hopped on three five-tons, some of the most dangerous vehicles in Baghdad, with canvas covers and no armor. Fifty soldiers in three vehicles was a tragedy waiting to happen. I prayed the whole way back to Mustang base.

Once again, the security guys stopped by. Romances were cropping up. Cooper and Phil-the-Australian started their whirlwind romance, Jack Parnell was interested in Saunders even though she had Michael Whited back home, and Mike Brown had begun to spend more time by my side. The night ended with night swimming in the pool.

The next morning, we took a load of things to our new home at Camp Falcon. Even though the base had countless barracks, we were sent to a row of tents. *So much for being in a safe location!* The hot summer was quickly approaching and tents offered no respite from the heat—even with the AC on full blast. The extension was getting worse by the moment.

That night—our last night at Mustang—the security guys brought an abundance of alcohol once again. I couldn't resist anymore. To hell with rules, I was going to let loose. That can of beer was my first lick of alcohol since we left the states. I was enjoying my brew, catching a nice buzz, and chatting with Mike when a rocket whistled overhead, too close for comfort. Mike and I froze with oh-shit expressions. *So that's why we shouldn't drink. If I had to drive, I would risk the lives of everyone in the convoy.* I sheepishly set the last bit of my beer can on the ground and quit consuming alcohol in the moment. It just wasn't worth it. I had a great time without catching a buzz.

Mike pulled me away from the circle of laughter to look at the stars. He flowered me with compliments and begged me to kiss him once we got out of earshot from the others. His sweet Irish accent, salt-and-pepper hair, and his sexy and refined personality wore me down. Thank goodness. When I finally caved in and stood on my tiptoes to meet his lips with my own, I was whisked away to a different place. We kissed under the Baghdad stars. He gazed into my eyes and whispered sweet sentiments into my ear. I melted in his arms. His kisses, his two-day-old stubble, his embraces, his tenderness—I was back in Wisconsin, a civilian, a woman. I was far away from war and all its ugliness. I had to say goodnight around 0300 because we had to get up early to move to Falcon. And that was the end of my intimacy with Mike.

MOVING DAY

Our morning routine was slow and groggy due to the prior evening's festivities and lack of sleep. We painstakingly packed up our few meager belongings that were still at Mustang base and headed to Camp Falcon. I whispered goodbye to our room, the basement, the building, our compound—a decrepit home, but it was home nonetheless.

We were in the throes of unpacking and organizing our stuff when Sfc. Phair called a meeting. "Our first mission," he said, "consists of escorting a convoy to a remote army base in the south—called Camp Duke—which is fifteen minutes north of Najif. We have to leave bright and early tomorrow morning. You need to find a working truck outfitted with a kit. Doesn't matter whose truck since we're the only convoy going out tomorrow. Load a three-day supply of food, water, and clothes, and be ready to go at 0700 tomorrow morning." Kits are American-made armored plates that are bolted onto our soft Humvees for added protection. Only about ten Humvees in our company received kits, and those vehicles were used for the dangerous missions when we didn't have up-armored Humvees.

The number of vehicles we took to Camp Duke was too large for a single chalk, or convoy of vehicles, so we broke up into two chalks. My Humvee rode in the second chalk, which left a half an hour after the first. We threw our three-day supply into the foreign vehicle, acclimated ourselves to its intricacies, and lined up, waiting for the go-ahead to drive south.

Shortly after we left, the first chalk came over the radio. "We've hit an IED and have a wounded soldier. Three trucks are going to turn back to take him to the medic's station. Proceed with caution; this roadway is not safe."

We groaned at the news and spent a little more time scanning the roadways for loose dirt, garbage, foreign vehicles, and potential terrorists across the landscape. We soon came to the first chalk's attack site and waited for over an hour until the road was clear. Thirty minutes later, we heard a loud compression blast toward the end of our convoy. My Humvee was about three vehicles behind the first Humvee. The IED had exploded next to the last vehicle and blew out their windshield, but no one was hurt. The minor damage didn't slow us down—we kept driving south. The rest of the ride passed without incident.

Camp Duke was a stark army base in its first phase of development. The base rose from the arid desert as if it were a mirage. Shimmering metal antennas, tan tents, and Humvees scuttling in all directions like ants on a disturbed nest began to display themselves the closer we got. Duke didn't have showers, a chow hall, running water, phones, or internet. The powdery sand, the electric energy in the air, the lack of vegetation, and the smells of sand and diesel fuel reminded me of Kuwait. And just like our convoy from Kuwait to Baghdad, we slept on cots under the stars as trucks drove past, blanketing us with powder.

MORTAR MADNESS

Back at Falcon, we were subjected to countless mortar attacks. Every night before I went to bed, I prayed:
Now I lay me down to sleep.
I pray the Lord my soul to keep.
If I should die before I wake,
I pray the Lord, my soul, to take.
And I meant every single word.

Our thin-skinned tents and the ceaseless attacks left me wondering if I would wake in the morning. We were never safe. When tents a few hundred yards away were destroyed on two different occasions, I questioned when our time would come.

We debated whether or not we should jump out of bed and run for the bunkers or stay in bed, waiting for the impacts to subside. Either way didn't seem safe, since the bunkers were shaped like a wide upside-down U and only had two sides. The mortar attacks were usually done by the time we made it the 50 yards to the bunker anyway. Most of the time we stayed in our beds and used the power of prayer.

The explosions were intense enough to scare Kirking out of her top bunk in mid-sleep. I would wake from the mortars and see her flailing body fly past my line of vision onto the floor. I laughed hysterically both times it happened. She was not too happy with me on the occasion that she hurt herself.

A few weeks into our stay at Falcon, explosions erupted and woke us up minutes after we fell asleep. Gray said, "Everyone up! Let's get to the bunker *now*!"

"Wait," I said under my breath to Courtney. "I think that's thunder."

"Really?" she responded. "Whoa, I think you're right. Hey! LT! It's thunder!"

She slowed, "It is? Ha! Oh, my god; you're right! Never mind, everyone. Go back to sleep."

Great, now thunderstorms remind me of war; just great.

Partway through a gym workout, I ran outside to use the porta-potty and returned to my sit-ups and push-ups. We were bombarded with mortars less than five minutes later. The mortars were close. Very close. I thought they were going to land in the gym. My comrades looked like chickens with their heads cut off. Some were yelling for us to get to the center of the gym and under whatever equipment we could find, some were ordering us to stand against the walls, others were shell-shocked and stuck in place—frozen like the living statues on Times Square. Within seconds, the bombing subsided and I ran outside to see what I could to do to help since I was a combat lifesaver. I stopped dead in my tracks—in a stupor. The porta-potty I had just been in was destroyed. There wasn't a semblance of the plastic blue porta-potty left, just a hole in the ground. Shouting in the distance got me out of my trance. They were yelling for a medic. One ran out of the gym—over to their destination to find a dead mechanic under a vehicle in the motor pool. That could have been me, had I taken more time going to the bathroom.

Two mortars had crashed into our compound on a different day while my squad was walking back from chow. A square-foot chunk of shrapnel skidded to a stop by Phair and Verbsky's feet. Watching the monsters explode in plain sight left me sick to the stomach. *How are we still alive? This luck can't last forever. On the flip side, too bad we're not allowed to take pieces of mortars home— that would be a sweet memento.*

Olinger and I were talking in a bunker one night. He was sitting to my right. Our backs were against the cement wall, our bottoms sitting on a bench. We were relaxed and enjoying each other's company. He asked, "What's one of the first things you're going to do when you get home?"

"Ahhh...When I get home...I think I'm most excited about night driving with my music blaring. Putting on Dave Matthews and cruising to nowhere. I want to be alone. I don't want anyone else to know where I'm going. What about you?"

"Hmm..." While he was in mid-thought, we heard and felt three rockets fly a few feet above us. They were close enough to hear the whizzing sound. We embraced each other. The conversation turned from longing thoughts of home to survival.

"How are we going to survive this place until it's time to go home?" I asked. "I feel like I can see death knocking on my door."

"I think about that all the time, too. At least we have each other. You have Kirking and I have Seifert as well. We'll get home; don't worry."

"Yeah, thanks. I don't know what I would do without you right now."

A flickering flashlight woke me up at 0100 on one of our many nights at Falcon. I propped myself up and turned toward the door to see where the light was coming from. A male soldier stood next to my bunk, peering over me. Without my glasses on, I didn't recognize him. I asked, "Can I help you?"

He didn't say anything. I thought he might be an administrative soldier with a Red Cross message or a team leader informing us of a mission.

When the man didn't reply, it dawned on me that this United States soldier was not supposed to be in our all-female tent. He stopped staring, turned around, and glided toward the door. I grabbed my glasses and slid on my sandals. When he heard me, he picked up the pace. With a slam of the door, he was gone. I burst through the door a second later, but he was already too far away for me to catch.

I went straight to the TOC to tell them what happened. They said they would keep an eye out for him. The TOC had soldiers that roamed our AO throughout the night to fend off events like this, but apparently they weren't paying attention at the time of the intruder.

When my fellow tent-mates found out what happened the next morning, they were pissed that I didn't wake them to retaliate against the scrawny stalker. Their anger and hostility from months of combat flared, and they wanted to take it out on the pathetic soldier who preyed on women. I explained to them that I was groggy from my deep sleep, and he was too quick to grab. He may not have survived our fury, seeing as how we all slept with knives taped to the sides of our bunks. The tent's waterproofing agent was highly flammable, making the easily accessible knives necessary to cut our way through the tent in case of a fire.

The same scrawny soldier was caught sneaking into our coed showers by our First Sergeant, and he followed a lone female soldier from my company into the female shower trailer. When she spotted him, he took off running. We identified him as an infantry soldier who lived in a set of tents adjacent to ours. I'm hoping he received some consequences for his actions, but I never found out either way.

BACK TO TRAINING

My squad was given our next and final mission on 28 April. Instead of working as gate guard and escort—as previously told— we were tasked to monitor the Iskandaria and Musayib police stations, which were located at least an hour and sometimes two hours south of Falcon. The stations were full of corrupt officers, many affiliated with Al Sadr. Al Sadr had become a prominent political figure in Iraq, and his followers fought constantly with those who opposed him. He did not agree with our occupation, and his strongholds were treacherous anti-coalition locations. The other two squads in my platoon assisted us when needed and helped with escort missions. Our mission was to win the IPs hearts and minds, train them to be upstanding officers, and provide them with the necessary gear to execute their work to our standards.

Our first southern training mission included Cpt. Glenn accompanying my team. Before we entered a more dangerous part of the country—as if any part is more dangerous than another—we stopped at Camp Chosen, which was an hour south to pick up two Bradleys as escorts. Al Musayib police station was our first destination. The station resembled Bab al Sham with its small, decrepit, and failing architecture. Next, we stopped by the area's police headquarters, then went to the Iskandaria Police Station, and the Mahmudiyah Police Station. The day passed without incident. Most insurgent attacks were aimed at weaker convoys because they knew the retaliation would be less severe. Perhaps that's why we didn't run across an attack. After dropping off the Bradleys at Camp Chosen, we headed home.

We spent the next couple of months driving south, visiting two to four stations a day, adding Hilla, Haswa, and Turir stations to our route. I was tasked to sit in fighting positions and wait for an attack, or I assisted in the training while we were in the stations. More times than not, I found myself on the rooftops, watching the Iraqis live in their meager dwellings and coexist with sand and garbage-laden rivers and canals. Our stations were all in close proximity to the Euphrates or a canal diverted from the main body of the river. Our mental and emotional investment for these stations was a fraction of what we put into Al Sha'ab. We stayed at each station for a maximum of five hours a day, sometimes only stopping by for a few minutes. We didn't get to know too many of the officers personally, and we certainly didn't have lasting relationships. The energy we put into doing our jobs right, driving to the stations, and wishing that everything would work out, felt like enough of an investment. The hope was that we could show the IPs we cared and were there to support them.

Our time at the southern stations continued to provide cultural surprises and laughable moments. Par for the course, I peed while standing between my open Humvee door and my seat with my PUD while at the Mahmudiyah PD. When I finished, I turned around to see an IP stare at me in disbelief. He shouted Arabic with a bewildered tone. When I showed him my funnel, a light bulb turned on. He smiled, nodded, and laughed.

One day, 15 kids on a street corner tried to get my attention by yelling out any English word they knew—ice cream, hello, orange, banana, and what's your name? I laughed; none of what they said made sense. One of their mothers stormed out of a local mud and straw hut, grabbed a stick off of the dirt ground, slapped their behinds, and yelled at them to go home. The kids whined and scampered off.

Some kids were playing in the Euphrates River on a different day. Ten yards upstream, a man was shoveling his garbage into the river. The boys were swimming in his filth. It was a dismal sight.

We issued copious amounts of gear to the many stations—night-vision goggles, CS spray, vests, weapons, uniforms, whistles, flashlights, flashlight holders, magazine pouches, first-aid kits, uniforms, jackets, flexicuffs, handcuffs, cuff holders, and belts. We escorted two five-tons and a deuce carrying the equipment. Most of the gear was taken for granted and squandered. The gear was either sold on the black market or destroyed because the IPs assumed we would give them more when they needed it. American tax dollars well-spent. What was the purpose of it all? The U.S. military must have known that the gear would fall into corrupt hands, yet they continued to issue hundreds of thousands of dollars worth of brand-new items. Were they assuming positive intentions? Were they too removed from the situation to understand the gravity of what was happening? Or just following orders, regardless of the outcome? It reminds me of our training at Ft. McCoy. We trained for a Vietnam-like war because that's what they've always done, even though we *all* knew our war in Iraq would look very different. The military emulates a long train—it's nearly impossible to stop once it's in motion, and by the time the caboose arrives, the engine is ready to move on. The idiocy of it all drove me crazy.

Al Sha'ab was guilty of ruining equipment as well. The IPs had blown out the transmission in two of their squad cars within a few months. Additionally, a few Glocks that we issued the IPs were found on the black market.

We only issued CS spray to the IPs who were brave enough to get sprayed. They weren't allowed to carry it otherwise. Only 13 out of 70 IPs were up to the challenge. Our post-spray directions got lost in translation. Verbsky said to the interpreter, "Tell the IPs to stand in a well-ventilated area and rinse the CS spray off with water. Do not rub the area, because that makes the burning sensation worse." We laughed so hard when the IPs did the opposite of what we told them to do, just like we laughed at each other after the basic training gas chambers. They rubbed their eyes, walked into a tiny room to get away from us, avoided the wind, and pushed the water away that we were trying to offer them. Made me wonder what else the interpreters got wrong throughout our deployment.

Our pre-mission briefings were getting more and more dire as the coalition casualty rates were increasing. According to the Iraq Coalition Casualty Count from 2009, there were 580 total deaths in 2003 and by June of 2004, there were already 401. My company had many brushes with danger, and we continued to acquire purple hearts, 23 in total by the end of our deployment, according to the Racine, Wisconsin, *Journal Times*. Luckily, my squad was unscathed up to this point, but we knew our number would be up soon. We were minutes shy of hitting an IED on the drive to Haswa and Iskandaria. The U.S. convoy that had gone through right before us was hit, and we waited for two hours while they cleared the exploded IED and filled in the crater to make the road drivable.

On some days, a helicopter escorted us on the dangerous stretches. We bestowed a strong military presence onto the insurgents, yet they continued to attack coalition convoys. If I were a ragtag bunch of insurgents, I'm not sure I would have the confidence to wage war against the strongest army in the world.

Our luck ran out on 25 May. We were driving home and were a mile away from the Haswa station when I *thought* Murray had slammed something metal onto the Humvee roof while sitting in the turret. That man was like a bull in a china shop, and I often thought I heard a nearby bomb, but it was only him banging his gun or ammo around. I was about to yell at him to stop slamming things down that sounded like IEDs, but the words never left my mouth. Another Humvee flew past the convoy, shattered a wooden cigarette stand, and slammed into an Iraqi garage 50 feet to the left of my Humvee. *Oh, my God; what just happened? Was that actually an IED?*

Our convoy screeched to a halt. Without a word, we dismounted from the vehicles. Gregory ran to the disabled Humvee, Murray stayed in the turret, and I joined the crew on the perimeter. I wanted the bastard that ignited the IED. I wanted him badly, but my search was fruitless. I returned to Murray seconds later and asked, "You OK?"

He scanned his body and gear. "Everything's fine. And you?"

"Yup. I just wish we could get the assholes for once. Looks like Gregory had another one of his leadership lapses, huh? Didn't even check to see if we were OK before he took off to play hero."

"Ha! Yup, go figure."

"So what the hell happened? I thought you made that noise and I was about to yell at you until I saw the Humvee fly past."

"No; wasn't me. Spooner's vehicle was the one hit. That explosion was damn loud out here. I thought I was a goner."

"Wait, Korb's vehicle? No! Is she OK?" *Please God, let her be OK!*

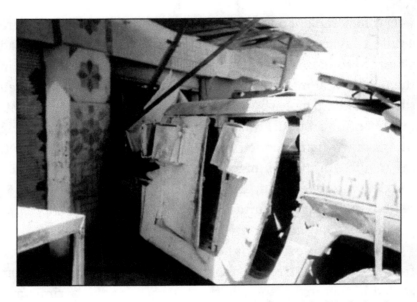

This is the explosion side of the Humvee. This is also where the truck found its final resting place after slamming into the garage. 5/25/04

Sgt. Spooner, who was sitting shotgun in the bombed vehicle, walked out from the dusty garage toward the convoy. He had jumped out of the moving Humvee when he noticed they were about to collide with the garage. Then a gray zombie lurched toward my truck screaming, "I'm OK, I'm OK!" It was Sgt. Springsteen, the driver. She was *not* OK. She had been sucked out of the vehicle as the explosive pressure receded. Her Kevlar was missing, and her short pixie haircut was caked with dust and sticking straight out. Her clothes were tattered and gray from the explosive material. When her adrenaline wore off, she couldn't move. Her entire left side was bruised internally and externally.

To my horror, someone yelled, "We're missing a soldier! It's Korb! Where's Korb? We can't find her."

My heart skipped a beat. I felt like the ground had fallen out from beneath me. *No! You can't tell me she's gone—please don't tell me she's gone. I can't survive here without her.* Ten seconds later, they found her. She was unconscious, in the fetal position, and in the back of the Humvee. She regained consciousness when they dragged her out of the vehicle. Her forearm was dripping blood onto the sand below, and she had scrapes, cuts, and bruises on her face and chest. They thought she had two compound fractures in her left arm, but it was shrapnel.

Ssg. Caldwell was sitting behind the driver when the IED exploded. He was knocked unconscious for a few seconds and received damage to his leg and elbow, but was doing all right otherwise. Again, they assumed he had a compound fracture in his left leg, but it, too, was shrapnel.

A medevac chopper arrived ten minutes after the explosion to take Springsteen, Korb, and Caldwell to the closest CSH.

Our attention turned to the damaged vehicles. We had two on our hands—the IED vehicle and another one that it had clipped—popping the back left tire. Camp Chosen brought a wrecker for the IEDed Humvee and a mechanic to fix the flat.

Ssg. Fox came walking down the road 30 minutes later with two Iraqi men in flexcuffs. He had stayed on the trail of the insurgents and spotted two guilty-looking Iraqis. He found traces of explosives on their hands. We apprehended them and took them into custody.

Korb and Caldwell returned to our compound from the CSH later that night. Korb was put on so many painkillers that she didn't remember most of the night. I took a picture of Korb with her disfigured weapon, and she had no recollection of me taking the photo. A piece of shrapnel had taken off the tip of her barrel. If Korb would have been leaning forward a few more inches, she would not have survived the explosion.

The night Korb came back full of painkillers. You can see the tip of her SAW is missing and she has small abrasions all over her face. 5/25/04

Springsteen returned a couple of days later. Her internal bruising kept her off of missions for a month or so.

On 5 June, insurgents drove to the Turir station in stolen IP vehicles. They killed the front gate guard, rushed inside, attacked the IPs, and ignited a VBIED, which leveled the police station. Seven IPs were killed, one was missing, and two were injured. The insurgents left a bomb in the debris and IEDs near the station entrance to attack the next shift of IPs. The time and work we put into the station were for naught. Everything we touched was being destroyed. Regardless of the IP's personal affiliation with us or Al Sadr, they had become the insurgents' enemy. Anyone who received payment from the U.S. government was under attack. Even the people who worked in our laundry service at

Camp Falcon were getting attacked on the way to work, causing our laundry service to close for weeks at a time.

Every station that we had worked in was attacked by insurgents, either while we were deployed or after we returned home. I read about how station after station had crumbled as I drank my coffee in the comfort of my home.

END OF MISSIONS

Our last day working at the southern stations was 21 June. After that, I played copious amounts of volleyball, worked out, avoided incoming mortars, wrote letters, loaded our conexes, and spent endless hours talking to Olinger and Kirking while we waited to convoy south.

June 30th was the official changeover of power to the Iraqi government. We mentally prepared for another extension, because we anticipated the turnover to crash and burn. When the day transpired with barely a shifting wind, we finally put our hope into returning home.

Our company had a huge 4th of July party. The family support group sent us luau materials, including neon-colored t-shirts that said *32nd MPs 4th of July Luau*. My parents sent a kiddie pool, which is where I spent the majority of my day when I wasn't playing volleyball, dancing, or balloon tossing.

In the afternoon, my company had an awards ceremony. Glenn and the 4 LTs received Bronze Stars. I watched, with the rest of the enlisted soldiers, when the CSM gave the Bronze Stars to the LT who put our lives in unnecessary danger. I no longer believed that award had any merit.

My platoon left for BIAP on 9 July. We were tasked to escort another company to Kuwait before we demobilized.

Enjoying the kiddie pool that my parents gave us. I'm wearing the shirt that our family support group sent over with other luau material. Taylor used her fashion design background to alter our t-shirts and make them more feminine. I donated mine to the Wisconsin Veterans Museum in Madison. 6/28/04

The rest of our company drove straight from Camp Falcon to Kuwait to begin the process home. There was no definitive word on when my platoon was leaving BIAP. We sat around all day on the 9th, anticipating an order to pack up and move out. Ten July—more hurry up and wait. Gray, Korb, Bentler, and I played cards for hours, I skyped with my whole family for the first time, and then played full-court basketball with 11 other soldiers. There was still no word on when we were leaving.

We were jacked around again on the 11th. At first, we were supposed to leave at 0300 the next morning, but at 1630 that mission was canceled. My platoon played another raucous game of basketball where we left our ranks on the sidelines.

Our mission on the 12th was canceled in the morning but was back on an hour later. Same dance, different day. Then, we were supposed to leave at 1500 and at 1415. Lt. Gray told us we weren't leaving until 0500 on the 13th, so we unloaded our stuff. A half an hour later, Lt. Gray told us the original mission was back on and that we were leaving in 30 minutes, at 1500.

At last, our convoy rolled out at 1630 on the 12th. I was in the second chalk of the convoy, but beat the first chalk because they broke down twice. Once again, the impregnable dust made driving treacherous. We had the pleasure of night-driving, which was even more difficult to navigate through thick clouds of swirling sand. We reached Cedar at 0100 and stayed the night.

PART IV
MY RETURN

Our final leg to Kuwait was uneventful, except for a blown radiator. After hooking the Humvee to the tow truck, we moved on. I was thankful for the quiet ride because the heat and heinous insects had only allowed for four hours of sleep.

We crossed the life-altering border into Kuwait at 1300. Without the crushing weight of war, I could sit up straighter, my vest didn't seem to suffocate me as much, and my head cleared as the stress and anxiety fluttered away. *I am done with war.*

We dismounted a quarter mile down the road. "Welcome to Kuwait!" said Captain Doscher. "First, you'll drive to Camp Victory to drop off your garbage and extra baggage. Next, you will report to Camp Arifjon, where you will demobe. My counterpart—Captain Stoltenberg—will be your rep in Arifjon and will walk you through the necessary steps to return home. You should be leaving within a week. Good luck with the rest of your journey, and I want to be the first to congratulate you on a job well-done. Thirty-second MPs, you have left your mark on Iraq. That is all I need from you at this location. Mount up!"

Kuwait's Camp Victory was less than an hour away. We unloaded our garbage, spare tires, fuel cans, and extra ammo. Our fantasy return home was turning into a reality. My steps were lighter, and I was more confident that we were about to leave this dreaded place. My comrades shared my sentiment. If I didn't know better, I would have thought we were at a college party for the next few hours. We were giddy, with smiles on our faces and rapid-fire jokes. Soldiers were running back and forth to one another's Humvees, laughing and whooping. I was dizzy with excitement.

Camp Arifjon—our new home for the next week and a half—was another few hours south. We arrived at 2030, unloaded our personal gear in our new home—an airplane hangar—and then drove to a dump to unload the rest of our garbage. That night, July 13th, I officially resumed my life as a female. I said goodbye to my PUD when I pitched it over the side of the dumpster. I teetered on the edge. *Should I do it? Should I really throw away this piece of equipment that has made my life easier?* Before I could change my mind, I tossed it over the edge of the dumpster, like Rose throwing The Heart of the Ocean over the boat's side in the movie *Titanic. It is time to return to my feminine side, to become a civilian again, to shed my military persona.* A twinge of regret stayed with me. As liberating as it was, I would have loved to have kept that blue funnel with its camo spray-paint peeling off the sides. The Wisconsin Veterans Museum in Madison also wanted it for their artifact warehouse. But to me, it symbolized my time to evolve back into my civilian self.

The next day, we took our truck to the wash rack. Per military fashion, we were supposed to start washing it at 1300, but we got booted to 2145. When we got there, we waited in line until 0100—twelve hours after our original start time. We sprayed, scrubbed, and cleaned every crevice of the truck until 0430. Every speck of dirt, contaminant, and dollop of grease had to be wiped away so that the inspectors could run a white glove over every inch without getting dirty. We had it checked twice by the customs official before it met the daffy standards. When we finished, the sun was rising over the Persian Gulf. The pink and orange sky reflecting off the salt-scented water, the palm trees, the sandy beach, and the distant call of birds made up for my lack of sleep. We passed inspection at 0700, and then we drove to the sterile area. I slept most of the day away after being up all night.

That night, Korb, Kirking, Boutilier, Taylor, and I sat in a circle on our bunks and packed our gear for the trip home. We each had a pair of boots and a uniform nearby. We debated on packing them or pitching them. We wouldn't need it anymore. What was the point of lugging the grungy rags home?

In April 2004, insurgents succeeded in stealing five Humvees from a military base called Anaconda. They wore U.S.-issued DCUs and vests that they had recovered from the garbage. From that point on, all U.S. soldiers had to shred or burn their uniforms if they chose to leave them behind. The thought brought a mischievous grin to our faces. We wanted the satisfaction of using our bare hands to shred the prison-like uniform. The symbolism was another nail in our proverbial time-at-war-coffin. Peace and optimism burst through my finger tips with every tear I made. My hatred and sorrow subsided when the splitting of fabric resonated through my body.

During the following few days, we got our new National Guard IDs—which ended our full-time Army status. Sfc. Phair met with us individually to review our sensitive items, and I spent time with Olinger and my fellow females at the pool.

Korb ran up to me as I was resting on the pool deck during one of my many visits. "Naylor, Gregory is calling you on the radio."

"Ugh, what now. I just want to relax," I said to Korb. Then over the handheld, "Go for Naylor."

"Naylor, where have you been? I've been calling you for forever. Get back to the hangar, now!" Gregory barked.

"Yes, Sergeant," I hissed. I looked at Korb and asked, "How long has he been calling me?"

"He just started. It's been less than a minute, I swear."

I found Gregory on his bunk. His face contorted when he saw me and said, "Naylor, you are grounded for the next 24 hours."

"What? I responded a few minutes late. You knew exactly where I was, and we didn't have a mission. You were just testing me. How can you ground me? What does that even mean in this hellhole?"

"You're grounded because I say so. You can go to chow and sit in your bunk. End of discussion."

I was too dumbfounded to speak. *What an egotistical prick! I am 23, he is 24, and I have never been grounded in my life. What the hell kind of surreal planet am I on? I wasn't doing anything wrong!* I knew he wasn't worth the breath. I walked away and dealt with my ridiculous consequence.

We ended our time at Camp Arifjon with customs inspections. After laying our personal gear on the ground outside of our hangar, we waited hours for the customs officials to comb through our things. We couldn't take anything home that might be detrimental to North America's environment and ecosystem. Palmer had to hand over the bullet that bounced off the ground and hit him in the balls. The 130-degree temps and Persian Gulf humidity baked our stuff. We had to wait until our scalding-hot gear was in the buildings' shadows before we packed our bags.

We left for the Camp Doha airport at 1430 on July 24th. We boarded our plane at 2330 and took off for home at 0230. I attempted to sleep, but the adrenaline and thrill of going home kept me wired and awake. I shut my eyes and relaxed, but my mind was imagining the comforts of home: civilian outfits, family time, soft beds, driving in a quiet and relaxing car, solo walks, long conversations with my best friend, Sam, and even the act of studying and learning.

We refueled at the Shannon airport in Ireland. Cpt. Glenn granted us permission to consume one alcoholic beverage. It was our first permissible drink in 15 months. The dark, malty flavor and subtle carbonation tasted like freedom when they hit my lips. The sweet liquid coursed through my veins and gave my tired body a wave of bliss. The buzz felt heavenly. It didn't take a lot of Guinness to hit a weary soldier. Korb and a few others found a way to sneak a second brew before we took off. I was nearly intoxicated after only one drink and didn't need another. We left lush, green, vibrant Ireland and the natives' lovely accents at 0830.

The eight-hour flight over the Atlantic gave us time to process our return home. The plane was abuzz with chatter. "Do you think they'll make us turn the plane around? I heard that it happened to a different company as they were flying over the Atlantic."

"How many people do you think will be waiting for us when we land? Do you think the press will be there?"

"Ha! When was the last time we showered?"

"How long do you think we'll be able to stay with our family and friends before we head to Ft. McCoy?"

"I heard that we need to pretend like we didn't see much at war in order to get out of Ft. McCoy faster. Someone told me that their friend had to stay an extra month because they admitted to seeing dead people."

"I cannot wait to hug my kids."

"Do you think I can sneak somewhere with my wife quick?"

"Demobing at Ft. McCoy better be quick. I have to get my life in order before college starts back up."

"How many of us are going to suffer from PTSD, do you think?"

We were on the plane with another company from Kentucky and made a two-hour pitstop to drop them off at 1100. My fellow soldiers and I couldn't contain ourselves when we landed on American soil. Our cheers erupted like a volcano. My senses were in overdrive. *The sky is bluer than I remember. The green trees and grass pop like neon signs. The plane doors opened. Holy crap! I can smell the vegetation. Has the air ever smelled this aromatic before? I feel like I should be running through a valley in a Tide commercial.* We disembarked for a short time while the plane refueled and our flight crew switched. I was transported to my parents' backyard when the soles of my boots stepped onto the soft grass. I could see the baseball field my dad built and the times we played pick-up ball in high school, the fire pit where I spent the majority of my summer nights, the place where we always pitched the tent and slept among nature, the path that led us to the pond with beaver dams and roaming foxes. Murray's voice interrupted my daydream: "Are we ever going to get home? I feel like we've been here forever."

"I sure hope so," I responded. "It can't come soon enough." A wave of euphoria swept over my body in that moment. I jumped up and down like Rocky Balboa and punched Murray in the arm. "Dude! It's our turn! We're actually going home! Can you believe it?"

He laughed, rubbed his arm, and shook his head with a grin that spread across his face.

"Oh, my gosh! This is it!" Korb yelled across the aisle when the plane left the Kentucky tarmack.

"I know! I still can't believe we're going home. I'm worried I'm going to wake up any minute in my bunk in Baghdad with a stomachache from grief."

"Naylor, this time it's real. Want me to pinch you?"

"Ha!" I laughed. "Yes, please! Seriously. I can't believe it's actually happening. I want to crawl through this window the second we land to give my family hugs."

Korb nodded, "I hear ya, Nailz, I hear ya."

The plane erupted into a deafening applause when we landed—like a walk-off homerun at the ballpark. I looked at Korb and embraced her. "We're home!" I exclaimed, "we're really home!" I turned to Kirking, smiled, and hugged her as well.

When the plane veered toward the hangar, we laid eyes on our families and friends who were waiting for us. The massive crowd was about the size of a football field, big enough to cover the grounds outside of the hangars.

As if the months, weeks, hours, and minutes weren't a long enough wait, they made us lineup in alphabetical order before we could get off the plane. Groans, "Are they serious?" "This is ridiculous," and "Why the hell do we have to do this?" were sentiments echoing through the plane as we jostled for space to reach our alphabetical order destination. I was shaking, light-headed, and nauseous from the anticipation of seeing my family. It could have been from lack of sleep as well. I kept bending over and peering out the tiny windows to see if I could catch a glimpse of a familiar face.

When the First Sergeant determined we were in alphabetical order, they opened the doors. The University of Wisconsin marching band serenaded us while we walked down the airplane's steps. A long line of military honchos and Governor Doyle stood at the bottom of the steps to shake our hands. Their faces were like a blur. I gazed past their smiles, trying to see my family's instead, but to no avail. The crowd was too massive.

The buzz of our family and friends grew louder when they saw our single-file line come their way. People were yelling for their soldiers and holding homemade signs. Groups were chanting their loved one's name. Their increasing decibels reminded me of when a band enters the stage at a concert. The more soldiers who emerged from the plane, the louder the crowd got. Yet, before we could embrace our loved ones, we had to hand over our guns at the weapon's truck. For the first time in 16 months, I didn't have to watch, clean, and keep eyes on my weapons. This solitary act felt like a giant leap toward our own liberation from active duty. It meant more than when we received our new IDs, than when we flew over the Atlantic, than when we got the all-clear with our sparkling-clean Humvee. The weapons were like a tether to war that we were no longer bound to.

I wanted to skip with joy and weightlessness toward the waiting crowd after that freeing moment. Instead, I smiled so largely my face hurt while I followed the snaking line of soldiers through a gated fence and around a bend, and there was my smiling mom—at the front of the crowd. She screamed, "Laura! Laura! It's you!"

Our long walk from the plane to our families. We had to shake everyone's hand when we got off. I know Gov. Doyle was there, but the rest of them were a blur. The white truck is where we turned our weapons in, and the crowd on the top right of the photo was our family and friends waiting for us. 7/23/04

I screeched with joy when I saw her and ran to her. I embraced her small frame, lifted her off the ground, and spun her around. Then my twin brother, Andy, emerged from the depths of the crowd and joined the embrace. When we unlocked our grip, I saw my dad standing there with a stoic smile on his face and tears streaming from his eyes. We hugged. The second we let go, I reached into my front pocket and handed him the two-dollar bill that he gave me prior to the deployment. "Dad, I kept this in the front pocket of my uniform every single day. It was a reminder of your love and guidance. I want you to have it back now that I'm home."

He shook his head with a crooked smile on his face, pride in his smiling eyes, and accepted it with joyful tears. That same two-dollar bill found its way into Andy's hands a few years later as he embarked on a Peace Corps mission to South Africa.

Grandma Naylor, Grandma and Grandpa Shanks, my friends—Ashley, Dan, Inez, and Hannah—and my aunt and uncle, Kathy and Bill, were there as well.

My parents and I the day I got home. This picture is testament that my dad wouldn't stop looking at me. 7/23/04

A whirlwind of conversation, pictures, and even a Wisconsin Public Radio interview consumed my next two hours. I had a hard time navigating the attention and physical contact. I flinched when my parents put their arms around me. The intimacy was foreign to my war-hardened body. I kept my mouth shut to spare their feelings, but it was surreal to want to deflect familiar touch. I forced myself to relearn the benefits of physical contact.

I crashed hard when my exhausted and weak body hit the mattress at 2100 after my company found its way via buses to Ft. McCoy.

We out-processed and partied during the next five days. I napped, ate Chinese food, drank at McCoy's, and lied to the mental-health officials about my well-being. The rumors on the plane were true. Soldiers who had previously demobilized told us not to release information about the carnage we witnessed. If we fessed up to seeing death and destruction, they could hold us at Ft. McCoy even longer to verify our mental fitness before releasing us into civilian life. I did everything in my power to get home, regardless of the after-effects.

The doctor asked, "Did you see combat?"

"Yes, but it wasn't too often and we got out of the kill zone immediately."

"Did you see any dead bodies?"

"Only from afar. I couldn't even really tell they were dead."

"Did you suffer prolonged periods of sadness?"

"No."

"Do you feel fully prepared to reintegrate into civilian life?"

"Absolutely."

On the 502nd day of our deployment, my company rode a coach bus in our nicest uniforms—a loose term—to the Minor League Baseball stadium in Madison. We were treated like celebrities. The bus itself felt like the VIP treatment after our uncomfortable military modes of transportation. Our family, friends, and fellow Wisconsinites filled the stadium while we were secretly bused to the main entrance. We were welcomed with a standing ovation as we marched into the stadium. The Governor and a couple military bigwigs said a few words, and then our commander stood on the pedestal and thanked us for serving. After standing in formation for less than 30 minutes, our commander declared the three most beautiful words I had ever heard. "You. Are. Released."

...You are released...

They released us!

We were done.

We were free to go.

Free for the first time in 16 months.

Free to do *as* we please *when* we please without a whisper to another human being.

Free!

The joy! The elation! The bliss!

We were free, but my first instinct was not to run to my parents, not to run away from the company formation, but to go to my fellow females, my new family, my lifeblood. We were overtaken by emotion. We stood in a circle and gave each other a bittersweet hug. Our eyes were blurry with tears. We were all trying to talk at the same time. "I love you guys."

"I never would have gotten through this without you."

"What will we do when we don't see each other?"

"We better have get-togethers often."

"Damn, I already miss you so much."

"Let's email phone numbers to each other right away, OK?"

"One last group hug. Love you all!"

It was the end of our adventure together.

To this day, there are few people who understand my complexities. My sisters-at-war know why I shed tears, know the difference between my smiles, and they know my happiness based on the glint in my eye. They can comprehend the torment I went through both during and after our deployment. They see through the cracks of my wrinkles and know what caused my premature aging. They know where I've been and what I've seen. We can cry on one another's shoulders and not a whisper needs to be spoken because we know. We know that the night-mares, demons, aggression, and anxiety will never end, but the edge softens as time goes by.

When we ran out of words and knew our families were anxiously waiting, we separated. I rushed over to my parents and gave them a strong embrace. I collected my swag bag and a case of Madison's finest beer and hopped in the car. At the very first gas station we saw, I ran to the bathroom and changed into a beautiful, comfortable, and glorious civilian outfit—a red Hawaiian-style dress. I was done with the heavy, crappy, make-me-feel-like-a-man clothes. Before I left the bathroom, I sat down for a delightful pee, knowing that I would never have to stand or squat again unless it was on my own accord. I was done with war.

Even though my time at war concluded, I still reported for drill weekends for the next two-and-a-half years, got promoted to sergeant, and acquired my own team. I finished my National Guard contractual obligations in 2007 and continued inactive ready reserve until 2009 when I got my honorable discharge.

PART V
POST TRAUMATIC STRESS

The return from the killing fields is more than a debriefing...it
is a slow ascent from hell.
~ *SGT Hart Hillman "A Terrible Love of War"*

"If you're a good soldier, you'll be a bad civilian....When
you get home, you have to start from scratch because it is a
different world and you are a different person....The worst
thing is that you don't fit. You don't fit anywhere when you
get home."
~ *The Ground Truth*

When I returned home, I looked on my parents' bookshelf
and saw a book entitled *Vietnam: The Tragedy*. My first thought
was, *Thank God Iraq wasn't a tragedy*, but the longer I thought
about it, the more I realized that it was a tragedy. I had given
my blood, sweat, and tears for what? Sixteen months of
my life for what? My innocence and happiness for what?
That tragedy unfolded during the next few years while I lived
with disabling PTSD. Every morning, I diligently read the
newspaper, and almost every day there was a section about Iraq.
Within those two years, that section outlined how every single
one of our police stations and territories was destroyed by insurgents. In the end, all was lost. Everything was a tragedy.

I have suffered immeasurable and, most times, unspoken
pain and torture since my return home. When I was at war, my
life back home felt like heaven. I only pictured the good, not the
bad. This made my return more difficult, since life can be hard
under any circumstance.

For the first six months, I couldn't find the joy I thought
would come naturally. The world was gray. My emotions were
low. I wanted to be alone, but when I was alone, I wanted to

be with people. The people in my life couldn't empathize with my emotional needs. I didn't know how to talk to them, how to relate to them, and they didn't know how to talk to me either. My roommates and I threw parties, but I felt like I was only half present. I went to my classes, but I didn't have a passion for learning and teaching. I tried to laugh at Andy's jokes, but I mostly half-smiled and shrunk into myself. *How can this be? I am home. I am free. It's not supposed to be like this.* I couldn't understand where my depression was coming from, which made me even more depressed.

That winter, the girls in my platoon and I had a gathering. When we talked about PTSD and how each of us had succumbed to the same dark state of mind, it soothed my soul. Instead of feeling isolated, I had solitude among my comrades. The veil of depression started to disappear, and that spring and most of the summer brought many joyous times. I thought I was cured.

Military psychologists told us that upon our return we may suffer PTSD, and they explained the different symptoms such as guilt, mistrust, irritability, social isolation, hypervigilance, flashbacks, anxiety, loss of interest, and/or nightmares. I refused to admit that war had a long-term impact on my life. I was an intelligent, strong, and determined person. I was not going to let the war beat me. I had made it out of my initial funk and thought that I had made it through the worst of it.

At the end August 2005, I was at Ft. McCoy for a two-week sergeant school. We reenacted war scenarios and took turns leading the platoon of troops while wearing MILES gear. Before Iraq, I lived for these moments. I kicked ass at laser tag and felt high from the adrenaline-fueled fun. Now I could not dredge up those positive and motivational emotions. I was huffing it in the middle of a single-file ruck march when simulated grenades and staccato M16 bursts boomed a few meters away. My heart rate increased a little, then a lot, then the tears welled up, and the thoughts of war wouldn't get out of my head. *Laura, the scenario is fake, you're going to be OK.* Images of Iraq flashed through my mind. *Breathe deep.* The horrid feeling of waking up in a war zone made my stomach queasy. *Think of something else.* The smell of explosives reminded me of Al Sha'ab's car bomb. *I can't breathe. Holy crap, everything is going black. I can't take another step.* The intrusive thoughts were taking over my mind. I lost control over my own thoughts. *What is happening to me? How can I go crazy like this?*

Simultaneously, Hurricane Katrina was tearing New Orleans apart. The cyclone was bearing down on the Big Easy just like my own dark cloud spun around me and tore apart my sense of safety, my sanity, and my fortitude. I was hyperventilating. I tried to holler for help, but couldn't. When I collapsed during the road march, my fellow troops rushed over and tried to take my clothes off because they thought I was suffering from heat stroke. I forced, "PTSD...PTSD! Where's Korb? I need Korb!" through my suffocating lungs.

Korb, who was at the training with me, raced over to provide her support. She said, "Back off. Naylor is not suffering from heat stroke. She has PTSD. Can't you see it? This temp is nothing compared to the Iraq heat. Let her chill out. Give her some space."

I was taken away from the war scenario for two hours to rest and get my mind back on track. During the break, a medic said, "Stop crying. It's not going to help the situation."

He got my death-look and I inquired through gritted teeth and clenched fists, "You ever been overseas?"

He shook his head with a smug look.

Blood rushed to my face. I was a bull seeing red. He hit a nerve I didn't know existed. I said, "Fuck off and stop trying to help when you have no idea what I've been through." *As if I can stop crying with a snap of a finger. Does he honestly believe I want to*

be in this state of mind? That I get joy out of feeling out of control?
That I want my world as I know it to be ravaged by this PTSD twister?

After a two-hour respite, my heart rate and breathing steadied.
I finished sergeant school among the top three soldiers in my
class of over 100. Once again, I thought the worst part of my
PTSD was over.

I survived the next couple of weeks without so much as a
raised pulse. But just like food coloring in a bowl of water, the
intrusive thoughts bled into my being and consumed my life. I
didn't need a trigger; I didn't need to be awake. I was on edge
24-hours a day, regardless of where I was and what I was doing.
My blood pressure, which used to be regular, skyrocketed to
190 over 120. My once-healthy self was deteriorating, because
I couldn't get my mind straight. I was working out and eating
healthy, but it didn't matter. My mental health was ruining my
physical health. I had a hard time concentrating while in school,
student teaching, and even while cooking dinner. If I wasn't
suffering from intrusive thoughts, my mind festered with worry
about when my next intrusive thought might occur. Similar to
when you're about to fall asleep and think *Oh, good; I'm almost*
asleep and then you're wide awake again. *Oh, good; I've gone an*
hour without thinking of war. Then war consumed me for the
next hour. My mind was overtaken.

I lost my happiness. I didn't have control over my thoughts
and was tormented day and night with visions of war. It wasn't
just war that I saw; it was me in my DCUs, it was the children of
Baghdad, the sandy sky, and the deadening grass. A smell, sight,
or sound could bring me into a state of insanity. When I visited a
friend's house and smelled the same hand soap we used in Iraq,
images flew back to me. Images I will never be able to get out
of my head. Sometimes the images aren't bad, but I still get the
sick, heinous, hopeless, fearful feeling of being extended, of
never returning home, of dread.

The thought of being happy sent me into a whirlwind of guilt. I had the convoluted idea that I didn't deserve to be happy. Anytime I caught myself smiling or laughing, a rush of guilt took the moment away. I felt bad for feeling bad, I felt sad for feeling happy, and I felt terrible for losing my cheerful self. My friends ostracized me because I ostracized myself. I worried about my family because they worried about me.

Dreams plagued my sleep. Mortars—I always saw mortars. Sometimes they exploded on impact, sometimes they were duds that skidded across the ground, but the mortars were always flying. I was never alone, either. My fellow soldiers and I dodged the incoming mortars. I saw my fellow soldiers incinerated by the mortars, family members destroyed by mortars, I saw myself die from mortars. I saw Korb shot point-blank in her face. I saw dead bodies. I saw war. I would wake up panicked.

War.

Mortars.

Day and night.

War.

PTSD was a downward cycle to a place I had never been before and never want to reach again. A normal life felt impossible with PTSD.

On my drive to school, a month after my first panic attack, I was living in a fog. My prior life was an unreachable dream. I would float in out of reality. I was caught in a layer of dirt where the earthworms burrowed and the moles sniffed around. No one wanted to touch my darkness, and I couldn't figure out which way was up. I clawed at the dirt, hoping to find daylight. Once in a while, I saw a glimpse of my old self, but it slid through my mud-caked fingers just out of reach. I gasped for fresh air, for freedom and joy. My air was dank, putrid, and smelled of earth and decay. The tears blinded my eyes, my breathing was on the verge of hyperventilation, my nose was like a faucet, and the thoughts wouldn't stop. I was gripped with fear. A roaring siren pulsed through my head, getting louder and louder until I couldn't hear my own thoughts. My ears rang so loudly I felt like I was in a fire truck rushing to the nearest emergency at full speed. I pulled over at the nearest park and called my older brother. "Joe," I sobbed, "I need you right now. I can't drive and get my mind straight. Can you pick me up at Vilas Park and take me to the VA to see someone in the mental-health department?"

"Oh, my God, Laura! Are you serious? Yes, I'll be there right away. I had no idea it was this bad."

"Joe, it's that bad. I need a professional. I can't get out of this on my own."

Joe lived less than five minutes away and found me within that time. He drove me directly to the VA, took me to the third floor, and with one look at me, the employees knew the urgency of the situation. Dr. Amy saw me immediately. She become my savior. My hero. I can never thank her enough for what she did for me. For talking to me straight, for testing out different meds, for letting me cry and swear and laugh, for giving me my life back.

I continued to see a therapist and a psychiatrist for the next five months following my initial visit to the VA. With time and patience, I was able to overcome my anxiety, my blood pressure returned to normal, and I found my cheery disposition.

Unfortunately, PTSD is something I will never fully overcome. I've had some rough patches since my final therapy session and since I stopped taking anti-anxiety pills, but I've been able to overcome those feelings on my own.

In some regards, I'm not surprised PTSD consumed my life. We were warned not to become too complacent with war. It was beneficial to have a sense of fear—to be surprised and scared when bombs exploded. But being on edge for 16 months wreaked havoc on my internal system. Stomachaches, headaches, the shakes, nightmares, and lack of trust in any situation were a few traits my fellow soldiers and I acquired while being overseas. We were never safe, not even in our compound. We went on hundreds of missions without knowing the consequences. The enemy could have been an IP, a translator, or civilian walking through the street.

It was impossible to stop those feelings after returning home. I was on edge for a long time. I suffered from war's aftermath for months. I even had to retrain my brain for civilian driving. My neural pathways were telling me to go through intersections as quickly as possible; never stop, try not to slow down, keep moving. For at least six months, I only yielded at red lights instead of stopping until the light turned green. Whenever I had a passenger in the car, I explained, "Thank goodness you're here. You need to help me watch for red lights. If they're red, remind me to stop and stay stopped." A few passengers laughed it off, thinking I was joking. After running a red light, they knew my request was legit.

Garbage and upturned roadsides also threw me for a loop. I almost had a head-on collision when I drove into the oncoming lane. I was veering away from a bag of garbage that was on the side of the road. It wasn't until I was a split-second away from impact that I realized I was home, that this incoming car was not going to get out of my way, and that the garbage was *not* an IED.

> There was enough baggage from tours in Afghanistan and Iraq that made coming home a place of uncertainty, anger, and confusion, not, as I had been led to believe, a warm celebration of safety.
> ~ *Benjamin Sledge*

THE CANNONS AT KING

King is a residential veterans home about five miles from my parents' house. A week after I returned home from war—well before my downward spiral—my parents and I went to King to visit my aunt and uncle who lived there. A French and Indian War reenactment was occurring in the field next to King. We had been sitting outside, enjoying the warm sun, low humidity, and the hum of the distant boats on the Chain O'Lakes. Then cannons from the reenactment boomed to life. The first couple of bombs made me jump, and I could feel my heart in my throat, but I thought that was a normal reaction to a simulated bomb. By the third, fourth, and fifth, I felt electric waves of fear coursing through my system. My body shook with anxiety. I could barely hear over the rushing noise in my ears. I knew my parents were looking at me—concerned—but I couldn't make eye contact. I was too ashamed of what was happening to me. *Where is my bravado? How can other veterans enjoy the show while I'm trying to crawl inside myself to hide?* As the staccato bangs continued, my fear intensified. "We have to get out of here. Now!" I heard myself say.

I was frozen in place. My body wouldn't move under my command. My parents stood on both sides of me and helped me walk to the car. I could barely stand on my own. *I'm safe, I'm safe, I'm safe,* repeated in my head, but my body wouldn't listen until the cannons were out of earshot. My parents were dumbstruck. "Are you OK, Laura? What can we do?"

Their questions continued on the drive home.

I shook my head—unsure of what to tell them. This had never happened to me before. I had no idea how powerful a simple noise could be. It had driven me into a semi-conscious state.

"I'll be fine," I said. "Not a big deal," I said. "See, I'm better already," I said. Little did we know how bad it would get.

"Civilians are lucky that we still have a sense of naiveté about what the world is like. The average American means well, but what they need to know is that these [military] men and women are seeing incredible evil, and coming home with that weighing on them and not knowing how to fit back into society."

~ Amy Amidon, a Navy psychologist

THUNDER AT EMILY'S

A couple of days later, I was at my friend Emily's cabin playing drinking games as a storm was creeping in. When the thunder rumbled, I heard bombs. I heard explosions. I heard death. I heard destruction. I heard *war*.

I wanted to hide under the table. I know that my eyeballs were popping out of my head in fear every time the thunder clapped. Rachael Murray looked at me like I was crazy. She didn't know how to react to what I was going through. She laughed when I physically jumped out of my seat in fear. I wanted to wrap my hands around her neck and strangle her for mocking me. *I have to go home. I have to get away from these people who don't understand. I need to talk to my Army girls—I need someone who understands.*

Despite my anxiety and fear and newfound hatred toward their ignorance, I stayed. I beat the storm. I beat the thunder. I beat my hatred. I won *that* time.

FIREWORKS

Once my older brother got home, we had a welcome-home party for the both of us. My neighbor naively shot off fireworks to celebrate. I looked at my mom with dread in my face and shaking hands. "What is going on?" I pined, "How can they be shooting off fireworks and making those noises after I was at war for sixteen months. What the hell?" My voice quivered. My breathing shortened. I scratched at my flesh. Tears fell from my eyes. My face reddened and blotched as I tried to enjoy the show, but my mind was not present.

As my fingers are typing these keys, my body is returning to its state from 14 years ago. I'm raw. I'm weak. I'm filled with trepidation. The fear is still real and present and powerful. Tears are running down my cheeks as I type. My vision is blurred, yet I persevere because *this* is part of my story. This is who I am. I will walk away from my computer tonight and lie down next to my loving husband and go to sleep and dream and wake up and continue on because that is my life. That is my fate. This is me. I am still suffering. I am a survivor. I am strong. I. Will. Go. On.

A few years ago, my older brother—whose PTSD manifests itself in different ways than my own—shot off fireworks while my immediate family was visiting my parents. I asked, "Are they loud? Are they boomers?"

"Naw," he responded, "They're just ground fireworks. Nothing too loud."

"You sure? Because if they're loud, please don't shoot them off. I'm not in a good place right now."

"Laura, relax. They're fine. You'll be OK."

He walked into the dark field, flicked his lighter, ignited the *mortar*, and continued to light more and more and more. I was not fine. I was staring into the dark sky, hearing the screeches before the blasts. I rocked in my chair and hugged myself. Then I covered my ears, praying for it to end. When it didn't, I got up and walked away into my own darkness—away from the fireworks. Away from my family. My bare feet kept putting one foot in front of the other. I couldn't stop until I reached only the chirping of crickets and the croaking of frogs. I could hear my mom calling my name. *They're looking for me. I have to go back.*

I can't go back. Joe betrayed me. He blatantly lied to me. He disregarded me. My own fellow veteran didn't care. How am I supposed to return? My own parents allowed it to happen. My husband didn't follow me. No one can understand my pain at this moment. I am alone.

I can't do this alone. It's too scary and sad and dismal. Should I keep walking?

Should I end it? This weight is so heavy sometimes. It would be so easy to quit this life. NO! I have children. I have a family. They love me. They really do. They just don't understand. It'll be OK. I love them, I love my life. This is a fleeting moment.

My mom's call was closer. It broke through my thoughts. In a slow and hesitant manner, I turned around and silently meandered the half mile back home. My mom embraced me first. "I'm sorry, baby," she said, "I'm sorry."

I buried my face in her neck and shuddered in grief. Damn my post-traumatic stress. Damn the fireworks. Damn my anxiety. Damn it all. My husband, who was right behind her, enveloped us both. It will be OK. I will be OK.

FULL MOON

Something as innocent as the full moon has turned my disposition upside down. While I was on night shift at Al Sha'ab in August of '03, I stared at the moon every night—memorizing its craters, its size, its shape, and its transformation as it waxed and waned. The moon became my connection to home. It was the same moon my parents had seen hours before and would see hours after me. It kept me grounded. I wasn't on a foreign planet, as it had often felt. I was still alive and real.

Fast forward four years. I was living in Fargo and had just had a great time out at the bars. I was slightly inebriated on the walk home. It was a perfect summer night for a walk. I was comfortable in a t-shirt, the wind was barely blowing, I was holding hands with my boyfriend, still feeling the flutters of new love. The stars were shimmering above and the moon lit our path as it danced among the clouds. *The moon.* Bam! PTSD hit me. *The moon from the Al Sha'ab roof. I feel sick. Despair. Exhaustion. Homesickness. That pining for peace and normalcy, of freedom, of sleeping for more than four hours in a stretch.* My stomach lurched. I was going to throw up. "Jay, I can't take it," I said as I covered my face in my hands. "I can't take this shit creeping up on me. I was fine a second ago and now I can't stop thinking of Iraq because of the frickin' moon. What the hell am I supposed to do? It's been four years, for God's sake. When will this torture end?"

"I don't know," he said softly. "We'll figure it out."

We stood there for a while as the shifting clouds covered and uncovered us from the moon's glow. I hid in his chest until my breathing returned to normal.

BALLOONS

If you would have told me that balloons were scary, I would have laughed at the absurdity of the comment. That was until I was on the tube station in London in 2007. A quirky lady with wildly crazy, curly hair and vibrant rainbow-colored clothes sat down across from me. She had a balloon figure in her hands. *Oh great, a balloon. Why the hell does she have a balloon? God, I hope she doesn't mess around with it. If that thing pops, I'm in trouble.*

Why is she twisting it? Argh, that squeaky rubbery noise is driving me insane. It's like fingernails down a chalkboard. My spine stiffened and my face contorted. I couldn't look away from that balloon. *It's going to pop. I know it. If it pops, I'm done for. Should I get off? No, I can't afford the wasted time. But I can't stay on here either. Man, this is like a frickin' torture chamber.*

Holy cow! Why is she playing with it so much? My teeth were grinding against each other. *Maybe I should ask her to stop. No, she'll never understand and then she'll think I'm the crazy one. What do I do? I can't take it anymore. My skin is crawling. Dammit, my mind is spinning out of control. Stop. Playing. With. The. Frickin'. Balloon!* I screamed in my head. *Stop! That's it. I have to get off.*

I jumped out of the car the second the doors opened. "Mind the gap," blared the loudspeaker. *Mind the gap...Mind...Did I have control over my mind? Would I eventually lose control? Would I be an insane person playing with my own balloons on the tube someday? Go away, PTSD! Leave me alone!*

SUMMING IT UP

Next time you're about to slam a door, pop a balloon, or create a loud bang, make sure you know your audience. It's imperative that civilians understand that veterans are everywhere and you never know their level of agony.

There are dozens of more examples I could add. I live in a state of fear and anxiety and have accepted it as my fate. That being said, no veteran is affected the same way. You may come across a veteran who saw more turmoil than I did, but is doing fine.

You may meet a veteran who has an increased temper, a drinking problem, or a drug problem.

You may see a veteran living on the street, too afraid, unable, or unwilling to ask for help.

One who has detached from the world known prior to the war.

One who feels like fighting in a war is the only way to be happy.

Our minds work in strange ways to overcome the craziness we went through. Among the 12 other women I worked with, almost all of us have dealt with PTSD in a different way. Depression is the strongest form of PTSD, but there are many other forms that take us away from our former selves and send us into a state-of-being we never thought possible.

When I look back at war, I see myself as someone completely different than who I am today or who I was before I left. I had a different state of mind, a shell of who I currently am. I am a civilian and I am a soldier—I am not one and the same—I am two separate entities. The soldier will do things the civilian deems immoral and insane. The civilian is able to accomplish things the soldier only dreamed about. The soldier was a slave to the military; the civilian is a free soul trying to make a positive impact in this crazy world. I became a wanderer until I met my husband—searching for the happiness that I had before my return from the killing fields.

I've found happiness by exploring the world, by affecting people's lives positively, by spreading peace, smiles, joy, and by building my wonderful family. I take nothing for granted. If something goes wrong, I know it could always be worse.

Would I sign up if I were given a second chance? Yes. I know that combat was part of my destiny. It was God's master plan. Many of my accomplishments and joys are due to my enlistment on that fateful March day in 2001.

I have been able to travel to my heart's content without fretting over money because I live a debt-free life.

I have deeper empathy for others.

I understand mental-health disorders from my firsthand experience.

I understand how vast cultural differences can be, and I respect those differences.

I am a new person. I can wake up and enjoy the simple pleasures of hearing a bird sing or a ray of sun warming my bed. I know what it feels like to be unhappy and will not settle for that unhappiness anymore. Life is too short and too fragile for complacency. I went through hell and back, and it has made me a better, stronger, and wiser person.

Would I ever go back to war? Never. Not for any money in the world. My life has no monetary value. Thank goodness my time in the military ended before the 32nd MPs were sent back to Iraq.

I want to make a positive difference in this world, not add to its strife. I would love to explore the same streets when and if Iraq is a safe place. To walk in the resort I lived in, to experience the Iraqi culture without restraint. I want to share my experience with my husband and children. Do I think that this will happen? No, I don't. We started something in Iraq that's going to take decades to end. War has always been a part of the Middle East. We stirred the pot of unrest and have unleashed the demons. I'm afraid for what is to come.

The first thing my students typically ask me is, "Did you kill anyone?" The answer to this question has three different parts.

1.   Did I *want* to kill someone? Yes! Undeniably, the answer is yes. I wanted nothing more than to retaliate against the culprits who put me into in harm's way. Every time a mortar landed, an IED blew up, a gun fired, I wanted to take out the instigator. How could I be in a war and not kill another human being after being subjected to so much torment?

2.   Did I have a chance to kill someone? No, not like you would think. We never found the people who launched the mortars. We never knew who detonated the IED. We never found the hole where the small-arms fire came from. Almost half of the civilians carried guns, making it impossible to figure out who the culprit was. We couldn't shoot aimlessly into the crowd, killing civilians. Additionally, my job was to get my team out of the kill zone as the driver of the Humvee, and a moment of hesitation meant the difference between life and death.

3.   How do I feel about not killing anyone now that I'm home? I am relieved that I didn't take another human life. I know I was trained for war, trained to kill. I wanted an eye for an eye, but there is no way I could come home after killing someone

with the same amount of sanity I now possess. I live without the guilt of killing another human being.

EPILOGUE

WHERE I'VE BEEN AND WHAT I'VE SEEN

When I returned from Iraq in August 2004, I went straight to my parents' house, sorted through my old life, and packed for college.

Once August hit, I moved to a house off campus and finished my last two years of college. I traveled when I was done, calling 2006 *The Year of Laura*. Every penny I made in Iraq was dedicated to filling 2006 with the most joy I could muster. I road-tripped to Maine and down the East Coast, visited Honduras, and backpacked through Europe for a month-and-a-half.

Once I returned home, I helped my dad run for State Assembly in my hometown's district in Wisconsin and then stayed with my cousin in Florida for a couple of weeks.

I received a physical education teaching job at a secondary school in Aylesbury, England. Even though I intended to live their indefinitely, I stayed for only six short months. I went home on summer holiday and decided to move to Fargo to be with my then-boyfriend, Jay. I got a job as an activities director for people with special needs. Jay and I stayed in Fargo until he was done with his master's degree, and then we moved to Madison so that I could be closer to my friends and family. I worked as a physical education teacher at West High School in Madison.

Jay and I broke up in March 2011. A couple of months later, I bought my own house and enjoyed the freedoms of single life until I met my husband, Garrett, in January on Friday the 13th, 2012. That February 25th we got engaged and were married on the 26th of May. Yes, your math is correct; we knew each other for only four-and-a-half months. I knew he was the one on our first date. We have had many adventures since. We have moved twice since we got married. From Madison, we moved to a small town called Columbus, Wisconsin, because we fell in love with and renovated a 1902 Victorian home. We took a lot of pride in the changes we made and wished we could have brought the house with us when I got a new job as assistant principal in my hometown of Waupaca. Instead, we live on a calm, blue-green, crystal-clear lake. The serenity, peace, and never-ending outdoor activities allow us and our three children to enjoy nature to its fullest. Our three joyful, vibrant, and caring children are Lily Ellamae, Lincoln Zachary, and Easton Garrett. My husband works in real estate and owns his own handyman business.

My parents still live in my hometown of Waupaca a mere six miles from my house. Andy joined the Peace Corps in 2007 and worked in South Africa. Ten months later, he returned to be with the love of his life, Ann. They married and now have two captivating daughters, Mallory Elizabeth and Kiersten Autumn. Andy is now a detective in the Madison, Wisconsin, police department. Joe, who still watches ESPN, is married to Tasha, and they have two athletic children—a daughter, Morgan Grace, and a son, James Joseph. Joe works for the Veterans Affairs and is currently planning the Veterans Golden Age Games. And I am now the principal of the middle school.

MEMORIAL DAY

Memorial Day is no longer a holiday, a time to have a cookout and party. It's a day to commemorate fallen soldiers. I remember Michelle Witmer and Daniel Thompson. Thompson was one of the soldiers in my team once I got my sergeant stripes. He died in Afghanistan in February 2009. I also remember the soldiers I lived and worked with for over a year. I think about the person I turned into while I was deployed. The blood, sweat, and tears I gave to serve our country. The despair, pride, love, hate, fear, and joy I felt for 16 long months. Memorial Day—one more thing in my life that is forever changed because of my time in service.

I read the following paragraphs at the end of the presentation that I give. It is a perfect summary of how I feel.

There was a time when I could obtain unadulterated happiness. A time when my life was innocent and carefree.

I was desecrated by the horrendousness of war.

A piece of me was left behind somewhere in desolate Iraq. Some days that piece feels like it's a tiny hole in my heart. Other days it feels like it sucks me in whole—leaving me with nothing but the darkness to stare at and relish. I was no longer innocent or happy.

Through time, this hole has become manageable, and that happiness I felt before the killing fields is creeping its way back into my being. I am becoming the person I once was, but it's been a difficult journey.

From now on, take a second to consider the veteran. The person who gave everything to serve their country only to return home ostracized, changed beyond recognition, and afraid of their new internal war.

A sound, sight, or smell can trigger intrusive thoughts, flashbacks, and the pure agony of war. The war a veteran faces is not over once the soldier steps on American soil. It will always be there, lingering.

Personally, it's the sound of thunder, fireworks, a door slamming, a gunshot, the smell of specific hand soap, the full moon, a piece of garbage on the road, a song on the radio, the list can go on and on.

Triggers are elusive yet real.

Veterans are everywhere and are affected differently by war.

Be cognizant of them, always.

ACKNOWLEDGMENTS

This book would not have been possible without the support of my friends and family. I am indebted to you all for your encouragement and patience. Garrett, my love, you know what this book took to finish and the time it took away from our relationship and our family. Thanks for your constant support and patience. Mom and Dad, your unconditional love and guidance are unmatchable. Andy and Joe, my brothers, thanks for supporting me in my times of hardship and for assisting me in my healing. Hannah, thanks for seeing me out of my darkest moments. I owe you so much because you never gave up on me. Patrick Fairbanks, Julia Steege-Reimann, Jay Delmedico, Nancy Pulvermacher, and Mark Nepper, you are my motivation for perfection because of your help along the way. Your support and suggestions motivated me like no others. Julia Dye, thank you for teaching me how to write. This humbling experience could not have been possible without your faith in my story. Speaking of faith, thanks to God for being my foundation before, during, and after my time at war. And to the rest of you who have touched my life, offered support, guidance, and never gave up on me: Thank you!

ABOUT THE AUTHOR

As a daughter of a Vietnam War Military Police officer and a sister to an Army Infantry Medic, Laura joined the Army National Guard as a Military Police officer in 2001 during her freshman year of college at the University of Wisconsin–Madison and received her Honorable Discharge in 2009. She served 16 months on active duty, spending over a year in Baghdad, Iraq.

Laura's love of travel, living abroad, and serving others brought her to her current position as a small business consultant where she helps leaders boost their employee buy-in, belonging, and collaboration so that they can build productive teams to take their organizations to new heights. She treasures spending time with her husband and three children. Nature is her oasis. She also loves to read, socialize, remodel homes, and learn, as attested to in her two master's degrees: Experiential Education and Educational Leadership.

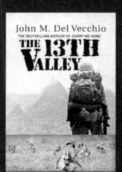

CPSIA information can be obtained
at www.ICGtesting.com
Printed in the USA
JSHW032021230222
23226JS00001B/5